CAMBRIDGE TEXTS IN THE
HISTORY OF POLITICAL THOUGHT

ARISTOTLE
The Politics
and
The Constitution of Athens

CAMBRIDGE TEXTS IN THE
HISTORY OF POLITICAL THOUGHT

Series editors

RAYMOND GEUSS
Lecturer in Philosophy, University of Cambridge

QUENTIN SKINNER
Regius Professor of Modern History in the University of Cambridge

Cambridge Texts in the History of Political Thought is now firmly established as the major student textbook series in political theory. It aims to make available to students all the most important texts in the history of western political thought, from ancient Greece to the early twentieth century. All the familiar classic texts will be included, but the series seeks at the same time to enlarge the conventional canon by incorporating an extensive range of less well-known works, many of them never before available in a modern English edition. Wherever possible, texts are published in complete and unabridged form, and translations are specially commissioned for the series. Each volume contains a critical introduction together with chronologies, biographical sketches, a guide to further reading and any necessary glossaries and textual apparatus. When completed the series will aim to offer an outline of the entire evolution of western political thought.

For a list of titles published in the series, please see end of book

ARISTOTLE

The Politics
and
The Constitution of Athens

EDITED BY
STEPHEN EVERSON
University of Michigan

CAMBRIDGE
UNIVERSITY PRESS

PUBLISHED BY THE PRESS SYNDICATE OF THE UNIVERSITY OF CAMBRIDGE
The Pitt Building, Trumpington Street, Cambridge, United Kingdom

CAMBRIDGE UNIVERSITY PRESS
The Edinburgh Building, Cambridge CB2 2RU, UK   http://www.cup.cam.ac.uk
40 West 20th Street, New York, NY 10011–4211, USA   http://www.cup.org
10 Stamford Road, Oakleigh, Melbourne 3166, Australia
Ruiz de Alarcón 13, 28014 Madrid, Spain

© in the translation and editorial matter
Cambridge University Press 1996

The translation of *The Politics* used in this edition is taken from
Jonathan Barnes, ed., *The Complete Works of Aristotle:
The Revised Translation*, Volumes One and Two, Bollingen Series 71:2.
Copyright © 1984 by the Jowett Copyright Trustees.
Published by Princeton University Press.
'The Politics' reprinted with permission
of Princeton University Press.

The extract from the *Nicomachean Ethics* Book x, Chapter 9, also
taken from *The Complete Works of Aristotle,* is likewise reprinted by kind
permission of Princeton University Press.

The text of *The Constitution of Athens* used in this edition is taken from
J. M. Moore, *Aristotle and Xenophon on Democracy and Oligarchy*, pp. 147–207,
© 1975 J. M. Moore. Reprinted by kind permission of University of California
Press, Berkeley and Chatto and Windus, London.

This edition of Aristotle: *The Politics* and *The Constitution of Athens* succeeds
and replaces Aristotle: *The Politics*, first published by Cambridge University
Press 1988 and reprinted several times (ISBN 0 521 35449 8 hardback,
0 521 35731 4 paperback).

This edition first published 1996
Reprinted 1998, 1999

Printed in the United Kingdom at the University Press, Cambridge

A catalogue record for this book is available from the British Library

A catalogue record for this book is available from the Library of Congress

ISBN 0 521 48243 7 hardback
ISBN 0 521 48400 6 paperback

WV

Contents

Contents

Acknowledgements

Benjamin Jowett's translation of the *Politics* was important both because it rendered Aristotle's treatise into clear and elegant prose and because it initiated the project of translating the whole of Aristotle's works into English. The Oxford Translation of Aristotle, which involved most of the leading scholars of ancient philosophy of the time and took until 1954 to complete, became the standard English version of Aristotle's works. Since the publication of Jowett's translation, however, much work has been done on the text of Aristotle and scholars have achieved a better understanding of Aristotle's works themselves. In 1984, Jonathan Barnes published a revision of the entire Oxford translations, including Jowett's *Politics*. The revised translation of the *Politics* is not only elegant and lucid but now firmly in keeping with advances in scholarship. Until now it has only been available as part of the complete translation of Aristotle and it was felt that it was important to make it more readily available to students of the history of political thought. I am grateful both to the Jowett Trustees and to the Princeton University Press for allowing the revised translation to be used in this series.

As far as the introduction itself goes, I am grateful for comments and discussions to Jonathan Barnes, Julia Annas, John Robertson and the general editors of the series. I should also like to thank Robert Peden for his help in proof-reading.

S.E.

Acknowledgements for the second edition

The introduction has been considerably changed for this new edition. I am grateful to David Charles, Thomas Harrison, Hugh Johnstone and Oswyn Murray for helping me to avoid the introduction of fresh errors.

S.E., August 1995

Introduction

The *Politics* is to be ranked amongst the greatest works of political philosophy. Not only does Aristotle provide a theory of the nature and the function of the state and an analysis of possible constitutional structures, but he also gives us detailed discussions of such subsidiary topics as equality, justice, property, citizenship and the causes of political stability and revolution. No philosopher before him had attempted to provide such a coherent and systematic study of the science of politics. Even more striking than the range and originality of the *Politics* is the consistent rigour and precision of its argument. Although there is indeed a powerful political theory to be found in the *Politics*, Aristotle rarely, if ever, allows the attraction of providing a systematic theory to lead him into smudging arguments or ignoring inconvenient evidence. As a pioneering natural as well as political scientist, Aristotle shows a proper respect for evidence and for precision in its analysis. The combination of this quality with an unsurpassed ability to see the philosophical implications of his subject-matter makes Aristotle a rare political theorist indeed.

It cannot be said, however, that the *Politics* is an easy work. Aristotle's style is terse and economical. The very precision and complexity of its arguments place demands on the reader which Aristotle makes little attempt to palliate. It is widely believed – and may very well be true – that the surviving works of Aristotle, including the *Politics*, are lecture notes and that he would have been able, as he lectured, to expand on points which may seem obscure on the page. Even if this is true, its effect should not be over-emphasised. The argument of the *Politics* may lack rhetorical presentation, but the general effect of this is that the details of the argument are to be seen without a distorting polish. If the *Politics* is a difficult work, this is because the problems with which it deals are not such as to allow solutions that are both simple and true.

There is a more important factor which may obscure Aristotle's account of the state to the reader who comes to the *Politics* for the first time, and this is the fact that Aristotle's political theory is closely related to claims and types of explanation which he uses and justifies elsewhere in his works. It is not that one cannot understand the *Politics* without reading other works, but rather that the nature of Aristotle's argument is more easily grasped if one has at least a tentative understanding of what he has to say, for instance, in the *Physics* about nature or the *Ethics* about human flourishing. In this introduction, as well as providing an outline of what I take to be Aristotle's general political theory, I shall also try to describe, briefly, its connection with what he has to say elsewhere.

Aristotle

Aristotle was born in 384 BC in Stagira in Macedon. His father, Nicomachus, was physician to the family of Amyntas, the king of Macedon. It seems that Nicomachus died when Aristotle was young and that Aristotle was brought up under the guardianship of a man called Proxenus. In 367, when Aristotle was seventeen, he went to Athens to join the Academy, the school of Plato. He stayed there until Plato's death in 347, when he left for Assos in Asia Minor, where he seems to have pursued the study of natural history in earnest, before moving to Lesbos. In 343, he returned to Macedon and was appointed by Amyntas' son Philip, now himself king, to be tutor to Philip's son Alexander. In 336 Philip was assassinated and was succeeded by Alexander, who continued to pursue his father's ambitions for Macedonian hegemony in Greece. Aristotle returned to Athens in 335 to found his own school, the Lyceum. He remained in Athens until 322 and died in Chalcis a year later.

Although Aristotle spent most of his life in Athens, his Macedonian origin prevented him from being a citizen there. There is a striking contrast between Aristotle's political theory and his own status and associations. For Aristotle, as we shall see, citizenship in a state and participation in its political life was a precondition of achieving human flourishing – a precondition denied to Aristotle himself. Given the emphasis which he places upon the importance of citizenship, one cannot but be struck by his matter-of-fact description of the position of resident aliens within the state: 'we call them citizens only in a qualified sense, as we might apply the term to children who are too young to be on the register, or to old men who are to be relieved of civic duties' (III.1, 1275a14–16).

Striking also is that, despite his association with Philip and Alexander the Great, Aristotle takes the *polis* to be the perfect political unit. There is no support to be found in the pages of the *Politics* for the Macedonian kings' ambition to rule Greece and to found an empire. Aristotle does remark that if the Hellenic race were 'formed into one state it would be able to rule the world' (VII.7, 1327b32–3), but it is evident from what he has already said that he does not regard this as a desirable or a proper ambition: 'Yet to a reflecting mind it must appear very strange that the statesman should always be considering how he can dominate and tyrannize over others, whether they are willing or not' (VII.2, 1324b 22–6).

Aristotle's interests were all-encompassing. His surviving writings range from a systematic study of deductive inference to detailed descriptions of animal species. His work is scientific in that he is concerned to describe and explain the natural world – of which man is a part – and to provide the conceptual tools with which to do this. In the *Politics* itself, we find a typical Aristotelian combination of conceptual analysis and attention to the facts. At the end of the *Nicomachean Ethics*, when Aristotle announces his move to the study of the state, he says that he will do so 'in the light of the constitutions we have collected' (1181b16–20). Underlying the theory of the *Politics* are not just the ethical and scientific doctrines of the *Ethics* and *Physics* but the collection of 158 constitutions compiled by Aristotle and his colleagues in the Lyceum.

The *Politics* must also be seen as part of a series of works in which Aristotle is concerned with human affairs. The most studied of these, at least in modern times, has been the *Nicomachean Ethics*

(*NE*). There is also a work called the *Eudemian Ethics* (*EE*) which has traditionally received less scholarly attention. In the nineteenth century it was considered to be by Aristotle's pupil Eudemus rather than Aristotle himself but is now generally accepted as a genuine member of the Aristotelian corpus and, indeed, as important for the study of Aristotle's ethical theory as the *NE*.

Only one of the constitutions collected by Aristotle's school has survived – the *Constitution of Athens*. This contains both a political history of Athens and a description of the constitution as it stood at the time of writing – although there is some reason to think that the work was updated to keep up with further constitutional changes. According to a recent and major commentary, 'as a historian [the author] is mediocre (though by no means useless to us), but as a describer of constitutional practice he is first in the field'.[1] The *Constitution of Athens* has not come down to us with the other works of Aristotle but exists on two papyri. On neither is the text explicitly attributed to Aristotle, and its identification as the Aristotelian *Constitution of Athens* was made at the end of the nineteenth century. Whilst there is no serious doubt that it did indeed form part of the Lyceum's collection of constitutions, it is not clear whether it was written by Aristotle himself or one of his students. This does not affect its usefulness. Whether or not Aristotle wrote all 158 constitutions, he certainly authorised them and made use of them in the writing of the *Politics*.

Aristotle's method and the collection of constitutions

Indeed, Aristotle's interest in the work of earlier legislators is motivated by more than the desire to provide historical examples to illustrate his arguments. In the *Politics*, as throughout the Aristotelian corpus, he takes the beliefs of his predecessors, along with people's ordinary beliefs, to have evidential value, and this is central to his method of inquiry. He gives an explicit statement of this method at the start of his discussion of *akrasia* in Book VII of the *NE*:

---

[1] P. J. Rhodes, *A Commentary on the Aristotelian 'Athenaion Politeia'* (Oxford, 1981), p. 60.

We must, as in all other cases, set the appearances before us and, after first discussing the difficulties, go on to prove, if possible, the truth of all the opinions about these affections or, failing this, of the greatest number and the most important; for if we both resolve the difficulties and leave the opinions undisturbed, we shall have proved the case sufficiently.

(VII.1, 1145b1–7)

The starting-points of Aristotle's inquiry are provided by experience – the appearances – and by what people have believed about the matter in question. Taken together, of course, these may contain inconsistencies and so present the difficulties which the theorist must resolve. People may have disagreed, for instance, about the nature of *akrasia* or what constitution the state should have, and particular theoretical claims may conflict with what is obviously the case. Indeed, as one's beliefs become more theoretical and thus less immediately grounded in experience, in the way things appear, so there is greater vulnerability to error. As his criticism of Plato in *Politics* II makes clear, Aristotle himself is perfectly aware that too unguarded an enthusiasm for theorising is quite as likely to take one away from the truth as it is to help one to attain it.

Theoretical success consists in resolving the difficulties presented by the appearances and people's existing beliefs: 'the solution of the difficulty is the discovery of the truth' (*NE* VII.2, 1146b6–8). This is not because Aristotle thinks that evaluative or normative beliefs are capable only of some lesser type of truth than, say, scientific beliefs. The method of 'saving the appearances' is one he follows in the physical and psychological treatises as well as in the *Ethics* and *Politics*. Rather, Aristotle believes that human beings are naturally sensitive to the way things are and so accepts that there is a presumption that our experience, and the beliefs to which it gives rise, will be true. He does not, of course, take that presumption to be indefeasible and does not deny that the world can be other than it appears or that we can hold false beliefs about it. He does accept, however, that if something is generally believed, or is believed by someone who has thought seriously about an issue, this is at least a sign of its truth – and this is why he makes it a requirement on the theorist who would deny the truth of some such belief that he should explain why someone should have held that belief in the first place (see *Physics* IV.4, 211a7–11).

A good example of this occurs in *Politics* III.9, where Aristotle discusses justice and has to deal with the fact that there are differences between oligarchic and democratic conceptions of justice. He begins by claiming that 'all men cling to justice of some kind', but notes that there is disagreement concerning what justice is: 'their conceptions are imperfect and they do not express the whole idea'. Whereas some think that justice is equality, others think it lies in inequality. Aristotle must thus resolve this contradiction and, importantly, he also seeks to explain why such disagreement should occur at all. In this case, people disagree 'because they are bad judges in their own affairs' and also 'because both the parties to the argument are speaking of a limited and partial justice, but imagine themselves to be speaking of absolute justice' (1280a20–2).

Thus, Aristotle's motivation for generally beginning his works by canvassing, and criticising, the views of his predecessors is not simply an antiquarian one. He regards them as having been engaged in the same inquiries as he is himself and so takes it that their conclusions will deserve to be assessed seriously to see if they are true. Even when they do go wrong, determining precisely where and why they go wrong will itself help in seeing where the truth lies.

Whilst earlier thinkers had written a great deal about many of the subjects which Aristotle deals with, political science had been comparatively neglected by earlier Greek thinkers. So, at the end of what is in effect the prologue to the *Politics*, the final chapter of the *Nicomachean Ethics*, he says that 'our predecessors have left the subject of legislation unexamined' (1181b12–13). This is an exaggeration, as Aristotle's criticism of Plato and others in *Politics* II itself makes evident. Nevertheless, what he goes on to say is revealing of what he takes his sources to be for the examination of existing beliefs about his subject:

> First, then, if anything has been said well in detail by earlier thinkers, let us try to review it; then in the light of the constitutions we have collected let us study what sorts of influence preserve and destroy states, and what sorts preserve or destroy the particular kinds of constitution, and to what causes it is due that some are well and others ill administered. When these have been studied we

shall perhaps be more likely to see which constitution is best, and how each must be ordered, and what laws and customs it must use.

(1181b13–22)

This is echoed at the start of *Politics* II, when Aristotle says that his purpose is 'to consider what form of political community is best of all for those who are most able to realise their ideal of life', and so he must 'examine not only [the perfect state] but other constitutions, both such as actually exist in well-governed states, and any theoretical forms which are held in high esteem, so that what is good and useful may be brought to light' (1260b25–31).

Politics II indeed provides the clearest example of the method, for it consists precisely of an examination of Plato's two differing accounts of the ideal state in the *Republic* and the *Laws*, and of the theoretical constitutions developed by Phaleas and Hippodamus as well as the actual constitutions of Sparta and Crete. The project in the *Politics* is to determine what is the best constitution: how the state should be set up if it is best to fulfil its purpose. Existing states are seen to be attempts at doing this, and the study of these has the additional advantage that the political scientist can find out the actual effects of different kinds of constitution and law. The *Constitution of Athens* duly falls into two parts: in the first half the author provides a history of the development of the Athenian state and, in the second, a description of the constitution as it then was. Although we do not possess the other constitutions collected by Aristotle's school, it seems likely that they too contained both historical and constitutional material. Certainly, the *Politics* deploys both kinds of information in the development of its theory of the state.

The *polis* and the state

I have described Aristotle as providing a theory of the nature and function of the state. Some would contest this claim on the grounds of anachronism: Aristotle's subject, they would say, is not the state, but the historically specific 'city-state' – the *polis*.[2] If

---

[2] Plural: *poleis*.

this complaint were true, it would certainly have the effect of limiting the interest of the *Politics*, as the practical purpose Aristotle intends for it would be not be one which we could any longer pursue ourselves. His discussion might tell us a great deal about the government of ancient cities but it will not cast light, other than accidentally, upon the nature and proper authority of later political institutions.

The idea that Aristotle's political interests are historically constrained in this way is not unmotivated. Not only were the societies which Aristotle knew, and whose constitutions he collected, generally cities, but he himself actually denies that a *polis* can function effectively if it becomes too large – where too large seems to be the size where a herald cannot make himself heard to all (1326b6) or the citizens are too numerous to know each other's characters (1326b14–15). If a *polis* consists of too many people, it will be self-sufficient only as a nation, an *ethnos*, since it will be 'almost incapable of constitutional government' (1326b4–5). If these claims were part of the definition of the *polis*, then we would have to accept that the *Politics* provides a theory of a political institution which has now all but died out. In fact, however, as Aristotle's acknowledgement at 1326b11 that deciding the possible size of the *polis* is a matter of experience suggests, these claims about size of population are quite contingent, and it is clear from Aristotle's formal account of the *polis* in Book III that his theory is not restricted in its application to those *poleis* that happen to be cities.

In III.3 Aristotle raises the question of how *poleis* are to be individuated. This has both theoretical and practical significance. It is theoretically important because it is clearly a basic requirement of a theory of the state that it should specify what it is for something to be a state. Its practical importance lies in the fact that, as Aristotle recognises, when there is dispute over whether one state is the same as another (after a revolution, for instance), it becomes a matter of dispute whether contracts in which the original state had been a party are still valid.

Aristotle considers and rejects two possible answers. According to the first, a *polis* is identified by its place and on the second by its inhabitants. The first will not do because it is too vague:

When are men, living in the same place, to be regarded as a single *polis* – what is the limit? Certainly not the wall of the *polis*, for you might surround all Peloponnesus with a wall.

(1276a24–7)

One can mark out a place which contains a group of people but the society which occupies that place will not thereby have the unity needed for a *polis*. Nor can one identify a *polis* with its citizens, as these can change without bringing about the demise of the *polis*.

Aristotle's own answer is that the *polis* should be identified with its constitution:

Since the *polis* is a partnership, and is a partnership of citizens in a constitution, when the form of government changes, and becomes different, then it may be supposed that the *polis* is no longer the same ... And in this manner we speak of every union or composition of elements as different when the form of their composition alters.

(1276b1–4; 6–8)

A *polis* is a composition of elements – the citizens – but, as a composition, its identity is determined not by reference to its constituents but to the way in which they are structured: we speak of the same state by attending to its constitution (1276b9–11).

Aristotle's analysis here is a particular application of his more general distinction between the form of a substance and its matter. The form of an object is given by specifying what it is to be the sort of thing it is, and the matter is what instantiates that form. Thus, to take an example from the *Metaphysics*, the form of a particular bronze sphere is being spherical and its matter is the bronze. Even this simple example, however, highlights an apparent difficulty in Aristotle's identification of the *polis* with its constitution – which is that it is in principle possible for two different *poleis* to share the same constitution. Clearly, two different particular spheres will instantiate the same form: what will distinguish them will be that that form is instantiated by different matter. Similarly, two different states could have the same form – the same constitution – but be different because each is differently instantiated, i.e. has a different citizenry.

It is perhaps to allow room to deal with this difficulty that Aristotle claims only that the state is chiefly determined by its constitution, thus allowing other factors to be brought in. If this leaves a gap in the account, it is one that is easily filled: at any one time, one can identify a particular *polis* as the instantiation of a constitution by a particular set of citizens. Once this identification has been made, it is not necessary for the citizenry to remain constant if the *polis* is to persist, but it is necessary that its form of government should not change. This provides the necessary asymmetry between the constitution and the citizenry to support Aristotle's giving priority to the former rather than the latter.

It is because any *polis* is a particular governmental arrangement of citizens that Aristotle is so concerned both to provide an account of the various possible kinds of government and also, at the beginning of III, to establish what it is to be a citizen:

> He who would inquire into the essence and attributes of various types of government must first of all determine what a *polis* is . . . But a *polis* is composite, like any other whole made up of many parts – these are the citizens who compose it. It is evident, therefore, that we must begin by asking, Who is the citizen, and what is the meaning of that term?
>
> (1274b32–4; 1274b38–1275a2)

This again turns out to be a less straightforward matter than one might at first have thought. So, one cannot, for instance, just take a citizen of a *polis* to be an inhabitant of the territory occupied by the *polis*, otherwise resident aliens and slaves would count as citizens (1275a7–8). What, on Aristotle's view, is distinctive of the citizen of a state, as opposed to a member of some society, is the right to participate in the administration of justice and government (1275a22–33). Thus, he concludes, 'he who has the power to take part in the deliberative or judicial administration of any state is said by us to be a citizen of that *polis*; and, speaking generally, a *polis* is a body of citizens sufficing for the purposes of life' (1275b18–21).

There is obviously nothing in this definition of the *polis* which is such as to restrict it in principle to the *city*-state. Any association will count as a *polis*, so long as it has a constitution, i.e. it is unified under a government. If Aristotle would not count modern states as *poleis*, this would not just be because they are not cities. If what it is for something to be a *polis* is for it to be a society unified by a single constitution, then there is no reason in principle why a much larger society than a city should not be a *polis*. Aristotle's subject in the *Politics* is neither the nature of the city, nor even of the 'city-state', but of a society unified under a government – and the closest notion we have to capture this is that of the state.

The state and nature

To be a citizen is to be a citizen of some particular state, which is why, for instance, 'he who is a citizen in a democracy will often not be a citizen in an oligarchy' (III.1, 1275a3–5). A state is thus, as Aristotle claims more than once, prior to its citizens, as 'the whole is of necessity prior to the part' (I.2, 1253a20). This claim is actually used in Book VIII to justify the state's rather than parents' taking charge of the education of children, since 'the neglect of education does harm to the constitution' and 'the training in things which are of common interest should be the same for all' (1337a13–14; 26–7): we must not 'suppose that anyone of the citizens belongs to himself, for they all belong to the state, and are each of them a part of the state, and the care of each part is inseparable from the care of the whole' (1337a27–9). Now, it is one thing to maintain that the state is definitionally prior to its citizens but quite another to claim that it is prior to the people who are its citizens. Any club is prior to its members but this does not itself entitle it to direct their lives – and certainly not the lives of their children. The difference, for Aristotle, is that whilst it will be a contingent matter whether people are members of types of association such as clubs, they are naturally, and hence necessarily, such as to be citizens of a state. Thus, the state is actually '*by nature* prior to the family and the individual' (I.2, 1253a18–19). To see why this is so, one needs to see how Aristotle justifies what is perhaps the central thesis of the *Politics* – that the state is itself a natural institution.

Aristotle's first move is to provide an account of the development of human society, claiming that 'he who thus considers things in their first growth and origin, whether a state or anything else, will obtain the clearest view of them' (1242a24–5). The state is presented as the culmination of a series of human associations, each of which is the natural successor to the one before.

The first stage of the process leading to the state consists of two necessary relations: marriage and slavery. These are necessary because they are between 'those who cannot live without each other' (1252a26). Marriage is not the result of choice but of instinct: 'in common with other animals and with plants, mankind has a natural desire to leave behind them an image of themselves' (1252a29–30). In contrast, the relation between master and slave is strictly necessary only for the slave, since the 'natural slave' does not himself possess reason, and so needs to be directed by those who do, whereas those people who cannot afford slaves can make do with animals instead.

The two relations of marriage and slavery are treated as basic and together they constitute the first type of association – the family. Since the family consists of natural relations, it is itself a natural association: 'The family is the association established by nature for the supply of men's everyday wants' (1252b12–14). As the population expands through reproduction, so the next type of association arises – the village. This, which is simply the combination of several families, is also a natural association and the first one which 'aims at something more than the supply of daily needs' (1252b15–16). The end of this process of social development is the state itself, which comes into existence when 'several villages are united in a single complete community, large enough to be nearly or quite self-sufficing' (1252b28).

Now, it might seem that it is this developmental account of the state which is supposed to justify the claim that the state is natural:

> And therefore, if the earlier forms of society are natural, so is the state, for it is the end of them, and the nature of a thing is its end. For what each thing is when fully developed, we call its nature, whether we are speaking of a man, a horse, or a family. Besides, the final cause and end of a thing is the best, and to be self-sufficing is the end and the best. Hence it is evident that the state is a creation of nature, and that man is by nature a political animal.
>
> (1252b30–1253a3)

If this is Aristotle's argument, however, it is problematic. He argues that the state is a natural society if the earlier social forms were natural – but the implication here is far from obvious. It is plausible enough to claim that the family comes about as the result of natural human instincts and needs, and that villages will arise as families multiply. In other words, the simple desire for sex or reproduction will indeed lead to the growth of families and then of villages. The state, however, is more than a collection of villages. What is distinctive of the state is, at least in part, that it has a constitution. This, however, is something which is indeed the result of deliberation and choice, and so a matter of artifice rather than nature. Indeed, if states were institutions which just happened to come about without planning, the project of the *Politics* would itself be beside the point.

Of course, Aristotle does not claim in I.2 that the state arises spontaneously – and the purpose of the argument in I.2 might be taken to be precisely to secure the naturalness of the state despite the fact that it is the result of deliberation. The state would be natural because it constitutes the end of the process of social development – a process whose origins are natural. As the culmination of a natural process, the state could be seen to be natural, even though the particular move from a collection of villages to the state is one which takes thought. In fact, however, Aristotle could not deploy this argument without begging the question. For although the state is indeed natural because it is the 'end', the *telos*, of the process of social development and 'what each thing is when fully developed, we call its nature', it is not the end in virtue of constituting the necessary finishing-point of that process. As Aristotle acknowledges, states can themselves proceed to degenerate into unnatural associations, such as empires. This does not count against the claim that the state is the *telos* of human society, since in fact that term signifies not the final point of the process of change but its culmination. The nature of a thing is what it is when fully developed – 'whether we are speaking of a man, a horse, or a family' – and what it is for something to be 'fully developed' is not for it to have reached its final stages. To see why this is so, it is important to recognise the role which natures play in Aristotelian explanation.

The question of how to specify the nature of a substance is raised in *Physics* II. Aristotle canvasses two opposed answers:

Some identify the nature or substance of a natural object with that immediate constituent of it which taken by itself is without arrangement, e.g. the wood is the nature of the bed, and the bronze the nature of the statue . . . Another account is that nature is the shape or form which is specified in the definition of the thing.

(193a10–12; 30–1)

As his refusal to identify the state with its citizenry will already have made clear, Aristotle accepts the second of these – 'the form indeed is nature rather than the matter' (193b7). His preference here is well motivated, if not uncontroversial. Simply, his thought is that to understand the behaviour of complex natural things, we cannot simply describe them in terms of their constitutive stuffs but must treat as basic the fact that they are particular types of thing.

This is apparent in the treatment of growth:

What grows *qua* growing grows from something into something. What, then, is growing? Not that from which it arose but that to which it tends.

(193b16–17)

What *is* the substance that starts off as an acorn and grows into an oak tree? Aristotle's answer is that it is an oak tree. If we want to understand why the acorn changes as it does, we have to explain it in terms of its potential for becoming the oak tree. A substance's nature, on Aristotle's view, is an *inner principle of change*. The acorn changes as it does because it has the nature it does – and that nature cannot be understood other than as a potential oak tree. So, when Aristotle claims in *Politics* I.2 that the state is natural because it is the end of the process of social development, he is placing his theory of the state in the context of his general account of natural change.

It is the fact that one will need to appeal to a substance's nature in order to explain its development which allows Aristotle to distinguish between something's *telos* and the condition in which it happens to end up. Many people's eyes, for instance, deteriorate with age, but we will not make reference to defective eyes in giving an account of what it is to be an eye: we will explain the development of the eye by reference to its function, and a fully developed eye will be one which performs this function properly. The notion of an 'end' here is teleological rather than temporal – natural change will not be properly explained unless its purpose is made clear.

> For those things are natural which, by a continuous movement originated from an internal principle, arrive at some end . . . It is absurd to suppose that purpose is not present because we do not observe the agent deliberating . . . If, therefore, purpose is present in art, it is also present in nature.
>
> (*Physics* 199b16–17; 26–7; 29–30)

The *telos* is not the point at which the process of growth happens to finish, it is that point which the whole process was *for*: we will not understand the process without seeing it as aiming towards that point. It is not, of course, that Aristotle imagines the work of some external or divine agent. The 'nature' here is just the – quite non-conscious – nature of the thing in question. It is the nature of an acorn to grow into an oak tree and so, Aristotle believes, we can properly talk of such growth as purposeful. Its changes take place for the sake of its becoming an oak tree and cannot be understood otherwise.

There is, however, an obvious difference between an institution such as the state and a natural substance such as an oak tree. When an acorn grows into an oak tree, there is a persisting subject of change throughout the process – and there is nothing in the development of the state which is analogous to this. Aristotle takes it to be a good of the acorn to realise its nature – to fulfil its potential to mature into an oak tree. The development of the oak tree is to be explained by reference to the good of the oak tree itself. The coming into being of the state, in contrast, is to be explained by reference to the good of its citizens: its claim to be a natural institution is justified because it can and should be explained by reference to *human* nature. What secures the status of the state as the *telos* of the process of social development is that it is the state rather than any other type of association which is able to allow its members to achieve the best life of which they are naturally capable.

The process of social development originates 'in the bare needs of life' and continues in existence 'for the sake of a good life' (1252b30). Each association in the process leading to the state is marked out by what it provides for the members of that association. The family supplied everyday wants. The village 'aimed' at 'something more than the supply of daily needs' and, now, the state exists for the sake of the good life. Aristotle's view of social and political association is firmly teleological: each type of association is explained by reference to what it is *for*, where this is some human good. It does not matter for the naturalness of the state that it is instituted through deliberation and choice – it is because humans are by nature political animals that the state is a natural institution. So, that a particular person's health may be a product of the doctor's skill – and so in some sense artificial – does not mean that his healthy condition is an unnatural one. Similarly, whilst the fact that the state has to be instituted by means of political skill means that in one sense states are artificial, its necessary role in allowing the proper development of its citizens entitles its claim to be a natural association.

The state and *eudaimonia*

Aristotle's argument for the claim that the state is natural does not, then, rely on the account of its development but is rather derived from his view of human nature, according to which people are necessarily such as to be citizens, and hence parts of a state. The state is prior to the individual *by nature* because humans must be part of a state if their needs are to be met. That the state is natural is evident because

> the individual, when isolated, is not self-sufficing; and therefore he is like a part in relation to the whole. But he who is unable to live in society, or who has no need because he is sufficient for himself, must be either a beast or a god: he is no part of a state.
>
> (1253a26–9)

Self-sufficiency (*autarkeia*) here is evidently not a purely economic notion. In *NE* 1.7, Aristotle defines the self-sufficient as 'that which when isolated makes life desirable and lacking in nothing' (1097b14–15) and claims that this is what *eudaimonia* – traditionally translated as 'happiness' or 'the good life' – must be. Humans are not self-sufficient since they need the company of other people and membership of the state if they are to achieve a life that is self-sufficient. Since that life must be complete, and so must not lack determinate types of good, and since not all goods are economic goods, the state's self-sufficiency requires more than that it meet the economic needs of its citizens.

In *Politics* VII.5, when Aristotle is discussing how much land the state should own, he lays down the general condition that it should have the sort of land which will enable it to be most self-sufficient and concludes that 'in extent and magnitude the land ought to be of a size that will enable its inhabitants to live a life of liberal and prudent leisure' (1326b31–3). Thus, a state will be self-sufficient when it can produce enough to enable its citizens to have *leisure*. In VIII.3, Aristotle contrasts leisure with business – the latter is pursued for the sake of the former since it is leisure which contains pleasure and happiness (1338a2–3). A state will certainly need to be self-sufficient economically, but full self-sufficiency will consist in its enabling its citizens to achieve the wide range of goods necessary for *eudaimonia*.

It is part of the definition of the state that it has the purpose of securing the happiness of its citizens. This may seem an anodyne claim to modern ears, to which talk of the pursuit of 'happiness' can sound rather vacuous. There are two aspects of Aristotles' theory, however, which together save it from vacuity and at the same time give the state a proper interest in promoting its citizens' virtue. The first is that Aristotle takes the *purpose* of the state to enable its citizens to lead the good life, and the second is his account of the good life itself.

The reason why it can seem trivial to claim that everybody desires happiness, and that the state has an interest in promoting the happiness of its citizens, is that we now tend to think of happiness as involving merely the satisfaction of desires which the individual already has or happens to acquire. What counts as happiness for one person can differ from what counts as happiness for another and happiness will thus be more or less difficult to achieve depending on the particular aspirations of the individual. If, for instance, someone sees no reason to be virtuous and does not want to act virtuously, then whatever reason there will be for legislating so as to encourage him to act virtuously, this will not be derived from a concern for securing his happiness.

Aristotle duly recognises that people disagree about the nature of happiness. Although everyone agrees that *eudaimonia* is indeed the highest good, there is disagreement about what it actually is:

> For the [general run of men] think that it is some plain and obvious thing, like pleasure, wealth or honour; they differ, however, from one another – and often even the same man identifies it with different things, with health when he is ill, with wealth when he is poor.
>
> (*NE* 1.4, 1095a21–5)

Such disagreement, moreover, is naturally reflected in disagreement about what makes a state a good state:

> those who hold that the well-being of the individual consists in his wealth, also think that riches make the happiness of the whole city, and those who value most highly the life of a tyrant deem that city the happiest which rules over the greatest number; while they who approve an individual for his excellence say that the more excellent a city is, the happier it is.
>
> (*Politics* VII.2, 1324a8–13)

There are two possible responses to such disagreement. One is to take it to be an indication that the question at issue does not admit of an objective answer; the other is to treat the disagreement as something which should be resolved and so to maintain that at least one of the disputing parties must be in error. In most cases of disagreement it will be fairly obvious which of these responses will be the correct one. In the case of evaluative disagreement, however, it is much less obvious – or at least much more controversial – which response is correct.

According to a certain kind of subjectivism, someone is happy if they are contented and they will be contented if (sufficiently many of) the desires they have are satisfied. Rather than things being desirable because they are valuable, they are taken to be valuable just because they are desired – and what things are desired will depend upon the particular circumstances and character of each person. For Aristotle, on the other hand, the question of what is worth pursuing is an objective one, and this is of the greatest importance for his whole political theory. It will be obvious that the state will have a very different function if its purpose is to enable, and encourage, its citizens to lead the good life – where what such a life consists in is taken to be objective and determinable – than if its role is merely to ensure certain economic essentials and to help its citizens to live as they want.

It is important to recognise that Aristotle's project in the *Politics* begins in the ethical treatises. Even though there is, for instance, little or nothing in the *NE* about the organisation and structureof political communities, Aristotle treats the enquiry in which he is engaged there as part of political science. This is precisely because the primary object of that enquiry is the concern of the political scientist: determining the nature of the 'highest end' of action, *eudaimonia*, is the business of 'that which is most truly the master art'; political science.

> For even if the end is the same for a single man and for a state, that of the state seems at all events something greater and more complete both to attain and to preserve; for though it is worthwhile to attain the end merely for one man, it is finer and more godlike to attain it for a nation or for states. These, then, are the ends at which our enquiry, being concerned with politics, aims.
>
> (*NE* I.2, 1094b7–12)

The *NE*, whose task is to determine what it is for an individual to achieve the good life, is thus a prolegomenon to the *Politics*, where Aristotle takes up the question of how to institute the state so as to attain *eudaimonia* for all its citizens. Knowing what the good life consists in is a necessary part of political science. If the very purpose of the state is to enable its citizens to achieve *eudaimonia*, one could hardly properly engage in the project of instituting the state if one were ignorant of what it is to achieve.

In Book I of the *NE*, Aristotle argues that there is a 'final end' of human action and that this is *eudaimonia*. He points out that whilst all actions are performed in order to achieve some good, some goods are merely instrumental, i.e. are desirable only as a means to some further end. Not everything can be chosen for the sake of something else, however, or 'at that rate the process would go on to infinity, so that our desire would be empty and vain' (1094a20–1). So, although we desire some things only because they will be instrumental in achieving other things, there must be some goods which are desired in themselves. To put it in slightly different terms: unless there is *something* which is intrinsically valuable, then nothing will be of any value at all, even instrumentally.

To claim that there must be something which is worth doing or having for itself, however, is one thing. To claim that there is a highest end of action for the sake of which everything else is done is quite another – and it has seemed to some that Aristotle fails to distinguish these claims. The fallacy which threatens is obvious enough, just as if one were to move, for instance, from the proposition that every person has a father to the conclusion that there is only one father and he is the father of everyone.

Fortunately, the threat of fallacy is averted once we understand what Aristotle's claim that *eudaimonia* is the final end of actions amounts to. One way – no doubt the most obvious – of taking such a claim would be to treat it as similar, say, to the hedonist's claim that everything is done for the sake of pleasure. Here the hedonist postulates a simple goal for all actions: take any action at all and one will discover that it was performed in order to get pleasure. If this is the sort of thing which Aristotle intends then he certainly provides us with no reason at all to believe it. In fact, his thesis is not like this at all. He does not need, or intend, to deny that there is a plurality of things which are desirable in themselves. Nor, to support the thesis that all actions are done for the sake of *eudaimonia*, does he need, or intend, to claim that there is only one type of motivation for human action.

Consider this passage from *NE* 1.7:

> We call complete without qualification that which is always desirable in itself and never for the sake of something else. Now such a thing *eudaimonia* is held to be; for this we choose always for itself and never for the sake of something else, but honour, pleasure, reason, and every virtue we choose indeed for themselves (for if nothing resulted from them we should still choose each of them), but we choose them also for the sake of *eudaimonia*, judging that through them we shall be happy.
>
> (1097a35–b5)

Aristotle explicitly allows here that honour, pleasure, reason and the other virtues are chosen for themselves – that if an action will achieve honour or pleasure or is a virtuous action, this is *reason enough* to do it. This is compatible with the thesis that there is a single highest end of action precisely because that end, *eudaimonia*, is not a simple good in the way that, say, pleasure is. *Eudaimonia* is the good *life* and, as such, it is composite, not simple. Honour, pleasure and the rest are parts of the good life because they are themselves of intrinsic value.

Eudaimonia is not something else over and above these things but rather a unified life constituted by them. To achieve it is to attain a life which is 'complete' and lacking in nothing of value. Someone who pursued honour, say, or pleasure to the exclusion of other genuine goods would not achieve happiness because his life would lack those goods and so be incomplete. To lead a happy life, one needs both to recognise what things are of value and to unify the pursuit of these into a coherent whole. This requires the exercise of what Aristotle calls *phronesis* – 'practical wisdom' – which is 'a rational disposition to act with regard to human goods' (*NE* VI.5, 1140b20–1): 'it is thought to be a mark of a man of practical wisdom to be able to deliberate well about what is good and expedient for himself, not in some particular respect, e.g. about what sorts of thing conduce to health or strength, but about what sorts of thing conduce to the good life in general' (1140a25–8).

Determining what is the good life is something about which people can go wrong – most often, perhaps, because they fail to see the value in some class of goods. Practical wisdom requires experience: one cannot judge properly what is valuable and what is not unless one has been suitably trained. For instance, those who cannot see the reason to act virtuously, and so cannot see the value in virtuous action, have not received a proper moral education – just as those who cannot see the value in music or painting have not received a proper aesthetic education. The life of both the vicious person and the philistine will be diminished because there are things of value in which they cannot participate precisely because they are blind to their value. In neither case can one offer an argument to them in order to show their evaluative blindness – what they lack is the ability to understand what it is for something to be just or elegant or whatever, and thus also the appreciation of why it is good to act justly rather than unjustly or for something to be elegant rather than clumsy. The acquisition of such cognitive abilities comes not through argument but through training and experience.

This is why Aristotle lays such stress on the role of the state in determining the education of children: 'since the whole city has one end, it is manifest that education should be one and the same for all, and that it should be public, and not private – not as at present, when everyone looks after his own children separately, and gives them separate instruction of the sort which he thinks best' (VIII.1, 1337a21–6). Since it is better to be virtuous than to be vicious, and so virtue is of value, one cannot be happy unless one is virtuous. A child who is not educated to see the value in virtuous activity will thus be incapable of achieving the good life. Given that anyone's primary interest is to be happy, the interests of the child require that its education should not be left entirely to the vagaries of its parents' evaluative abilities.

Since moral education involves not the inculcation of rules of behaviour but rather the acquisition of evaluative concepts, it needs to be directed by those who already possess those concepts. What is important is not that the child learns to act in certain predetermined ways but that he should come to understand the reasons for virtuous actions and recognise when they are relevant to action. Once he has achieved this, habituation will lead him to take pleasure in virtuous activity for its own sake. It is at this point that he will have become a virtuous agent and so be capable of the good life. Aristotle does not think that virtue is either identical with or sufficient for happiness, but it is its central component.

This is why the state, since its purpose is to enable the happiness of its citizens, has a proper interest in shaping their character rather than simply in directing their actions. It is in doing this that it allows them properly to realise their natures, since the distinctive feature of human nature is the capacity for *phronesis* and thus for virtue. What distinguishes us from other 'gregarious creatures' is that we have speech – and 'the power of speech is intended to set forth the expedient and the inexpedient, and therefore likewise the just and unjust' (I.2, 1253a14–15):

> It is a characteristic of man that he alone has any sense of good and evil, of just and unjust, and the like, and the association of living beings who have this sense makes a family and a state.
>
> (1253a15–18)

Although the capacity to acquire this sense is indeed natural and innate, its realisation requires participation in an association whose very 'principle of order' is the administration of justice (1253a37–9). Only those who are not capable of virtue have no need of the state – which is why if there were anyone who was actually self-sufficient, he would be either 'a beast or a god' (1253a29). Animals are not capable of moral perception and the only activity of the gods is that of the theoretical intellect. Only humans have both social dealings and the ability to regulate their behaviour in accordance with virtue.

For Aristotle, then, the question of how to live well is one which admits of an objective answer and, since the purpose of the state is to enable its citizens to achieve well-being, the best government will be one whose members are best equipped to know how to fulfil that purpose. The role of the government of a state is to act in the interests of the citizens but this need not be the same as acting according to their wishes, since those in power may have a better idea of what is in the interest of the citizens than they do themselves. So, whilst Aristotle is not unsympathetic to allowing 'the many' to take executive decisions, this is not because he thinks that each person has the right to participate in the administration of the state but because, although the individuals of the many may not be good men, 'when they meet together they may be better than the few good men, if regarded not individually but collectively' (III.11, 1281b1–2). A large collection of individuals may exercise better judgement than a small group, even if the individual members of the latter are each wiser than those of the former. Their claim to authority rests on their collective expertise, however, and not on their forming a majority of the citizenry. When it turns out that 'a whole family, or some individual, happens to be so pre-eminent in excellence as to surpass all others, then it is just that they should be the royal family and supreme over all, or that this one citizen should be king' (III.17, 1288a15–19). In practice, however, 'kings have no marked superiority over their subjects' (VII.14, 1332b24–5) and so in the ideal state, 'it is obviously necessary on many grounds that all the citizens alike should take their turn of governing and being governed' (1332b25–7). This accords with the principle of justice that equals should be treated similarly.

Whether the government of the state is in the hands of one person, a few or the many, its function is the same. That is why the true forms of government are monarchy, aristocracy and 'constitutional government': what is crucial is not who rules but that they rule justly, that is, in accordance with the common interest. A constitution is perverted if the rulers govern in their own interests rather than those of the citizens as a whole. This is as possible when everyone participates in government as when only a few do. What is important is not how the government is chosen but rather that those who form the government should have the expertise to govern in the common interest of the citizens.

Political science and the structure of the *Politics*

In *Physics* II.3, Aristotle says that in order to achieve understanding of something, one needs to be able to provide four different types of explanation for it: what its form is, what it is made of, what it is for and what brings it about. In the *Politics*, as we have seen, Aristotle provides three of these explanations for the state. The form of the state is its constitution, its matter is its citizenry and its purpose is the well-being of its citizens. For Aristotle, however, political science is not just a 'science' (an *epistēmē*) but an 'art' (a *technē*[3]). According to *NE* VI.4, a *technē* is 'a productive disposition involving a true account' (1140a10). To acquire the political art, then, is to acquire a productive disposition – that is, a disposition to produce something. All arts are concerned with 'contriving and considering how something may come into being which is capable of either being or not being' (*NE* VI.4, 1140a10–13). In possessing an art, someone is capable of producing something: a doctor can produce health because he possesses the art of medicine, someone who knows the art of building can produce houses – and the political scientist can produce states. The acquisition of that disposition is the result of coming to understand the relevant subject-matter, which is why an art involves the possession of a true account. The political scientist must have an account of his subject-matter, the state, and so needs to know what it is for something to be a state, what constitutes it and, crucially, what its purpose is. He does not, of course, need to study the cause of the state, since it is the political scientist himself

---

[3] Plural: *technai*.

who brings states into existence – although he *does* need to know the causes of changes to states, especially those which bring about their destruction.

This helps us to understand how the structure of the *Politics* is determined by the requirements of political science. For, although its status as a work of Aristotle has never been seriously questioned, many have doubted that it constitutes a single, coherent work. Certainly, the text as we now have it breaks off abruptly, suggesting at least that the last part of the work has been lost. In the current edition, the books are given in the order in which they are preserved in the manuscripts – but it is quite possible that this order is not Aristotle's own, and determining how the books might be arranged so as to provide the best argumentative shape has provided a focus for scholarly ingenuity since the Renaissance.

What has seemed most worrying has been the inclusion of Books IV–VI after Book III, thus postponing the discussion of the ideal state promised at the end of that book. Some have suggested placing Books VII–VIII after Book III, so that the latter's closing announcement of the intention to consider the nature of the ideal state can be immediately fulfilled. Against this, however, Aristotle has, in his account of monarchy in Book III provided the beginnings of a classification of different types of constitution and it is not unnatural to see a continuation of this in Books IV and VI. Given this, one might contemplate transposing Books V and VI so that the constitutional taxonomy is not interrupted by the discussion of revolution, but this appears to be blocked by the reference back in VI.I to the discussion of 'the destruction and preservation of states'.

One influential explanation for these apparent difficulties in the text as it has come down to us was provided by Werner Jaeger in his attempt to chart the development of Aristotle's thought. Whereas most Aristotelian scholarship has operated on the principle that, as far as possible, one should read Aristotle's works so that they are consistent with one another, Jaeger's book was a systematic attempt to provide an account of Aristotle as a philosopher whose ideas developed over time. In his chapter on the *Politics*, Jaeger argued that the first version of the work was a treatise on the ideal state, in the tradition of Plato's *Republic* and *Laws*, and consisted of what are now Books II–III and VII–VIII. At a later stage, having conducted the research for the compilation of the various constitutions, Aristotle added the 'empirical' books IV–VI and a new introduction (Book I) for the resulting 'general theory of politics'. Whereas the earlier books are governed by the 'search for absolute norms and standards', the later books 'develop the theory of actual historical states, or rather of the manifold varieties, diseases and treatments of actual states'.[4]

Now, it is certainly true that there is much in Books IV–VI that is initially puzzling if we try to see the argument of those books as part of the project of determining how the state should be instituted if it is to enable all its citizens to attain well-being. At times, Aristotle's arguments can even be reminiscent of *The Prince*. He spells out, for instance, the measures that will be necessary if the tyrant is to maintain the stability of his tyranny:

> All that we have said may be said to be summed up under three heads, which answer to the three aims of the tyrant. These are the humiliation of his subjects, for he knows that a mean-spirited man will not conspire against anybody: the creation of mistrust among them; for a tyrant is not overthrown until men begin to have confidence in one another, and this is the reason why tyrants are at war with the good; they are under the idea that their power is endangered by them, not only because they will not be ruled despotically, but also because they are loyal to one another, and to other men: [third], he desires that his subjects shall be incapable of action . . .

> (V.II, 1314a14–23)

The tone of this chapter is not that of a theorist merely charting the behaviour of tyrants, but of a political scientist reporting what the tyrant must do if his rule is to survive. It would seem that the project of determining how to constitute the ideal state of virtuous and happy citizens is quite far from the front of Aristotle's mind in these middle books.

Nevertheless, whilst the argument of Books IV–VI does not bear directly on the question of what form the best state will have, there is still good reason why they should have a place in a treatise whose principal aim is to show how that goal is to be achieved.

[4] W. W. Jaeger, *Aristotle: Fundamentals of the History of his Development*, translated by R. Robinson, 2nd edition (Oxford, 1948), pp. 264; 269.

Aristotle himself provides a justification for the concerns of those books at the beginning of Book IV. 'It is the business of a single art or science', he says, 'to consider all that appertains to a single subject', and gives as an example of this the fact that the gymnastics trainer should not only be able to determine the correct mode of training for the man who desires the best form of body but also 'what common form of training is adapted to the great majority of men'. Indeed, 'if a man does not desire the best habit of body, or the greatest skill in gymnastics, which might be attained by him, still the trainer . . . should be able to impart any lower degree of either'. Similarly, not only should the political scientist consider 'what government is best and what sort it must be, to be most in accordance with our aspirations, if there were no external impediment' but he should know what would be the best state in particular circumstances, when these are not ideal. Moreover, just as the trainer will know what to do with someone who does not want to do even the best he can, the political scientist will also know, for any state, how it may be constituted 'under any given conditions and, when formed, how it may be longest preserved' – even when that state is not even the best under the circumstances, 'but of an inferior type'.

One can now place the *Politics* within Aristotle's general theory of *technai*. In the discussion of capacities in *Metaphysics* IX, he distinguishes between rational and non-rational capacities. Whereas something which possesses a non-rational capacity is thereby capable only of producing one sort of effect, someone who possesses an art, a rational capacity, can produce contrary effects: 'e.g. the hot is capable only of heating, but the medical art can produce both disease and health' (*Met.* IX.2, 1046b6–7). The reason for this, Aristotle explains, 'is that science is an account, and the same account explains both a thing and its privation, only not in the same way . . . therefore such sciences must deal with contraries, although the one in virtue of itself and the other accidentally' (1046b7–9; 10–11). This may sound obscure but its point is straightforward enough. A doctor is someone who knows the art of healing and so has such knowledge as will enable him to make people healthy. To have this, however, requires that he know how the human body works and such knowledge will enable him to affect it as he wishes. Of course, he only possesses this knowledge in order to be able to produce health and not to produce disease – and so the science is related to the first in itself and the second only accidentally – but the same body of knowledge will give him the capacity to produce either.

The political scientist's task, as we have seen, is to produce a state which will enable its citizens to achieve *eudaimonia. That* goal is set by the study of human well-being in the *NE* and is reinforced by the argument of the first book of the *Politics*. In order to achieve that goal, the political scientist must know how states work and, in particular, what are the causes of their preservation and destruction. Unless he has that knowledge, he will not be able to produce constitutional structures which will allow any created state to survive. This knowledge is gained, as one should expect, from the study of the behaviour of actual states – just as medical knowledge is obtained from studying the workings of actual bodies. The political scientist may not actually *use* the knowledge of how to institute a tyranny and keep the tyrant in power but, if he has the expertise to create the best state, or even the best state in any particular circumstances, then he will have that knowledge. Any insistence on distinguishing between the concerns of the outer books and those of the inner books distorts the nature of political science as Aristotle conceives it.

This allows us to accept the general structure of the work as it stands. In the first three books, Aristotle sets out the nature of the state in accordance with the requirements of the scientist: he cites its form, matter and purpose. In Book II, in accordance with his general method, he considers earlier attempts to specify what the state should be like and criticises these. Before starting out on his own account of the constitution and attributes of the ideal state, he canvasses the data provided by the study of the actual constitutions which his school had collected, and thereby offers material which is necessary for understanding how states work. With this done, he is able to proceed to work out how the state should be instituted if it is best to fulfil its function of providing the necessary context in which its citizens can achieve *eudaimonia*. Indeed, we can now see that the *Politics* does just what Aristotle says he will do at the end of *NE* x.9.[5] There is no conflict between

---

[5] Cited above, pp. xiv–xv.

the concerns of the middle books and those of the books which surround them. Throughout the *Politics* Aristotle is engaged in the single enterprise of understanding the workings of states, and of the people who are part of them, so that the political scientist can securely determine how the state should be constituted if it is to satisfy the purpose which human nature requires of it.

Note on the texts

The text of the *Nicomachean Ethics* is that provided by I. Bywater (Oxford, 1894). The text of the *Politics* is that of A. Dreizehnter, *Aristoteles Politik, eingeleitet, kritisch herausgegeben und mit Indices versehen* (Munich, 1970). The text of the *Constitution of Athens* is that of F. G. Kenyon (Oxford, 1920). Where a reading different from these texts has been preferred, this has been signalled.

Principal events

A guide to further reading

Aristotle

Two short introductions to Aristotle are
J. L. Ackrill, *Aristotle the Philosopher* (Oxford, 1981)
J. Barnes, *Aristotle* (Oxford, 1982).
Longer and more detailed accounts of his thought include
W. K. C. Guthrie, *Aristotle: an Encounter* (Cambridge, 1981)
J. Lear, *Aristotle: the Desire to Understand* (Cambridge, 1988)
and, most substantially,
T. H. Irwin, *Aristotle's First Principles* (Oxford, 1988).
Introductory articles on central aspects of his philosophy can be
found in
J. Barnes (ed.), *The Cambridge Companion to Aristotle* (Cambridge,
    1995).
Translations of all of Aristotle's surviving works are given in
J. Barnes (ed.), *The Complete Works of Aristotle: the Revised Oxford
    Translation* (Princeton, 1984).

Aristotle's ethical theory

Aristotle's political theory is secured upon the argument of his
ethical works. Two good translations of the *Nicomachean Ethics* are
W. D. Ross (revised by J. L. Ackrill and J. O. Urmson), *Aristotle's
    Nicomachean Ethics* (Oxford, 1980), and
T. H. Irwin, *Aristotle, Nicomachean Ethics* (Indianapolis, 1985).

A translation of, and commentary on, part of the *Eudemian Ethics* are given in

M. J. Woods, *Aristotle's Eudemian Ethics, Books I, II and VIII* (Oxford, 1982).

An important consideration of the relationship between Aristotle's ethical treatises is

A. Kenny, *The Aristotelian Ethics* (Oxford, 1978).

A much fuller guide to work on Aristotle's ethics can be found in the bibliography to

S. Everson (ed.), *Ethics* (Cambridge, 1966).

General studies of Aristotle's ethical theory include

W. F. R. Hardie, *Aristotle's Ethical Theory*, 2nd edition (Oxford, 1980)

S. Broadie, *Ethics with Aristotle* (Oxford, 1991).

Two collections of articles are

A. O. Rorty (ed.), *Essays on Aristotle's Ethics* (Berkeley/Los Angeles/London, 1980)

J. Barnes, M. Schofield and R. Sorabji (eds.), *Articles on Aristotle*, II, *Ethics and Politics* (London, 1977).

Discussions of Aristotle's method include

G. E. L. Owen, 'Tithenai ta phainomena', in his *Logic, Science and Dialectic* (London, 1986)

J. Barnes, 'Aristotle and the Methods of Ethics', *Revue Internationale de Philosophie* 34 (1980), 490–511

T. H. Irwin, 'Aristotle's Methods of Ethics', in D. J. O'Meara (ed.), *Studies in Aristotle* (Washington, 1981).

The relation between the *Politics* and Aristotle's ethical theory is discussed in

A. W. H. Adkins, 'The Connection between Aristotle's *Ethics* and *Politics*', *Political Theory* 12 (1984), 29–49.

Eudaimonia

Aristotle's account of *eudaimonia* has received an enormous amount of critical attention. Key discussions include

J. L. Ackrill, 'Aristotle on *Eudaimonia*', in Rorty, 15–33

R. Kraut, *Aristotle on the Human Good* (Princeton, 1989)

A. Kenny, *Aristotle on the Perfect Life* (Oxford, 1992)

T. Nagel, 'Aristotle on *Eudaimonia*', in Rorty, 7–14

J. McDowell, 'The Role of *Eudaimonia* in Aristotle's Ethics', in Rorty, 359–76

K. V. Wilkes, 'The Good Man and the Good for Man in Aristotle's *Ethics*', in Rorty, 341–57.

Virtue

J. O. Urmson, 'Aristotle's Doctrine of the Mean', in Rorty, 157–70

R. Hursthouse, 'A False Doctrine of the Mean', *Proceedings of the Aristotelian Society* 81 (1980–1), 57–72

D. S. Hutchison, *The Virtues of Aristotle* (London, 1986)

N. Sherman, *The Fabric of Character* (Oxford, 1989).

The *Politics*

A magisterial commentary on the *Politics* is

W. L. Newman, *The Politics of Aristotle*, 4 vols. (Oxford, 1887–1902)

R. Robinson, *Aristotle's Politics Books III and IV* (Oxford, 1962) contains both a translation of those books and a philosophical commentary on them.

Two introductions to the work are

E. Barker, *The Politics of Aristotle* (Oxford, 1946)

R. G. Mulgan, *Aristotle's Political Theory* (Oxford, 1977).

Many useful articles can be found in

D. Keyt and F. D. Miller (eds.), *A Companion to Aristotle's Politics* (Oxford, 1991).

G. Patzig (ed.), *Aristotle's Politik* (Göttingen, 1990) contains the proceedings of the 11th Symposium Aristotelicum, whose subject was the *Politics*.

A major general study of the work is

F. D. Miller, Jr, *Nature, Justice and Rights in Aristotle's Politics* (Oxford, 1995).

The structure of the *Politics* is discussed in

Werner Jaeger, *Aristotle: Fundamentals of the History of his Development*, translated by R. Robinson, 2nd edition (Oxford, 1948), ch. 10

W. D. Ross, *Aristotle* (Oxford, 1949), ch. 8

C. Rowe, 'Aims and Methods in Aristotle's *Politics*', in Keyt and Miller, 57-74

T. H. Irwin, 'Moral Science and Political Theory in Aristotle', in P. A. Cartledge and F. D. Harvey (eds.), *Crux* (London, 1985), 150–68

C. H. Kahn, 'The Normative Structure of Aristotle's *Politics*', in Patzig, 369–84.

The state

A. C. Bradley, 'Aristotle's Conception of the State', in Keyt and Miller, 13–56

C. Johnson, *Aristotle's Theory of the State* (London, 1990)

O. Murray, '*Polis* and *Politeia* in Aristotle', *Acts of the Copenhagen Polis Centre* 1 (Copenhagen, 1993).

Aristotle's arguments for the naturalness of the state are discussed in

D. Keyt, 'Three Basic Theorems in Aristotle's *Politics*', in Keyt and Miller, 118–41

S. Everson, 'Aristotle on the Foundations of the State', *Political Studies* 36 (1988), 89–101.

For the related claim that humans are political animals, see

R. G. Mulgan, 'Aristotle's Doctrine that Man is a Political Animal', *Hermes* 102 (1974), 438–45

W. Kullman, 'Man as a Political Animal in Aristotle', in Keyt and Miller, 94–117

J. M. Cooper, 'Political Animals and Civic Friendship', in Patzig, 220–41.

Property and distributive justice

T. H. Irwin, 'Aristotle's Defence of Private Property', in Keyt and Miller, 200–25

F. D. Miller, 'Aristotle on Property Rights', in J. Anton and A. Preus (eds.), *Essays in Ancient Greek Philosophy*, essay 4 (Albany, 1990)

H. Kelsen, 'Aristotle's Doctrine of Justice', in *What is Justice?* (Berkeley, 1957)

D. Keyt, 'Distributive Justice in Aristotle's *Ethics* and *Politics*', *Topoi* 4 (1985), 23–45

W. von Leyden, *Aristotle on Equality and Justice* (London, 1985)

M. C. Nussbaum, 'Nature, Function and Capability', in Patzig, 152–86, which contains a potent reply by David Charles.

The ideal state

J. Bluhm, 'The Place of the "Polity" in Aristotle's Theory of the Ideal State', *Journal of Politics* 24 (1962), 743–53

G. Huxley, 'On Aristotle's Best State', in P. A. Cartledge and F. D. Harvey (eds.), *Crux* (London, 1985), 139–49

P. A. Van der Waerdt, 'Kingship and Philosophy in Aristotle's Best Regime', *Phronesis* 30 (1985), 249–73.

Liberty

J. Barnes, 'Aristotle and Political Liberty', in Patzig, 249–63, which also contains a reply by Richard Sorabji

W. T. Schmid, 'Aristotle on Choice: Liberty and the *Polis*', *Paideia* 2 (1978), 182–95.

Law and natural law

M. Hamburger, *Morals and Law: the Growth of Aristotle's Legal Theory*, new edition (New York, 1971)

W. von Leyden, 'Aristotle and the Concept of Law', *Philosophy* 42 (1967), 1–19

F. D. Miller, 'Aristotle on Nature, Law and Justice', *University of Dayton Review*, Special Issue on Aristotle, 19 (1988–9), 57–69

D. N. Schroeder, 'Aristotle on Law', *Polis* 4 (1981), 17–31

M. S. Shellens, 'Aristotle on Natural Law', *Natural Law Forum* 4 (1959), 72–100.

Democracy

W. Kullman, 'Equality in Aristotle's Political Thought', in I. Kajanto (ed.), *Equality and Inequality of Man in Ancient*

Thought, *Commentationes Humanarum Litterarum* 75 (1984), 31–44

R. G. Mulgan, 'Aristotle and the Democratic Conception of Freedom', *Auckland Classical Studies Presented to E. M. Blaiklock* (Auckland, 1970), 95–111

R. G. Mulgan, 'Aristotle's Analysis of Oligarchy and Democracy', in Keyt and Miller, 307–22

D. Winthrop, 'Aristotle on Participatory Democracy', *Polity* 11 (1978), 151–71.

Citizenship

R. Develin, 'The Good Man and the Good Citizen in Aristotle's *Politics*', *Phronesis* 18 (1973), 71–9

C. Johnson, 'Who is Aristotle's Citizen?', *Phronesis* 29 (1984), 73–90.

Slavery

W. Ambler, 'Aristotle's Understanding of the Naturalness of the City', *Review of Politics* 47 (1985), 163–85

W. Fortenbaugh, 'Aristotle on Slaves and Women', in Barnes *et al.*, 135–9

M. Schofield, 'Ideology and Philosophy in Aristotle's Theory of Slavery', in Patzig, 1–27

N. D. Smith, 'Aristotle's Theory of Natural Slavery', in Keyt and Miller, 142–55.

Economics

M. I. Finley, 'Aristotle and Economic Analysis', in Barnes *et al.*, 140–58

T. J. Lewis, 'Acquisition and Anxiety: Aristotle's Case Against the Market', *Canadian Journal of Economics* 11 (1978), 69–90

S. Meikle, 'Aristotle and the Political Economy of the *Polis*', *Journal of Hellenic Studies* 99 (1979), 57–73

S. Meikle, 'Aristotle and Exchange Value', in Keyt and Miller, 156–81

K. Polanyi, 'Aristotle Discovers the Economy', in K. Polanyi,

C. M. Arensberg and H. W. Pearson (eds.), *Trade and Market in the Early Empires* (Glencoe, 1957), 64–94

J. Soudek, 'Aristotle's Theory of Exchange: an Enquiry into the Origin of Economic Analysis', *Proceedings of the American Philosophical Society* 96 (1952), 45–75.

The *Constitution of Athens*

P. J. Rhodes, *A Commentary on the 'Athenaion Politeia'* (Oxford, 1981)

K. von Fritz and E. Kapp, *Aristotle's 'Constitution of Athens' and Related Texts* (New York, 1950)

J. M. Moore, *Aristotle and Xenophon on Democracy and Oligarchy* (London, 1975)

J. J. Keaney, 'The Structure of Aristotle's *Athenaion Politeia*', *Harvard Studies in Classical Philology* 67 (1963), 115–46

J. J. Keaney, 'The Date of Aristotle's *Athenaion Politeia*', *Historia* 19 (1970), 326–36

K. von Fritz, 'The Composition of Aristotle's *Constitution of Athens* and the So-Called Draconian Constitution', *Classical Philology* 49 (1954), 73–93.

Other constitutions

R. E. De Laix, 'Aristotle's Conception of the Spartan Constitution', *Journal of the History of Philosophy* 12 (1974), 21–30

G. Huxley, 'Crete in Aristotle's *Politics*', *Greek, Roman and Byzantine Studies* 12 (1971), 505–15.

The *Nicomachean Ethics*
BOOK X, CHAPTER 9

If these matters and the excellences, and also friendship and pleasure, have been dealt with sufficiently in outline, are we to suppose that our programme has reached its end? Surely, as is said, where there are things to be done the end is not to survey and recognise the various things, but rather to do them; with regard to 1179ᵇ1 excellence, then, it is not enough to know, but we must try to have and use it, or try any other way there may be of becoming good. Now if arguments were in themselves enough to make men good, they would justly, as Theognis says, have won very great rewards, and such rewards should have been provided; but as 5 things are, while they seem to have power to encourage and stimulate the generous-minded among the young, and to make a character which is gently born, and a true lover of what is noble, ready to be possessed by excellence, they are not able to encourage the man to nobility and goodness. For these do not by nature obey 10 the sense of shame, but only fear, and do not abstain from bad acts because of their baseness but through fear of punishment; living by passion they pursue their own pleasures and the means to them, and avoid the opposite pains, and have not even a conception of what is noble and truly pleasant, since they have never tasted it. What argument would remould such people? It is hard, 15 if not impossible, to remove by argument the traits that have long since been incorporated in the character; and perhaps we must be content if, when all the influences by which we are thought to become good are present, we get some tincture of excellence.

Now some think that we are made good by nature, others by 20 habituation, others by teaching. Nature's part evidently does not depend on us, but as a result of some divine causes is present in those who are truly fortunate; while argument and teaching, we may suspect, are not powerful with all men, but the soul of the student must first have been cultivated by means of habits for 25 noble joy and noble hatred, like earth which is to nourish the seed. For he who lives as passion directs will not hear argument that dissuades him, nor understand it if he does; and how can we persuade one in such a state to change his ways? And in general passion seems to yield not to argument but to force. The character, then, must somehow be there already with a kinship to excellence, 30 loving what is noble and hating what is base.

But it is difficult to get from youth up a right training for

excellence if one has not been brought up under right laws; for
35 to live temperately and hardily is not pleasant to most people,
especially when they are young. For this reason their nurture and
occupation should be fixed by law; for they will not be painful
1180ᵃ1 when they have become customary. But it is surely not enough
that when they are young they should get the right nurture and
attention; since they must, even when they are grown up, practise
and be habituated to them, we shall need laws for this as well,
and generally speaking to cover the whole of life; for most people
5 obey necessity rather than argument, and punishments rather than
what is noble.

This is why some think that legislators ought to stimulate men to
excellence and urge them forward by the motive of the noble, on
the assumption that those who have been well advanced by the
formation of habits will attend to such influences; and that punishments and penalties should be imposed on those who disobey and
10 are of inferior nature, while the incurably bad should be completely banished. A good man (they think), since he lives with his
mind fixed on what is noble, will submit to argument, while a bad
man, whose desire is for pleasure, is corrected by pain like a beast
of burden. This is, too, why they say the pains inflicted should be
those that are most opposed to the pleasures such men love.

However that may be, if (as we have said) the man who is to
15 be good must be well trained and habituated, and go on to spend
his time in worthy occupations and neither willingly nor unwill-
ingly do bad actions, and if this can be brought about if men live
in accordance with a sort of intellect and right order, provided
this has force – if this be so, the paternal command indeed has
not the required force or compulsive power (nor in general has
20 the command of one man, unless he be a king or something
similar), but the law *has* compulsive power, while it is at the same
time an account proceeding from a sort of practical wisdom and
intellect. And while people hate *men* who oppose their impulses,
even if they oppose them rightly, the law in its ordaining of what
is good is not burdensome.

25 In the Spartan state alone, or almost alone, the legislator seems
to have paid attention to questions of nurture and occupations; in
most states such matters have been neglected, and each man lives
as he pleases, Cyclops-fashion, 'to his own wife and children deal-

ing law'.[1] Now it is best that there should be a public and proper care for such matters; but if they are neglected by the community it would seem right for each man to help his children and friends towards excellence, and that they should be able, or at least choose, to do this.[2]

It would seem from what has been said that he can do this better if he makes himself capable of legislating. For public care is plainly effected by laws, and good care by good laws; whether written or unwritten would seem to make no difference, nor whether they are laws providing for the education of individuals or of groups – any more than it does in the case of music or gymnastics and other such pursuits. For as in cities laws and character have force, so in households do the injunctions and the habits of the father, and these have even more because of the tie of blood and the benefits he confers; for the children start with a natural affection and disposition to obey. Further, individual education has an advantage over education in common, as individual medical treatment has; for while in general rest and abstinence from food are good for a man in a fever, for a particular man they may not be; and a boxer presumably does not prescribe the same style of fighting to all his pupils. It would seem, then, that the detail is worked out with more precision if the care is particular to individuals; for each person is more likely to get what suits his case.

But individuals[3] can be best cared for by a doctor or gymnastic instructor or anyone else who has the universal knowledge of what is good for every one or for people of a certain kind (for the sciences both are said to be, and are, concerned with what is common); not but what some particular detail may perhaps be well looked after by an unscientific person, if he has studied accurately in the light of experience what happens in each case, just as some people seem to be their own best doctors, though they could give no help to anyone else. None the less, it will perhaps be agreed that if a man does wish to become master of an art or science he must go to the universal, and come to know it as well

---

[1] *Odyssey*, IX 114.
[2] Placing καὶ δρᾶν αὐτὸ δύνασθαι after συμβάλλεσθαι.
[3] Reading καθ᾽ ἕνα.

as possible; for, as we have said, it is with this that the sciences are concerned.

25 And surely he who wants to make men, whether many or few, better by his care must try to become capable of legislating, if it is through laws that we can become good. For to get anyone whatever – anyone who is put before us – into the right condition is not for the first chance comer; if anyone can do it, it is the man who knows, just as in medicine and all other matters which give scope for care and practical wisdom.

Must we not, then, next examine whence or how one can learn
30 how to legislate? Is it, as in all other cases, from statesmen? Certainly it was thought to be a part of statesmanship. Or is a difference apparent between statesmanship and the other sciences and faculties? In the others the same people are found offering to teach the faculties and practising them, e.g. doctors or painters; but while the sophists profess to teach politics, it is practised not by any of them but by the politicians, who would seem to do so by
1181ᵃ1 dint of a certain faculty and experience rather than of thought; for they are not found either writing or speaking about such matters (though it were a nobler occupation perhaps than composing speeches for the law-courts and the assembly), nor again are they found to have made statesmen of their own sons or any other of
5 their friends. But it was to be expected that they should if they could; for there is nothing better than such a skill that they could have left to their cities, or could choose to have for themselves, or, therefore, for those dearest to them. Still, experience seems to contribute not a little; else they could not have become politicians
10 by familiarity with politics; and so it seems that those who aim at knowing about the art of politics need experience as well.

But those of the sophists who profess the art seem to be very far from teaching it. For, to put the matter generally, they do not even know what kind of thing it is nor what kinds of things it is about; otherwise they would not have classed it as identical with
15 rhetoric or even inferior to it, nor have thought it easy to legislate by collecting the laws that are thought well of; they say it is possible to select the best laws, as though even the selection did not demand intelligence and as though right judgement were not the greatest thing, as in matters of music. For while people experienced in any department judge rightly the works produced in it,

6

and understand by what means or how they are achieved, and 20
what harmonises with what, the inexperienced must be content if
they do not fail to see whether the work has been well or ill made –
as in the case of painting. Now laws are as it were the works of
the political art; how then can one learn from them to be a legis- 1181ᵇ1
lator, or judge which are best? Even medical men do not seem to
be made by a study of text-books. Yet people try, at any rate, to
state not only the treatments, but also how particular classes of
people can be cured and should be treated – distinguishing the
various states; but while this seems useful to experienced people, 5
to the ignorant it is valueless. Surely, then, while collections of
laws, and of constitutions also, may be serviceable to those who
can study them and judge what is good or bad and what enactments suit what circumstances, those who go through such collections without a practised faculty will not have right judgement
(unless it be spontaneous), though they may perhaps become more 10
intelligent in such matters.

Now our predecessors have left the subject of legislation to us
unexamined; it is perhaps best, therefore, that we should ourselves
study it, and in general study the question of the constitution, in
order to complete to the best of our ability the philosophy of
human nature. First, then, if anything has been said well in detail 15
by earlier thinkers, let us try to review it; then in the light of the
constitutions we have collected let us study what sorts of influence
preserve and destroy states, and what sorts preserve or destroy
the particular kinds of constitution, and to what causes it is due
that some are well and others ill administered. When these have 20
been studied we shall perhaps be more likely to see which constitution is best, and how each must be ordered, and what laws and
customs it must use. Let us make a beginning of our discussion.

The Politics

Politics

B. JOWETT

BOOK I

1 · Every state is a community of some kind, and every community is 1252^a1 established with a view to some good; for everyone always acts in order to obtain that which they think good. But, if all communities aim at some good, the state or political community, which is the highest of all, and which embraces all the rest, aims at good in a 5 greater degree than any other, and at the highest good.

Some people think that the qualifications of a statesman, king, householder, and master are the same, and that they differ, not in kind, but only in the number of their subjects. For example, the ruler 10 over a few is called a master; over more, the manager of a household; over a still larger number, a statesman or king, as if there were no difference between a great household and a small state. The distinction which is made between the king and the statesman is as follows: When the government is personal, the ruler is a king; when, according 15 to the rules of the political science, the citizens rule and are ruled in turn, then he is called a statesman.

But all this is a mistake, as will be evident to any one who considers the matter according to the method which has hitherto guided us. As in other departments of science, so in politics, the compound should always be resolved into the simple elements or least parts of the whole. We must therefore look at the elements of which the state is 20 composed, in order that we may see in what the different kinds of rule differ from one another, and whether any scientific result can be attained about each one of them.

2 · He who thus considers things in their first growth and origin,

25 whether a state or anything else, will obtain the clearest view of them. In the first place there must be a union of those who cannot exist without each other; namely, of male and female, that the race may continue (and this is a union which is formed, not of choice, but because, in common with other animals and with plants, mankind

30 have a natural desire to leave behind them an image of themselves), and of natural ruler and subject, that both may be preserved. For that which can foresee by the exercise of mind is by nature lord and master, and that which can with its body give effect to such foresight is a subject, and by nature a slave; hence master and slave have the same

1252^b1 interest. Now nature has distinguished between the female and slave. For she is not niggardly, like the smith who fashions the Delphian knife for many uses; she makes each thing for a single use, and every instrument is best made when intended for one and not for many

5 uses. But among barbarians no distinction is made between women and slaves, because there is no natural ruler among them: they are a community of slaves, male and female. That is why the poets say, –

> It is meet that Hellenes should rule over barbarians;[1]

as if they thought that the barbarian and the slave were by nature one.

10   Out of these two relationships the first thing to arise is the family, and Hesiod is right when he says, –

> First house and wife and an ox for the plough,[2]

for the ox is the poor man's slave. The family is the association established by nature for the supply of men's everyday wants, and the members of it are called by Charondas, 'companions of the cup-

15 board', and by Epimenides the Cretan, 'companions of the manger'. But when several families are united, and the association aims at something more than the supply of daily needs, the first society to be formed is the village. And the most natural form of the village appears to be that of a colony from the family, composed of the children and grandchildren, who are said to be 'suckled with the same milk'. And this is the reason why Hellenic states were originally governed by kings; because the Hellenes were under royal rule before they came

20 together, as the barbarians still are. Every family is ruled by the eldest, and therefore in the colonies of the family the kingly form of

---

[1] Euripides, *Iphigeneia in Aulis*, 1400.   [2] Hesiod, *Works and Days*, 405.

government prevailed because they were of the same blood. As Homer says:

> Each one gives law to his children and to his wives.[1]

For they lived dispersedly, as was the manner in ancient times. That is why men say that the Gods have a king, because they themselves either are or were in ancient times under the rule of a king. For they imagine not only the forms of the Gods but their ways of life to be like their own.

When several villages are united in a single complete community, large enough to be nearly or quite self-sufficing, the state comes into existence, originating in the bare needs of life, and continuing in existence for the sake of a good life. And therefore, if the earlier forms of society are natural, so is the state, for it is the end of them, and the nature of a thing is its end. For what each thing is when fully developed, we call its nature, whether we are speaking of a man, a horse, or a family. Besides, the final cause and end of a thing is the best, and to be self-sufficing is the end and the best.

Hence it is evident that the state is a creation of nature, and that man is by nature a political animal. And he who by nature and not by mere accident is without a state, is either a bad man or above humanity; he is like the

> Tribeless, lawless, hearthless one,[2]

whom Homer denounces – the natural outcast is forthwith a lover of war; he may be compared to an isolated piece at draughts.

Now, that man is more of a political animal than bees or any other gregarious animals is evident. Nature, as we often say, makes nothing in vain, and man is the only animal who has the gift of speech. And whereas mere voice is but an indication of pleasure or pain, and is therefore found in other animals (for their nature attains to the perception of pleasure and pain and the intimation of them to one another, and no further), the power of speech is intended to set forth the expedient and inexpedient, and therefore likewise the just and the unjust. And it is a characteristic of man that he alone has any sense of good and evil, of just and unjust, and the like, and the association of living beings who have this sense makes a family and a state.

25

30

1253ᵃ1

5

10

15

---

[1] Homer, *Odyssey*, IX 114–15.   [2] Homer, *Iliad*, IX 63.

Further, the state is by nature clearly prior to the family and to the
20 individual, since the whole is of necessity prior to the part; for
example, if the whole body be destroyed, there will be no foot or hand,
except homonymously, as we might speak of a stone hand; for when
destroyed the hand will be no better than that. But things are defined
by their function and power; and we ought not to say that they are the
same when they no longer have their proper quality, but only that they
25 are homonymous. The proof that the state is a creation of nature and
prior to the individual is that the individual, when isolated, is not self-
sufficing; and therefore he is like a part in relation to the whole. But
he who is unable to live in society, or who has no need because he is
sufficient for himself, must be either a beast or a god: he is no part of a
30 state. A social instinct is implanted in all men by nature, and yet he
who first founded the state was the greatest of benefactors. For man,
when perfected, is the best of animals, but, when separated from law
and justice, he is the worst of all; since armed injustice is the more
dangerous, and he is equipped at birth with arms, meant to be used by
35 intelligence and excellence, which he may use for the worst ends.
That is why, if he has not excellence, he is the most unholy and the
most savage of animals, and the most full of lust and gluttony. But
justice is the bond of men in states; for the administration of justice,
which is the determination of what is just, is the principle of order in
political society.

1253ᵇ1 3 · Seeing then that the state is made up of households, before
speaking of the state we must speak of the management of the
household. The parts of household management correspond to the
persons who compose the household, and a complete household
5 consists of slaves and freemen. Now we should begin by examining
everything in its fewest possible elements; and the first and fewest
possible parts of a family are master and slave, husband and wife,
father and children. We have therefore to consider what each of these
three relations is and ought to be: – I mean the relation of master and
servant, the marriage relation (the conjunction of man and wife has no
10 name of its own), and thirdly, the paternal relation (this also has no
proper name). And there is another element of a household, the so-
called art of getting wealth, which, according to some, is identical with
household management, according to others, a principal part of it; the
nature of this art will also have to be considered by us.

Let us first speak of master and slave, looking to the needs of 15 practical life and also seeking to attain some better theory of their relation than exists at present. For some are of the opinion that the rule of a master is a science, and that the management of a household, and the mastership of slaves, and the political and royal rule, as I was saying at the outset, are all the same. Others affirm that the rule of a 20 master over slaves is contrary to nature, and that the distinction between slave and freeman exists by convention only, and not by nature; and being an interference with nature is therefore unjust.

4 · Property is a part of the household, and the art of acquiring property is a part of the art of managing the household; for no man can live well, or indeed live at all, unless he is provided with 25 necessaries. And as in the arts which have a definite sphere the workers must have their own proper instruments for the accomplishment of their work, so it is in the management of a household. Now instruments are of various sorts; some are living, others lifeless; in the rudder, the pilot of a ship has a lifeless, in the look-out man, a living instrument; for in the arts the servant is a kind of instrument. Thus, 30 too, a possession is an instrument for maintaining life. And so, in the arrangement of the family, a slave is a living possession, and property a number of such instruments; and the servant is himself an instrument for instruments. For if every instrument could accomplish its 35 own work, obeying or anticipating the will of others, like the statues of Daedalus, or the tripods of Hephaestus, which, says the poet,

of their own accord entered the assembly of the Gods;[1]

if, in like manner, the shuttle would weave and the plectrum touch the lyre, chief workmen would not want servants, nor masters slaves. Now 1254ª1 the instruments commonly so called are instruments of production, whilst a possession is an instrument of action. From a shuttle we get something else besides the use of it, whereas of a garment or of a bed there is only the use. Further, as production and action are different 5 in kind, and both require instruments, the instruments which they employ must likewise differ in kind. But life is action and not production, and therefore the slave is the minister of action. Again, a possession is spoken of as a part is spoken of; for the part is not only a part of something else, but wholly belongs to it; and this is also true of 10

[1] Homer, *Iliad*, XVIII 369.

a possession. The master is only the master of the slave; he does not belong to him, whereas the slave is not only the slave of his master, but wholly belongs to him. Hence we see what is the nature and office of a
15 slave; he who is by nature not his own but another's man, is by nature a slave; and he may be said to be another's man who, being a slave, is also a possession. And a possession may be defined as an instrument of action, separable from the possessor.

5 · But is there any one thus intended by nature to be a slave, and for whom such a condition is expedient and right, or rather is not all slavery a violation of nature?
20 There is no difficulty in answering this question, on grounds both of reason and of fact. For that some should rule and others be ruled is a thing not only necessary, but expedient; from the hour of their birth, some are marked out for subjection, others for rule.
25 And there are many kinds both of rulers and subjects (and that rule is the better which is exercised over better subjects – for example, to rule over men is better than to rule over wild beasts; for the work is better which is executed by better workmen, and where one man rules and another is ruled, they may be said to have a work); for in all things which form a composite whole and which are made up of parts,
30 whether continuous or discrete, a distinction between the ruling and the subject element comes to light. Such a duality exists in living creatures, originating from nature as a whole; even in things which have no life there is a ruling principle, as in a musical mode. But perhaps this is matter for a more popular investigation. A living
35 creature consists in the first place of soul and body, and of these two, the one is by nature the ruler and the other the subject. But then we must look for the intentions of nature in things which retain their nature, and not in things which are corrupted. And therefore we must study the man who is in the most perfect state both of body and soul, for in him we shall see the true relation of the two: although in bad or
1254^{b}1 corrupted natures the body will often appear to rule over the soul, because they are in an evil and unnatural condition. At all events we may firstly observe in living creatures both a despotical and a
5 constitutional rule; for the soul rules the body with a despotical rule, whereas the intellect rules the appetites with a constitutional and royal rule. And it is clear that the rule of the soul over the body, and of the mind and the rational element over the passionate, is natural and

expedient; whereas the equality of the two or the rule of the inferior is always hurtful. The same holds good of animals in relation to men; for 10 tame animals have a better nature than wild and all tame animals are better off when they are ruled by man; for then they are preserved. Again, the male is by nature superior, and the female inferior; and the one rules, and the other is ruled; this principle, of necessity, extends 15 to all mankind. Where then there is such a difference as that between soul and body, or between men and animals (as in the case of those whose business is to use their body, and who can do nothing better), the lower sort are by nature slaves, and it is better for them as for all 20 inferiors that they should be under the rule of a master. For he who can be, and therefore is, another's, and he who participates in reason enough to apprehend, but not to have, is a slave by nature. Whereas the lower animals cannot even apprehend reason,[a] they obey their passions. And indeed the use made of slaves and of tame animals is not very different; for both with their bodies minister to the needs of 25 life. Nature would like to distinguish between the bodies of freemen and slaves, making the one strong for servile labour, the other upright, and although useless for such services, useful for political life in the 30 arts both of war and peace. But the opposite often happens – that some have the souls and others have the bodies of freemen. And doubtless if men differed from one another in the mere forms of their bodies as much as the statues of the Gods do from men, all would 35 acknowledge that the inferior class should be slaves of the superior. And if this is true of the body, how much more just that a similar distinction should exist in the soul? But the beauty of the body is seen, whereas the beauty of the soul is not seen. It is clear, then, that some 1255[a]1 men are by nature free, and others slaves, and that for these latter slavery is both expedient and right.

6 · But that those who take the opposite view have in a certain way right on their side, may be easily seen. For the words slavery and slave are used in two senses. There is a slave or slavery by convention as 5 well as by nature. The convention is a sort of agreement – the convention by which whatever is taken in war is supposed to belong to the victors. But this right many jurists impeach, as they would an orator who brought forward an unconstitutional measure: they detest

---

[a] Reading λόγου.

the notion that, because one man has the power of doing violence and
10 is superior in brute strength, another shall be his slave and subject.
Even among philosophers there is a difference of opinion. The origin
of the dispute, and what makes the views invade each other's territory,
is as follows: in some sense excellence, when furnished with means,
15 has actually the greatest power of exercising force: and as superior
power is only found where there is superior excellence of some kind,
power seems to imply excellence, and the dispute to be simply one
about justice (for it is due to one party identifying*a* justice with
goodwill, while the other identifies it with the mere rule of the
20 stronger). If these views are thus set out separately, the other views
have no force or plausibility against the view that the superior in
excellence ought to rule, or be master. Others, clinging, as they think,
simply to a principle of justice (for convention is a sort of justice),
assume that slavery in accordance with the custom of war is just, but at
the same moment they deny this. For what if the cause of the war be
25 unjust? And again, no one would ever say that he is a slave who is
unworthy to be a slave. Were this the case, men of the highest rank
would be slaves and the children of slaves if they or their parents
chanced to have been taken captive and sold. That is why people do
not like to call themselves slaves, but confine the term to foreigners.
30 Yet, in using this language, they really mean the natural slave of whom
we spoke at first; for it must be admitted that some are slaves
everywhere, others nowhere. The same principle applies to nobility.
People regard themselves as noble everywhere, and not only in their
own country, but they deem foreigners noble only when at home,
35 thereby implying that there are two sorts of nobility and freedom, the
one absolute, the other relative. The Helen of Theodectes says:

> Who would presume to call me servant who am on both sides
> sprung from the stem of the Gods?

What does this mean but that they distinguish freedom and slavery,
1255b1 noble and humble birth, by the two principles of good and evil? They
think that as men and animals beget men and animals, so from good
men a good man springs. Nature intends to do this often but cannot.

We see then that there is some foundation for this difference of
5 opinion, and that all are not either slaves by nature or freemen by
nature, and also that there is in some cases a marked distinction

---

a Reading τὸ . . . εὔνοιαν δοκεῖν.

between the two classes, rendering it expedient and right for the one
to be slaves and the others to be masters: the one practising
obedience, the other exercising the authority and lordship which
nature intended them to have. The abuse of this authority is injurious
to both: for the interests of part and whole, of body and soul, are the 10
same, and the slave is a part of the master, a living but separated part
of his bodily frame. Hence, where the relation of master and slave
between them is natural they are friends and have a common interest,
but where it rests merely on convention and force the reverse is true. 15

7 · The previous remarks are quite enough to show that the rule of a
master is not constitutional rule, and that all the different kinds of rule
are not, as some affirm, the same as each other. For there is one rule
exercised over subjects who are by nature free, another over subjects
who are by nature slaves. The rule of a household is a monarchy, for
every house is under one head: whereas constitutional rule is a 20
government of freemen and equals. The master is not called a master
because he has science, but because he is of a certain character, and
the same remark applies to the slave and the freeman. Still there may
be a science for the master and a science for the slave. The science of
the slave would be such as the man of Syracuse taught, who made 25
money by instructing slaves in their ordinary duties. And such a
knowledge may be carried further, so as to include cookery and
similar menial arts. For some duties are of the more necessary, others
of the more honourable sort; as the proverb says, 'slave before slave,
master before master'. But all such branches of knowledge are servile. 30
There is likewise a science of the master, which teaches the use of
slaves; for the master as such is concerned, not with the acquisition,
but with the use of them. Yet this science is not anything great or
wonderful; for the master need only know how to order that which the
slave must know how to execute. Hence those who are in a position 35
which places them above toil have stewards who attend to their
households while they occupy themselves with philosophy or with
politics. But the art of acquiring slaves, I mean of justly acquiring
them, differs both from the art of the master and the art of the slave,
being a species of hunting or war. Enough of the distinction between
master and slave.

8 · Let us now inquire into property generally, and into the art of 1256ᵃ1

getting wealth, in accordance with our usual method, for a slave has been shown to be a part of property. The first question is whether the art of getting wealth is the same as the art of managing a household or
5 a part of it, or instrumental to it; and if the last, whether in the way that the art of making shuttles is instrumental to the art of weaving, or in the way that the casting of bronze is instrumental to the art of the statuary, for they are not instrumental in the same way, but the one provides tools and the other material; by the material I mean the substratum out of which any work is made; thus wool is the material of
10 the weaver, bronze of the statuary. Now it is easy to see that the art of household management is not identical with the art of getting wealth, for the one uses the material which the other provides. For the art which uses household stores can be no other than the art of household management. There is, however, a doubt whether the art of getting wealth is a part of household management or a distinct art.
15 If the getter of wealth has to consider whence wealth and property can be procured, but there are many sorts of property and riches, then are husbandry, and the care and provision of food in general, parts of the art of household management or distinct arts? Again, there are many
20 sorts of food, and therefore there are many kinds of lives both of animals and men; they must all have food, and the differences in their food have made differences in their ways of life. For of beasts, some are gregarious, others are solitary; they live in the way which is best
25 adapted to sustain them, accordingly as they are carnivorous or herbivorous or omnivorous: and their habits are determined for them by nature with regard to their ease and choice of food. But the same things are not naturally pleasant to all of them; and therefore the lives of carnivorous or herbivorous animals further differ among them-
30 selves. In the lives of men too there is a great difference. The laziest are shepherds, who lead an idle life, and get their subsistence without trouble from tame animals; their flocks having to wander from place to place in search of pasture, they are compelled to follow them,
35 cultivating a sort of living farm. Others support themselves by hunting, which is of different kinds. Some, for example, are brigands, others, who dwell near lakes or marshes or rivers or a sea in which there are fish, are fishermen, and others live by the pursuit of birds or wild beasts. The greater number obtain a living from the cultivated
40 fruits of the soil. Such are the modes of subsistence which prevail among those whose industry springs up of itself, and whose food is

not acquired by exchange and retail trade – there is the shepherd, and 1256^b1
husbandman, the brigand, the fisherman, the hunter. Some gain a
comfortable maintenance out of two employments, eking out the
deficiencies of one of them by another: thus the life of a shepherd may 5
be combined with that of a brigand, the life of a farmer with that of a
hunter. Other modes of life are similarly combined in any way which
the needs of men may require. Property, in the sense of a bare
livelihood, seems to be given by nature herself to all, both when they
are first born, and when they are grown up. For some animals bring 10
forth, together with their offspring, so much food as will last until they
are able to supply themselves; of this the vermiparous or oviparous
animals are an instance; and the viviparous animals have up to a
certain time a supply of food for their young in themselves, which is
called milk. In like manner we may infer that, after the birth of 15
animals, plants exist for their sake, and that the other animals exist for
the sake of man,^a the tame for use and food, the wild, if not all, at least
the greater part of them, for food, and for the provision of clothing
and various instruments. Now if nature makes nothing incomplete, 20
and nothing in vain, the inference must be that she has made all
animals for the sake of man. And so, from one point of view, the art of
war is a natural art of acquisition, for the art of acquisition includes
hunting, an art which we ought to practise against wild beasts, and
against men who, though intended by nature to be governed, will not 25
submit; for war of such a kind is naturally just.

Of the art of acquisition then there is one kind which by nature is a
part of the management of a household, in so far as the art of
household management must either find ready to hand, or itself
provide, such things necessary to life, and useful for the community of 30
the family or state, as can be stored. They are the elements of true
riches; for the amount of property which is needed for a good life is
not unlimited, although Solon in one of his poems says that

> No bound to riches has been fixed for man.

But there is a boundary fixed, just as there is in the other arts; for the 35
instruments of any art are never unlimited, either in number or size,
and riches may be defined as a number of instruments to be used in a
household or in a state. And so we see that there is a natural art of

---

^a Retaining ζῷα τῶν ἀνθρώπων.

acquisition which is practised by managers of households and by statesmen, and the reason for this.

40   9 · There is another variety of the art of acquisition which is commonly and rightly called an art of wealth-getting, and has in fact
1257ᵃ1   suggested the notion that riches and property have no limit. Being nearly connected with the preceding, it is often identified with it. But though they are not very different, neither are they the same. The kind already described is given by nature, the other is gained by
5   experience and art.

Let us begin our discussion of the question with the following considerations. Of everything which we possess there are two uses: both belong to the thing as such, but not in the same manner, for one is the proper, and the other the improper use of it. For example, a
10   shoe is used for wear, and is used for exchange; both are uses of the shoe. He who gives a shoe in exchange for money or food to him who wants one, does indeed use the shoe as a shoe, but this is not its proper use, for a shoe is not made to be an object of barter. The same may be
15   said of all possessions, for the art of exchange extends to all of them, and it arises at first from what is natural, from the circumstance that some have too little, others too much. Hence we may infer that retail trade is not a natural part of the art of getting wealth; had it been so, men would have ceased to exchange when they had enough. In the
20   first community, indeed, which is the family, this art is obviously of no use, but it begins to be useful when the society increases. For the members of the family originally had all things in common; later, when the family divided into parts, the parts shared in many things, and different parts in different things, which they had to give in exchange for what they wanted, a kind of barter which is still practised
25   among barbarous nations who exchange with one another the necessaries of life and nothing more; giving and receiving wine, for example, in exchange for corn, and the like. This sort of barter is not part of the wealth-getting art and is not contrary to nature, but is
30   needed for the satisfaction of men's natural wants. The other form of exchange grew, as might have been inferred, out of this one. When the inhabitants of one country became more dependent on those of another, and they imported what they needed, and exported what they had too much of, money necessarily came into use. For the various
35   necessaries of life are not easily carried about, and hence men agreed

to employ in their dealing with each other something which was intrinsically useful and easily applicable to the purposes of life, for example, iron, silver, and the like. Of this the value was at first measured simply by size and weight, but in process of time they put a 40 stamp upon it, to save the trouble of weighing and to mark the value.

When the use of coin had once been discovered, out of the barter of 1257[b]1 necessary articles arose the other art of wealth-getting, namely, retail trade; which was at first probably a simple matter, but became more complicated as soon as men learned by experience whence and by what exchanges the greatest profit might be made. Originating in the 5 use of coin, the art of getting wealth is generally thought to be chiefly concerned with it, and to be the art which produces riches and wealth, having to consider how they may be accumulated. Indeed, riches is assumed by many to be only a quantity of coin, because the arts of getting wealth and retail trade are concerned with coin. Others 10 maintain that coined money is a mere sham, a thing not natural, but conventional only, because, if the users substitute another commodity for it, it is worthless, and because it is not useful as a means to any of the necessities of life, and, indeed, he who is rich in coin may often be in want of necessary food. But how can that be wealth of which a man 15 may have a great abundance and yet perish with hunger, like Midas in the fable, whose insatiable prayer turned everything that was set before him into gold?

Hence men seek after a better notion of riches and of the art of getting wealth, and they are right. For natural riches and the natural art of wealth-getting are a different thing; in their true form they are 20 part of the management of a household; whereas retail trade is the art of producing wealth, not in every way, but by exchange. And it is thought to be concerned with coin; for coin is the unit of exchange and the limit of it. And there is no bound to the riches which spring from this art of wealth-getting. As in the art of medicine there is no 25 limit to the pursuit of health, and as in the other arts there is no limit to the pursuit of their several ends, for they aim at accomplishing their ends to the uttermost (but of the means there is a limit, for the end is always the limit), so, too, in this art of wealth-getting there is no limit of the end, which is riches of the spurious kind, and the acquisition of 30 wealth. But the art of wealth-getting which consists in household management, on the other hand, has a limit;[a] the unlimited acquisi-

---

[a] Reading $\alpha \check{\upsilon}$ for $o\check{\upsilon}$.

tion of wealth is not its business. And, therefore, from one point of view, all riches must have a limit; nevertheless, as a matter of fact, we find the opposite to be the case; for all getters of wealth increase their
35 hoard of coin without limit. The source of the confusion is the near connexion between the two kinds of wealth-getting; in both, the instrument is the same, although the use is different, and so they pass into one another; for each is a use of the same property, but with a difference; accumulation is the end in the one case, but there is a further end in the other. Hence some persons are led to believe that getting wealth is the object of household management, and the whole
40 idea of their lives is that they ought either to increase their money without limit, or at any rate not to lose it. The origin of this disposition
1258ᵃ1 in men is that they are intent upon living only, and not upon living well; and, as their desires are unlimited, they also desire that the means of gratifying them should be without limit. Those who do aim at a good life seek the means of obtaining bodily pleasures; and, since the enjoyment of these appears to depend on property, they are
5 absorbed in getting wealth; and so there arises the second species of wealth-getting. For, as their enjoyment is in excess, they seek an art which produces the excess of enjoyment; and, if they are not able to supply their pleasures by the art of getting wealth, they try other
10 causes, using in turn every faculty in a manner contrary to nature. The quality of courage, for example, is not intended to make wealth, but to inspire confidence; neither is this the aim of the general's or of the physician's art; but the one aims at victory and the other at health. Nevertheless, some men turn every quality or art into a means of getting wealth; this they conceive to be the end, and to the promotion of the end they think all things must contribute.
15   Thus, then, we have considered the art of wealth-getting which is unnecessary, and why men want it; and also the necessary art of wealth-getting, which we have seen to be different from the other, and to be a natural part of the art of managing a household, concerned with the provision of food, not, however, like the former kind, unlimited, but having a limit.

10 · And we have found the answer to our original question,
20 Whether the art of getting wealth is the business of the manager of a household and of the statesman or not their business? – viz. that

wealth is presupposed by them. For as political science does not make men, but takes them from nature and uses them, so too nature provides them with earth or sea or the like as a source of food. At this stage begins the duty of the manager of a household, who has to order the things which nature supplies – he may be compared to the weaver who has not to make but to use wool, and to know, too, what sort of wool is good and serviceable or bad and unserviceable. Were this otherwise, it would be difficult to see why the art of getting wealth is a part of the management of a household and the art of medicine not; for surely the members of a household must have health just as they must have life or any other necessity. The answer is that as from one point of view the master of the house and the ruler of the state have to consider about health, from another point of view not they but the physician has to; so in one way the art of household management, in another way the subordinate art, has to consider about wealth. But, strictly speaking, as I have already said, the means of life must be provided beforehand by nature; for the business of nature is to furnish food to that which is born, and the food of the offspring is always what remains over of that from which it is produced. That is why the art of getting wealth out of fruits and animals is always natural.

There are two sorts of wealth-getting, as I have said; one is a part of household management, the other is retail trade: the former is necessary and honourable, while that which consists in exchange is justly censured; for it is unnatural, and a mode by which men gain from one another. The most hated sort, and with the greatest reason, is usury, which makes a gain out of money itself, and not from the natural object of it. For money was intended to be used in exchange, but not to increase at interest. And this term interest, which means the birth of money from money, is applied to the breeding of money because the offspring resembles the parent. That is why of all modes of getting wealth this is the most unnatural.

11 · Enough has been said about the theory of wealth-getting; we will now proceed to the practical part. Such things may be studied by a free man, but will only be practised from necessity. The useful parts of wealth-getting are, first, the knowledge of live-stock – which are most profitable, and where, and how – as for example, what sort of horses or sheep or oxen or any other animals are most likely to give a

15 return. A man ought to know which of these pay better than others,
and which pay best in particular places, for some do better in one
place and some in another. Secondly, husbandry, which may be either
tillage or planting, and the keeping of bees and of fish, or fowl, or of
20 any animals which may be useful to man. These are the divisions of
the true or proper art of wealth-getting and come first. Of the other,
which consists in exchange, the first and most important division is
commerce (of which there are three kinds – ship-owning, the
conveyance of goods, exposure for sale – these again differing as they
25 are safer or more profitable), the second is usury, the third, service for
hire – of this, one kind is employed in the mechanical arts, the other is
unskilled and bodily labour. There is still a third sort of wealth-
getting intermediate between this and the first or natural mode which
is partly natural, but is also concerned with exchange, viz. the
30 industries that make their profit from the earth, and from things
growing from the earth which, although they bear no fruit, are
nevertheless profitable; for example, the cutting of timber and all
mining. The art of mining itself has many branches, for there are
various kinds of things dug out of the earth. Of the several divisions of
wealth-getting I now speak generally; a minute consideration of them
35 might be useful in practice, but it would be tiresome to dwell upon
them at greater length now.

Those occupations are most truly arts in which there is the least
element of chance; they are the meanest in which the body is most
maltreated, the most servile in which there is the greatest use of the
body, and the most illiberal in which there is the least need of
excellence.

Works have been written upon these subjects by various persons;
1259ᵃ1 for example, by Chares the Parian, and Apollodorus the Lemnian,
who have treated of Tillage and Planting, while others have treated of
other branches; anyone who cares for such matters may refer to their
writings. It would be well also to collect the scattered stories of the
5 ways in which individuals have succeeded in amassing a fortune; for
all this is useful to persons who value the art of getting wealth. There
is the anecdote of Thales the Milesian and his financial scheme,
which involves a principle of universal application, but is attributed to
him on account of his reputation for wisdom. He was reproached for
10 his poverty, which was supposed to show that philosophy was of no
use. According to the story, he knew by his skill in the stars while it

was yet winter that there would be a great harvest of olives in the coming year; so, having a little money, he gave deposits for the use of all the olive-presses in Chios and Miletus, which he hired at a low price because no one bid against him. When the harvest-time came, 15 and many were wanted all at once and of a sudden, he let them out at any rate which he pleased, and made a quantity of money. Thus he showed the world that philosophers can easily be rich if they like, but that their ambition is of another sort. He is supposed to have given a striking proof of his wisdom, but, as I was saying, his scheme for 20 getting wealth is of universal application, and is nothing but the creation of a monopoly. It is an art often practised by cities when they are in want of money; they make a monopoly of provisions.

There was a man of Sicily, who, having money deposited with him, bought up all the iron from the iron mines; afterwards, when the 25 merchants from their various markets came to buy, he was the only seller, and without much increasing the price he gained 200 per cent. Which when Dionysius heard, he told him that he might take away his money, but that he must not remain in Syracuse, for he thought that 30 the man had discovered a way of making money which was injurious to his own interests. He made the same discovery as Thales; they both contrived to create a monopoly for themselves. And statesmen as well ought to know these things; for a state is often as much in want of money and of such schemes for obtaining it as a household, or even 35 more so; hence some public men devote themselves entirely to finance.

12 · Of household management we have seen that there are three parts – one is the rule of a master over slaves, which has been discussed already, another of a father, and the third of a husband. A husband and father, we saw, rules over wife and children, both free, but the rule differs, the rule over his children being a royal, over his 1259^b1 wife a constitutional rule. For although there may be exceptions to the order of nature, the male is by nature fitter for command than the female, just as the elder and full-grown is superior to the younger and more immature. But in most constitutional states the citizens rule and 5 are ruled by turns, for the idea of a constitutional state implies that the natures of the citizens are equal, and do not differ at all. Nevertheless, when one rules and the other is ruled we endeavour to create a difference of outward forms and names and titles of respect, which

may be illustrated by the saying of Amasis about his foot-pan.[1] The
10 relation of the male to the female is always of this kind. The rule of a
father over his children is royal, for he rules by virtue both of love and
of the respect due to age, exercising a kind of royal power. And
therefore Homer has appropriately called Zeus 'father of Gods and
15 men',[2] because he is the king of them all. For a king is the natural
superior of his subjects, but he should be of the same kin or kind with
them, and such is the relation of elder and younger, of father and son.

13 · Thus it is clear that household management attends more to
men than to the acquisition of inanimate things, and to human
excellence more than to the excellence of property which we call
20 wealth, and to the excellence of freemen more than to the excellence
of slaves. A question may indeed be raised, whether there is any
excellence at all in a slave beyond those of an instrument and of a
servant – whether he can have the excellences of temperance,
25 courage, justice, and the like; or whether slaves possess only bodily
services. And, whichever way we answer the question, a difficulty
arises; for, if they have excellence, in what will they differ from
freemen? On the other hand, since they are men and share in rational
principle it seems absurd to say that they have no excellence. A similar
30 question may be raised about women and children, whether they too
have excellences; ought a woman to be temperate and brave and just,
and is a child to be called temperate, and intemperate, or not? So in
general we may ask about the natural ruler, and the natural subject,
whether they have the same or different excellences. For if a noble
35 nature is equally required in both, why should one of them always
rule, and the other always be ruled? Nor can we say that this is a
question of degree, for the difference between ruler and subject is a
difference of kind, which the difference of more and less never is. Yet
how strange is the supposition that the one ought, and that the other
ought not, to have excellence! For if the ruler is intemperate and
1260ᵃ1 unjust, how can he rule well? if the subject, how can he obey well? If
he is licentious and cowardly, he will certainly not do what is fitting. It
is evident, therefore, that both of them must have a share of

---

[1] Herodotus, II 172. Amasis, a sixth-century king of Egypt, was despised by his subjects
because of his humble birth. He put up a statue of a god which they worshipped and then
told them that it had been made out of a foot-bath.

[2] Homer, *Iliad*, I 544.

excellence, but varying as natural subjects also vary among themselves. Here the very constitution of the soul has shown us the way; in it one part naturally rules, and the other is subject, and the excellence 5 of the ruler we maintain to be different from that of the subject – the one being the excellence of the rational, and the other of the irrational part. Now, it is obvious that the same principle applies generally, and therefore almost all things rule and are ruled according to nature. But the kind of rule differs – the freeman rules over the slave after another manner from that in which the male rules over the female, or the man 10 over the child; although the parts of the soul are present in all of them, they are present in different degrees. For the slave has no deliberative faculty at all; the woman has, but it is without authority, and the child has, but it is immature. So it must necessarily be supposed to be with the excellences of character also; all should partake of them, but only 15 in such manner and degree as is required by each for the fulfilment of his function. Hence the ruler ought to have excellence of character in perfection, for his function, taken absolutely, demands a master artificer, and reason is such an artificer; the subjects, on the other hand, require only that measure of excellence which is proper to each of them. Clearly, then, excellence of character belongs to all of them; 20 but the temperance of a man and of a woman, or the courage and justice of a man and of a woman, are not, as Socrates maintained, the same; the courage of a man is shown in commanding, of a woman in obeying. And this holds of all other excellences, as will be more clearly seen if we look at them in detail, for those who say generally 25 that excellence consists in a good disposition of the soul, or in doing rightly, or the like, only deceive themselves. Far better than such definitions is the mode of speaking of those who, like Gorgias, enumerate the excellence. All classes must be deemed to have their special attributes; as the poet says of women.

Silence is a woman's glory,[1] 30

but this is not equally the glory of man. The child is imperfect, and therefore obviously his excellence is not relative to himself alone, but to the perfect man and to his teacher, and in like manner the excellence of the slave is relative to a master. Now we determined that a slave is useful for the wants of life, and therefore he will obviously

---

[1] Sophocles, *Ajax*, 293.

35 require only so much excellence as will prevent him from failing in his function through cowardice or lack of self-control. Someone will ask whether, if what we are saying is true, excellence will not be required also in the artisans, for they often fail in their work through the lack of self-control. But is there not a great difference in the two cases? For

40 the slave shares in his master's life; the artisan is less closely connected with him, and only attains excellence in proportion as he

1260^{b}1 becomes a slave. The meaner sort of mechanic has a special and separate slavery; and whereas the slave exists by nature, not so the shoemaker or other artisan. It is manifest, then, that the master ought to be the source of such excellence in the slave, and not a mere possessor of the art of mastership which trains the slave in his

5 functions. That is why they are mistaken who forbid us to converse with slaves and say that we should employ command only, for slaves stand even more in need of admonition than children.

So much for this subject; the relations of husband and wife, father

10 and child, their several excellences, what in their intercourse with one another is good, and what is evil, and how we may pursue the good and escape the evil, will have to be discussed when we speak of the different forms of government. For, inasmuch as every family is a part of a state, and these relationships are the parts of a family, and the excellence of the part must have regard to the excellence of the whole,

15 women and children must be trained by education with an eye to the constitution, if the excellences of either of them are supposed to make any difference in the excellences of the state. And they must make a

20 difference: for the children grow up to be citizens, and half the free persons in a state are women.

Of these matters, enough has been said; of what remains, let us speak at another time. Regarding, then, our present enquiry as complete, we will make a new beginning. And, first, let us examine the various theories of a perfect state.

BOOK II

27 1 · Our purpose is to consider what form of political community is best of all for those who are most able to realize their ideal of life. We must therefore examine not only this but other constitutions, both

such as actually exist in well-governed states, and any theoretical ₃₀ forms which are held in esteem, so that what is good and useful may be brought to light. And let no one suppose that in seeking for something beyond them we are anxious to make a sophistical display at any cost; we only undertake this inquiry because all the constitu- ₃₅ tions which now exist are faulty.

We will begin with the natural beginning of the subject. The members of a state must either have all things or nothing in common, or some things in common and some not. That they should have nothing in common is clearly impossible, for the constitution is a community, and must at any rate have a common place – one city will be in one place, and the citizens are those who share in that one city. 1261ᵃ1 But should a well-ordered state have all things, as far as may be, in common, or some only and not others? For the citizens might conceivably have wives and children and property in common, as ₅ Socrates proposes in the *Republic* of Plato. Which is better, our present condition, or one conforming to the law laid down in the *Republic?*

2 · There are many difficulties in the community of women. And the ₁₀ principle on which Socrates rests the necessity of such an institution evidently is not established by his arguments. Further, as a means to the end which he ascribes to the state, the scheme, taken literally, is impracticable, and how we are to interpret it is nowhere precisely stated. I am speaking of the supposition from which the argument of ₁₅ Socrates proceeds, that it is best for the whole state to be as unified as possible.[1] Is it not obvious that a state may at length attain such a degree of unity as to be no longer a state? – since the nature of a state is to be a plurality, and in tending to greater unity, from being a state, it becomes a family, and from being a family, an individual; for the ₂₀ family may be said to be more one than the state, and the individual than the family. So that we ought not to attain this greatest unity even if we could, for it would be the destruction of the state. Again, a state is not made up only of so many men, but of different kinds of men; for similars do not constitute a state. It is not like a military alliance. The ₂₅ usefulness of the latter depends upon its quantity even where there is no difference in quality (for mutual protection is the end aimed at),

[1] Plato, *Republic,* v 462.

just as a greater weight depresses the scale more (in like manner, a state differs from a nation, when the nation has not its population organized in villages, but lives an Arcadian sort of life); but the
30 elements out of which a unity is to be formed differ in kind. That is why the principle of reciprocity, as I have already remarked in the *Ethics*,[1] is the salvation of states. Even among freemen and equals this is a principle which must be maintained, for they cannot all rule together, but must change at the end of a year or some other period of
35 time or in some order of succession. The result is that upon this plan they all govern; just as if shoemakers and carpenters were to exchange their occupations, and the same persons did not always continue shoemakers and carpenters. And since it is better that this should be so in politics as well, it is clear that while there should be continuance of the same persons in power where this is possible, yet where this is
1261ᵇ1 not possible by reason of the natural equality of the citizens, and at the same time it is just that all should share in the government (whether to govern be a good thing or a bad), – in these cases this is imitated.[a] Thus the one party rules and the others are ruled in turn, as if they
5 were no longer the same persons. In like manner when they hold office there is a variety in the offices held. Hence it is evident that a city is not by nature one in that sense which some persons affirm; and that what is said to be the greatest good of cities is in reality their destruction; but surely the good of things must be that which
10 preserves them. Again, from another point of view, this extreme unification of the state is clearly not good; for a family is more self-sufficing than an individual, and a city than a family, and a city only comes into being when the community is large enough to be self-sufficing. If then self-sufficiency is to be desired, the lesser degree of
15 unity is more desirable than the greater.

3 · But, even supposing that it were best for the community to have the greatest degree of unity, this unity is by no means proved to follow from the fact of all men saying 'mine' and 'not mine' at the same
20 instant of time, which, according to Socrates, is the sign of perfect unity in a state.[2] For the word 'all' is ambiguous. If the meaning be

[1] *NE*, v 5.   [2] *Rep.*, v 462c.

---

[a] The text is uncertain.

that every individual says 'mine' and 'not mine' at the same time, then perhaps the result at which Socrates aims may be in some degree accomplished; each man will call the same person his own son and the same person his own wife, and so of his property and of all that falls to his lot. This, however, is not the way in which people would speak who had their wives and children in common; they would say 'all' but 25 not 'each'. In like manner their property would be described as belonging to them, not severally but collectively. There is an obvious fallacy in the term 'all': like some other words, 'both', 'odd', 'even', it is ambiguous, and even in abstract argument becomes a source of 30 logical puzzles. That all persons call the same thing 'mine' in the sense in which each does so may be a fine thing, but it is impracticable; or if the words are taken in the other sense, such a unity in no way conduces to harmony. And there is another objection to the proposal. For that which is common to the greatest number has the least care bestowed upon it. Everyone thinks chiefly of his own, hardly at all of the common interest; and only when he is himself concerned 35 as an individual. For besides other considerations, everybody is more inclined to neglect something which he expects another to fulfil; as in families many attendants are often less useful than a few. Each citizen will have a thousand sons who will not be his sons individually, but anybody will be equally the son of anybody, and will therefore be 40 neglected by all alike. Further, upon this principle, every one will use 1262ª1 the word 'mine' of one who is prospering or the reverse, however small a fraction he may himself be of the whole number; the same boy will be my son, and so and so's son, the son of each of the thousand, or whatever be the number of the citizens; and even about this he will not 5 be positive; for it is impossible to know who chanced to have a child, or whether, if one came into existence, it has survived. But which is better – for each to say 'mine' in this way, making a man the same relation to two thousand or ten thousand citizens, or to use the word 'mine' as it is now used in states? For usually the same person is called by one man his own son whom another calls his own brother or cousin 10 or kinsman – blood relation or connexion by marriage – either by himself or of some relation of his, and yet another his clansman or tribesman; and how much better is it to be the real cousin of somebody than to be a son after Plato's fashion! Nor is there any way of preventing brothers and children and fathers and mothers from 15 sometimes recognizing one another; for children are born like their

parents, and they will necessarily be finding indications of their relationship to one another. Geographers declare such to be the fact;
20 they say that in part of Upper Libya, where the women are common, nevertheless the children who are born are assigned to their respective fathers on the ground of their likeness. And some women, like the females of other animals – for example, mares and cows – have a strong tendency to produce offspring resembling their parents, as was the case with the Pharsalian mare called Honest Wife.

25 4 · Other difficulties, against which it is not easy for the authors of such a community to guard, will be assaults and homicides, voluntary as well as involuntary, quarrels and slanders, all of which are most unholy acts when committed against fathers and mothers and near relations, but not equally unholy when there is no relationship.
30 Moreover, they are much more likely to occur if the relationship is unknown than if it is known and, when they have occurred, the customary expiations of them can be made if the relationship is known, but not otherwise. Again, how strange it is that Socrates, after having made the children common, should hinder lovers from carnal
35 intercourse only, but should permit love and familiarities between father and son or between brother and brother, than which nothing can be more unseemly, since even without them love of this sort is improper.[1] How strange, too, to forbid intercourse for no other reason than the violence of the pleasure, as though the relationship of
40 father and son or of brothers with one another made no difference.

This community of wives and children seem better suited to the
1262^{b}1 husbandmen than to the guardians, for if they have wives and children in common, they will be bound to one another by weaker ties, as a subject class should be, and they will remain obedient and not rebel. In a word, the result of such a law would be just the opposite of that
5 which good laws ought to have, and the intention of Socrates in making these regulations about women and children would defeat itself. For friendship we believe to be the greatest good of states and what best preserves them against revolutions; and Socrates particularly praises the unity of the state which seems and is said by him to be
10 created by friendship. But the unity which he commends would be like that of the lovers in the *Symposium*, who, as Aristophanes says,

[1] *Rep.*, III 403A–B.

desire to grow together in the excess of their affection, and from being two to become one, in which case one or both would certainly perish.[1] Whereas in a state having women and children common, love will be 15 diluted; and the father will certainly not say 'my son', or the son 'my father'. As a little sweet wine mingled with a great deal of water is imperceptible in the mixture, so, in this sort of community, the idea of relationship which is based upon these names will be lost; there is no reason why the so-called father should care about the son, or the son 20 about the father, or brothers about one another. Of the two qualities which chiefly inspire regard and affection – that a thing is your own and that it is precious – neither can exist in such a state as this.

Again, the transfer of children as soon as they are born from the 25 rank of husbandmen or of artisans to that of guardians, and from the rank of guardians into a lower rank, will be very difficult to arrange;[2] the givers or transferrers cannot but know whom they are giving and transferring, and to whom. And the previously mentioned assaults, 30 unlawful loves, homicides, will happen more often among them; for they will no longer call the members of the class they have left brothers, and children, and fathers, and mothers, and will not, therefore, be afraid of committing any crimes by reason of consanguinity. Touching the community of wives and children, let this be 35 our conclusion.

5 · Next let us consider what should be our arrangements about property: should the citizens of the perfect state have their possessions in common or not? This question may be discussed separately 40 from the enactments about women and children. Even supposing that the women and children belong to individuals, according to the 1263ᵃ1 custom which is at present universal, may there not be an advantage in having and using possessions in common? E.g. (1) the soil may be appropriated, but the produce may be thrown for consumption into the common stock; and this is the practice of some nations. Or (2), the 5 soil may be common, and may be cultivated in common, but the produce divided among individuals for their private use; this is a form of common property which is said to exist among certain foreigners. Or (3), the soil and the produce may be alike common.

When the husbandmen are not the owners, the case will be

---

[1] *Symposium*, 192c ff.   [2] *Rep.*, III 415B–D.

10 different and easier to deal with; but when they till the ground for themselves the question of ownership will give a world of trouble. If they do not share equally in enjoyment and toils, those who labour much and get little will necessarily complain of those who labour little
15 and receive or consume much. But indeed there is always a difficulty in men living together and having all human relations in common, but especially in their having common property. The partnerships of fellow-travellers are an example to the point; for they generally fall out over everyday matters and quarrel about any trifle which turns up.
20 So with servants: we are most liable to take offence at those with whom we most frequently come into contact in daily life.

These are only some of the disadvantages which attend the community of property; the present arrangement, if improved as it might be by good customs and laws, would be far better, and would
25 have the advantages of both systems. Property should be in a certain sense common, but, as a general rule, private; for, when everyone has a distinct interest, men will not complain of one another, and they will make more progress, because everyone will be attending to his own business. And yet by reason of goodness, and in respect of use,
30 'Friends', as the proverb says, 'will have all things common'. Even now there are traces of such a principle, showing that it is not impracticable, but, in well-ordered states, exists already to a certain extent and may be carried further. For, although every man has his own property, some things he will place at the disposal of his friends,
35 while of others he shares the use with them. The Lacedaemonians, for example, use one another's slaves, and horses, and dogs, as if they were their own; and when they lack provisions on a journey, they appropriate what they find in the fields throughout the country. It is clearly better that property should be private, but the use of it common; and the special business of the legislator is to create in men this benevolent disposition. Again, how immeasurably greater is the
1263^{b}1 pleasure, when a man feels a thing to be his own; for surely the love of self is a feeling implanted by nature and not given in vain, although selfishness is rightly censured; this, however, is not the mere love of self, but the love of self in excess, like the miser's love of money; for all, or almost all, men love money and other such objects in a measure.
5 And further, there is the greatest pleasure in doing a kindness or service to friends or guests or companions, which can only be rendered when a man has private property. These advantages are lost

by excessive unification of the state. The exhibition of two excellences, besides, is visibly annihilated in such a state: first, temperance towards women (for it is an honourable action to abstain from another's wife for temperance sake); secondly, liberality in the matter of property. No one, when men have all things in common, will any longer set an example of liberality or do any liberal action; for liberality consists in the use which is made of property.

Such legislation may have a specious appearance of benevolence; men readily listen to it, and are easily induced to believe that in some wonderful manner everybody will become everybody's friend – especially when someone is heard denouncing the evils now existing in states, suits about contracts, convictions for perjury, flatteries of rich men and the like, which are said to arise out of the possession of private property.[1] These evils, however, are due not to the absence of communism but to wickedness. Indeed, we see that there is much more quarrelling among those who have all things in common, though there are not many of them when compared with the vast numbers who have private property.

Again, we ought to reckon not only the evils from which the citizens will be saved, but also the advantages which they will lose. The life which they are to lead appears to be quite impracticable. The error of Socrates must be attributed to the false supposition from which he starts. Unity there should be, both of the family and of the state, but in some respects only. For there is a point at which a state may attain such a degree of unity as to be no longer a state, or at which, without actually ceasing to exist, it will become an inferior state, like harmony passing into unison, or rhythm which has been reduced to a single foot. The state, as I was saying, is a plurality, which should be united and made into a community by education; and it is strange that the author of a system of education which he thinks will make the state virtuous, should expect to improve his citizens by regulations of this sort, and not by philosophy or by customs and laws, like those which prevail at Sparta and Crete respecting common meals, whereby the legislator has made property common. Let us remember that we should not disregard the experience of ages; in the multitude of years these things, if they were good, would certainly not have been unknown; for almost everything has been found out, although

---

[1] *Rep.*, V 464B ff.

sometimes they are not put together; in other cases men do not use
the knowledge which they have. Great light would be thrown on this
subject if we could see such a form of government in the actual
process of construction; for the legislator could not form a state at all
without distributing and dividing its constituents into associations for
common meals, and into phratries and tribes. But all this legislation
ends only in forbidding agriculture to the guardians, a prohibition
which the Lacedaemonians try to enforce already.

But, indeed, Socrates has not said, nor is it easy to decide, what in
such a community will be the general form of the state. The citizens
who are not guardians are the majority, and about them nothing has
been determined: are the husbandmen, too, to have their property in
common? Or is each individual to have his own? and are their wives
and children to be individual or common? If, like the guardians, they
are to have all things in common, in what do they differ from them, or
what will they gain by submitting to their government? Or upon what
principle would they submit, unless indeed the governing class adopt
the ingenious policy of the Cretans, who give their slaves the same
institutions as their own, but forbid them gymnastic exercises and the
possession of arms. If, on the other hand, the inferior classes are to be
like other cities in respect of marriage and property, what will be the
form of the community? Must it not contain two states in one, each
hostile to the other?[1] He makes the guardians into a mere occupying
garrison, while the husbandmen and artisans and the rest are real
citizens. But if so the suits and quarrels, and all the evils which
Socrates affirms to exist in other states, will exist equally among them.
He says indeed that, having so good an education, the citizens will not
need many laws, for example laws about the city or about the markets;
but then he confines his education to the guardians. Again, he makes
the husbandmen owners of the property upon condition of their
paying a tribute. But in that case they are likely to be much more
unmanageable and conceited than the Helots, or Penestae, or slaves
in general. And whether community of wives and property be
necessary for the lower equally with the higher class or not, and the
questions akin to this, what will be the education, form of government, laws of the lower class, Socrates has nowhere determined:
neither is it easy to discover this, nor is their character of small

---

[1] *Rep.*, IV 422F.

importance if the common life of the guardians is to be maintained. 40

Again, if Socrates makes the women common, and retains private 1264ᵇ1
property, the men will see to the fields, but who will see to the house?
And who will do so if the agricultural class have both their property
and their wives in common? Once more: it is absurd to argue, from
the analogy of animals, that men and women should follow the same 5
pursuits, for animals have not to manage a household. The government, too, as constituted by Socrates, contains elements of danger;
for he makes the same person always rule. And if this is often a cause
of disturbance among the meaner sort, how much more among high-
spirited warriors? But that the persons whom he makes rulers must be 10
the same is evident; for the gold which the God mingles in the souls of
men is not at one time given to one, at another time to another, but
always to the same: as he says, God mingles gold in some, and silver in
others, from their very birth; but brass and iron in those who are 15
meant to be artisans and husbandmen. Again, he deprives the
guardians even of happiness, and says that the legislator ought to
make the whole state happy.[1] But the whole cannot be happy unless
most, or all, or some of its parts enjoy happiness. In this respect
happiness is not like the even principle in numbers, which may exist 20
only in the whole, but in neither of the parts; not so happiness. And if
the guardians are not happy, who are? Surely not the artisans, or the
common people. The Republic of which Socrates discourses has all
these difficulties, and others quite as great. 25

6 · The same, or nearly the same, objections apply to Plato's later
work, the *Laws*, and therefore we had better examine briefly the
constitution which is therein described. In the *Republic*, Socrates has
definitely settled in all a few questions only; such as the community of
women and children, the community of property, and the constitution 30
of the state. The population is divided into two classes – one of
husbandmen, and the other of warriors; from this latter is taken a
third class of counsellors and rulers of the state. But Socrates has not
determined whether the husbandmen and artisans are to have a share
in the government, and whether they, too, are to carry arms and share 35
in the military service, or not. He certainly thinks that the women
ought to share in the education of the guardians, and to fight by their

[1] *Rep.*, IV 419 ff.

side.[1] The remainder of the work is filled up with digressions foreign
to the main subject, and with discussions about the education of the
guardians. In the *Laws* there is hardly anything but laws; not much is
said about the constitution. This, which he had intended to make
more of the ordinary type, he gradually brings round to the other
form. For with the exception of·the community of women and
property, he supposes everything to be the same in both states; there
is to be the same education; the citizens of both are to live free from
servile occupations, and there are to be common meals in both. The
only difference is that in the *Laws*, the common meals are extended to
women, and the warriors number 5000, but in the *Republic* only 1000.

The discourses of Socrates are never commonplace; they always
exhibit grace and originality and thought; but perfection in everything
can hardly be expected. We must not overlook the fact that the
number of 5000 citizens, just now mentioned, will require a territory
as large as Babylon, or some other huge site, if so many persons are to
be supported in idleness, together with their women and attendants,
who will be a multitude many times as great. In framing an ideal we
may assume what we wish, but should avoid impossibilities.

It is said that the legislator ought to have his eye directed to two
points – the people and the country.[2] But neighbouring countries also
must not be forgotten by him, firstly because the state for which he
legislates is to have a political and not an isolated life. For a state must
have such a military force as will be serviceable against her neighbours, and not merely useful at home. Even if such a life is not
accepted, either for individuals or states, still a city should be
formidable to enemies, whether invading or retreating.

There is another point: Should not the amount of property be
defined in some way which differs from this by being clearer? For
Socrates says that a man should have so much property as will enable
him to live temperately, which is only a way of saying to live well; this is
too general a conception.[3] Further, a man may live temperately and
yet miserably. A better definition would be that a man must have so
much property as will enable him to live not only temperately but
liberally; if the two are parted, liberality will combine with luxury;
temperance will be associated with toil. For liberality and temperance
are the only eligible qualities which have to do with the use of

---

[1] *Rep.*, V 451D ff.   [2] *Laws*, IV 704 ff.   [3] *Laws*, V 737C–D.

property. A man cannot use property with mildness or courage, but
temperately and liberally he may; and therefore the practice of these
excellences is inseparable from property. There is an absurdity, too,
in equalizing the property and not regulating the number of citizens;
the population is to remain unlimited, and he thinks that it will be 40
sufficiently equalized by a certain number of marriages being unfruit-
ful, however many are born to others, because he finds this to be the
case in existing states. But greater care will be required than now; for
among ourselves, whatever may be the number of citizens, the 1265^b1
property is always distributed among them, and therefore no one is in
want; but, if the property were incapable of division as in the *Laws*, the
supernumeraries, whether few or many, would get nothing. One 5
would have thought that it was even more necessary to limit population than property; and that the limit should be fixed by calculating
the chances of mortality in the children, and of sterility in married 10
persons. The neglect of this subject, which in existing states is so
common, is a never-failing cause of poverty among the citizens; and
poverty is the parent of revolution and crime. Pheidon the Corinthian,
who was one of the most ancient legislators, thought that the families
and the number of citizens ought to remain the same, although
originally all the lots may have been of different sizes; but in the *Laws* 15
the opposite principle is maintained. What in our opinion is the right
arrangement will have to be explained hereafter.[1]

There is another omission in the *Laws*: Socrates does not tell us
how the rulers differ from their subjects; he only says that they should 20
be related as the warp and thc woof, which are made out of different
wools.[2] He allows that a man's whole property may be increased
fivefold, but why should not his land also increase to a certain extent?
Again, will the good management of a household be promoted by his 25
arrangement of homesteads? for he assigns to each individual two
homesteads in separate places, and it is difficult to live in two houses.[3]

The whole system of government tends to be neither democracy
nor oligarchy, but something in a mean between them, which is
usually called a polity, and is composed of the heavy-armed soldiers.
Now, if he intended to frame a constitution which would suit the 30
greatest number of states, he was very likely right, but not if he meant
to say that this constitutional form came nearest to his first state; for

---

[1] VII 5, 10, 16.　　　[2] *Laws*, V 734F. ff.　　　[3] *Laws*, V 745C.

many would prefer the Lacedaemonian, or, possibly, some other more aristocratic government. Some, indeed, say that the best
35 constitution is a combination of all existing forms, and they praise the Lacedaemonian because it is made up of oligarchy, monarchy, and democracy, the king forming the monarchy, and the council of elders the oligarchy, while the democratic element is represented by the
40 Ephors; for the Ephors are selected from the people. Others, however, declare the Ephorate to be a tyranny, and find the element
1266ᵃ1 of democracy in the common meals and in the habits of daily life. In the *Laws* it is maintained that the best constitution is made up of democracy and tyranny,[1] which are either not constitutions at all, or are the worst of all. But they are nearer the truth who combine many
5 forms; for the constitution is better which is made up of more numerous elements. The constitution proposed in the *Laws* has no element of monarchy at all; it is nothing but oligarchy and democracy, leaning rather to oligarchy. This is seen in the mode of appointing magistrates; for although the appointment of them by lot from among those who have been already selected combines both elements, the
10 way in which the rich are compelled by law to attend the assembly and vote for magistrates or discharge other political duties, while the rest may do as they like, and the endeavour to have the greater number of the magistrates appointed out of the richer classes and the highest officers selected from those who have the greatest incomes, both these are oligarchical features. The oligarchical principle prevails
15 also in the choice of the council, for all are compelled to choose, but the compulsion extends only to the choice out of the first class, and of an equal number out of the second class and out of the third class, but not in this latter case to all the voters but to those from the third or fourth class; and the selection of candidates out of the fourth class is only compulsory on the first and second. Then, from the persons so
20 chosen, he says that there ought to be an equal number of each class selected. Thus a preponderance will be given to the better sort of people, who have the larger incomes, because some of the lower classes, not being compelled, will not vote. These considerations, and
25 others which will be adduced when the time comes for examining similar constitutions, tend to show that states like Plato's should not be composed of democracy and monarchy. There is also a danger in

[1] *Laws*, v 756–7.

electing the magistrates out of a body who are themselves elected; for, if but a small number choose to combine, the elections will always go as they desire. Such is the constitution which is described in the *Laws*. 30

7 · Other constitutions have been proposed; some by private persons, others by philosophers and statesmen, which all come nearer to established or existing ones than either of Plato's. No one else has introduced such novelties as the community of women and children, 35 or public tables for women: other legislators begin with what is necessary. In the opinion of some, the regulation of property is the chief point of all, that being the question upon which all revolutions turn. This danger was recognized by Phaleas of Chalcedon, who was the first to affirm that the citizens of a state ought to have equal 40 possessions. He thought that in a new colony the equalization might 1266ᵇ1 be accomplished without difficulty, not so easily when a state was already established; and that then the shortest way of compassing the desired end would be for the rich to give and not to receive marriage portions, and for the poor not to give but to receive them.

Plato in the *Laws* was of the opinion that, to a certain extent, 5 accumulation should be allowed, forbidding, as I have already observed, any citizen to possess more than five times the minimum qualification.[1] But those who make such laws should remember what they are apt to forget – that the legislator who fixes the amount of 10 property should also fix the number of children; for, if the children are too many for the property, the law must be broken. And, besides the violation of the law, it is a bad thing that many from being rich should become poor; for men of ruined fortunes are sure to stir up revolutions. That the equalization of property exercises an influence 15 on political society was clearly understood even by some of the old legislators. Laws were made by Solon and others prohibiting an individual from possessing as much land as he pleased; and there are other laws in states which forbid the sale of property: among the Locrians, for example, there is a law that a man is not to sell his 20 property unless he can prove unmistakably that some misfortune has befallen him. Again, there have been laws which enjoin the preservation of the original lots. Such a law existed in the island of Leucas, and the abrogation of it made the constitution too democratic, for the

---

[1] *Laws*, V 744F.

rulers no longer had the prescribed qualification. Again, where there
25 is equality of property, the amount may be either too large or too
small, and the possessor may be living either in luxury or penury.
Clearly, then, the legislator ought not only to aim at the equalization
of properties, but at moderation in their amount. Further, if he
prescribe this moderate amount equally to all, he will be no nearer the
30 mark; for it is not the possessions but the desires of mankind which
require to be equalized, and this is impossible, unless a sufficient
education is provided by the laws. But Phaleas will probably reply that
this is precisely what he means; and that, in his opinion, there ought to
be in states, not only equal property, but equal education. Still he
35 should tell us what will be the character of his education; there is no
use in having one and the same for all, if it is of a sort that predisposes
men to avarice, or ambition, or both. Moreover, civil troubles arise,
not only out of the inequality of property, but out of the inequality of
40 honour, though in opposite ways. For the common people quarrel
1267ᵃ1 about the inequality of property, the higher class about the equality of
honour; as the poet says,

The bad and good alike in honour share.[1]

There are crimes for which the motive is want; and for these
Phaleas expects to find a cure in the equalization of property, which
will take away from a man the temptation to be a robber, because he is
5 hungry or cold. But want is not the sole incentive to crime; men also
wish to enjoy themselves and not to be in a state of desire – they wish
to cure some desire, going beyond the necessities of life, which preys
upon them; indeed this is not the only reason – they may desire to
enjoy pleasures unaccompanied with pain, and therefore they commit
crimes.

Now what is the cure of these three disorders? Of the first,
10 moderate possessions and occupation; of the second, habits of
temperance; as to the third, if any desire pleasures which depend on
themselves, they will find the satisfaction of their desires nowhere but
in philosophy; for all other pleasures we are dependent on others.
The fact is that the greatest crimes are caused by excess and not by
necessity. Men do not become tyrants in order that they may not
15 suffer cold; and hence great is the honour bestowed, not on him who

[1] Homer, *Iliad*, IX 319.

kills a thief, but on him who kills a tyrant. Thus we see that the institutions of Phaleas avail only against petty crimes.

There is another objection to them. They are chiefly designed to promote the internal welfare of the state. But the legislator should consider also its relation to neighbouring nations, and to all who are outside of it. The government must be organized with a view to military strength; and of this he has said not a word. And so with respect to property: there should not only be enough to supply the internal wants of the state, but also to meet dangers coming from without. The property of the state should not be so large that more powerful neighbours may be tempted by it, while the owners are unable to repel the invaders; nor yet so small that the state is unable to maintain a war even against states of equal power, and of the same character. Phaleas has not laid down any rule; but we should bear in mind that abundance of wealth is an advantage. The best limit will probably be, that a more powerful neighbour must have no inducement to go to war with you by reason of the excess of your wealth, but only such as he would have had if you had possessed less. There is a story that Eubulus, when Autophradates was going to besiege Atarneus, told him to consider how long the operation would take, and then reckon up the cost which would be incurred in the time. 'For', said he, 'I am willing for a smaller sum than that to leave Atarneus at once.' These words of Eubulus made an impression on Autophradates, and he desisted from the siege.

The equalization of property is one of the things that tend to prevent the citizens from quarrelling. Not that the gain in this direction is very great. For the nobles will be dissatisfied because they think themselves worthy of more than an equal share of honours; and this is often found to be a cause of sedition and revolution. And the avarice of mankind is insatiable; at one time two obols was pay enough; but now, when this sum has become customary, men always want more and more without end; for it is of the nature of desire to be unlimited, and most men live only for the gratification of it. The beginning of reform is not so much to equalize property as to train the nobler sort of natures not to desire more, and to prevent the lower from getting more; that is to say, they must be kept down, but not ill-treated. Besides, the equalization proposed by Phaleas is imperfect; for he only equalizes land, whereas a man may be rich also in slaves, and cattle, and money, and in the abundance of what are called his

movables. Now either all these things must be equalized, or some limit must be imposed on them, or they must all be let alone. It would appear that Phaleas is legislating for a small city only, if, as he
15 supposes, all the artisans are to be public slaves and not to form a supplementary part of the body of citizens. But if there is a law that artisans are to be public slaves, it should only apply to those engaged on public works, as at Epidamnus, or at Athens on the plan which Diophantus once introduced.
20 From these observations any one may judge how far Phaleas was wrong or right in his ideas.

8 · Hippodamus, the son of Euryphon, a native of Miletus, the same who invented the art of planning cities, and who also laid out the Peiraeus – a strange man, whose fondness for distinction led him into
25 a general eccentricity of life, which made some think him affected (for he would wear flowing hair and expensive ornaments; but these were worn on a cheap but warm garment both in winter and summer); he, besides aspiring to be an adept in the knowledge of nature, was the
30 first person not a statesman who made inquiries about the best form of government.

The city of Hippodamus was composed of 10,000 citizens divided into three parts – one of artisans, one of husbandmen, and a third of armed defenders of the state. He also divided the land into three
35 parts, one sacred, one public, the third private: – the first was set apart to maintain the customary worship of the gods, the second was to support the warriors, the third was the property of the husbandmen. He also divided laws into three classes, and no more, for he maintained that there are three subjects of lawsuits – insult, injury,
40 and homicide. He likewise instituted a single final court of appeal, to which all causes seeming to have been improperly decided might be
1268ᵃ1 referred; this court he formed of elders chosen for the purpose. He was further of the opinion that the decisions of the courts ought not to be given by the use of a voting pebble, but that everyone should have a tablet on which he might not only write a simple condemnation, or leave the tablet blank for a simple acquittal; but, if he partly acquitted
5 and partly condemned, he was to distinguish accordingly. To the existing law he objected that it obliged the judges to be guilty of perjury, whichever way they voted. He also enacted that those who discovered anything for the good of the state should be honoured, and

he provided that the children of citizens who died in battle should be maintained at public expense, as if such an enactment had never been heard of before, yet it actually exists at Athens and in other places. As 10 to the magistrates, he would have them all elected by the people, that is, by the three classes already mentioned, and those who were elected were to watch over the interests of the public, of strangers, and of orphans. These are the most striking points in the constitution of 15 Hippodamus. There is not much else.

The first of these proposals to which objection may be taken is the threefold division of the citizens. The artisans, and the husbandmen, and the warriors, all have a share in the government. But the husbandmen have no arms, and the artisans neither arms nor land, and therefore they become all but slaves of the warrior class. That 20 they should share in all the offices is an impossibility; for generals and guardians of the citizens, and nearly all the principal magistrates, must be taken from the class of those who carry arms. Yet, if the two other classes have no share in the government, how can they be loyal 25 citizens? It may be said that those who have arms must necessarily be masters of both the other classes, but this is not so easily accomplished unless they are numerous: and if they are, why should the other classes share in the government at all, or have power to appoint magistrates? Further, what use are farmers to the city? Artisans there 30 must be, for these are wanted in every city, and they can live by their craft, as elsewhere; and the husbandmen, too, if they really provided the warriors with food, might fairly have a share in the government. But in the republic of Hippodamus they are supposed to have land of their own, which they cultivate for their private benefit. Again, as to 35 this common land out of which the soldiers are maintained, if they are themselves to be the cultivators of it, the warrior class will be identical with the husbandmen, although the legislator intended to make a distinction between them. If, again, there are to be other cultivators distinct both from the husbandmen, who have land of their own, and from the warriors, they will make a fourth class, which has no place in the state and no share in anything. Or, if the same persons are to 40 cultivate their own lands, and those of the public as well, they will have a difficulty in supplying the quantity of produce which will maintain 1268^b1 two households:^a and why, in this case, should there be any division,

---

^a Reading οἰκίαις.

for they might find food themselves and give to the warriors from the same land and the same lots? There is surely a great confusion in all this.

5   Neither is the law to be commended which says that the judges, when a simple issue is laid before them, should make a distinction in their judgement; for the judge is thus converted into an arbitrator. Now, in an arbitration, although the arbitrators are many, they confer with one another about the decision; but in courts of law this is
10 impossible, and, indeed, most legislators take pains to prevent the judges from holding any communication with one another. Again, will there not be confusion if the judge thinks that damages should be given, but not so much as the suitor demands? He asks, say, for twenty minae, and the judge allows him ten minae (or in general the suitor asks for more and the judge allows less), while another judge allows
15 five, another four minae. In this way they will go on splitting up the damages, and some will grant the whole and others nothing: how is the final reckoning to be taken? Again, no one contends that he who votes for a simple acquittal or condemnation perjures himself, if the indictment has been laid in an unqualified form; and this is just, for
20 the judge who acquits does not decide that the defendant owes nothing, but that he does not owe the twenty minae. He only is guilty of perjury who thinks that the defendant ought not to pay twenty minae, and yet condemns him.

    To honour those who discover anything which is useful to the state is a proposal which has a specious sound, but cannot safely be enacted
25 by law, for it may encourage informers, and perhaps even lead to political commotions. This question involves another. It has been doubted whether it is or is not expedient to make any changes in the laws of a country, even if another law be better. Now, if all changes are inexpedient, we can hardly assent to the proposal of Hippodamus;
30 for, under pretence of doing a public service, a man may introduce measures which are really destructive to the laws or to the constitution. But, since we have touched upon this subject, perhaps we had better go a little into detail, for, as I was saying, there is a difference of opinion, and it may sometimes seem desirable to make changes. Such changes in the other arts and sciences have certainly been beneficial;
35 medicine, for example, and gymnastics, and every other art and craft have departed from traditional usage. And, if politics be an art, change must be necessary in this as in any other art. That improve-

ment has occurred is shown by the fact that old customs are exceedingly simple and barbarous. For the ancient Hellenes went 40 about armed and bought their brides from each other. The remains of ancient laws which have come down to us are quite absurd; for example, at Cumae there is a law about murder, to the effect that if 1269ᵃ1 the accuser produce a certain number of witnesses from among his own kinsmen, the accused shall be held guilty. Again, men in general desire the good, and not merely what their fathers had. But the primaeval inhabitants, whether they were born of the earth or were 5 the survivors of some destruction, may be supposed to have been no better than ordinary or even foolish people among ourselves (such is certainly the tradition concerning the earth-born men); and it would be ridiculous to rest contented with their notions. Even when laws have been written down, they ought not always to remain unaltered. As in other sciences, so in politics, it is impossible that all things 10 should be precisely set down in writing; for enactments must be universal, but actions are concerned with particulars. Hence we infer that sometimes and in certain cases laws should be changed; but when we look at the matter from another point of view, great caution would seem to be required. For the habit of lightly changing the laws is an evil, and, when the advantage is small, some errors both of 15 lawgivers and rulers had better be left; the citizen will not gain so much by making the change as he will lose by the habit of dis- obedience. The analogy of the arts is false; a change in a law is a very different thing from a change in an art. For the law has no power to 20 command obedience except that of habit, which can only be given by time, so that a readiness to change from old to new laws enfeebles the power of the law. Even if we admit that the laws are to be changed, are they all to be changed, and in every state? And are they to be changed 25 by anybody who likes, or only by certain persons? These are very important questions; and therefore we had better reserve the discus- sion of them to a more suitable occasion.

9 · In the governments of Lacedaemon and Crete, and indeed in all governments, two points have to be considered: first, whether any particular law is good or bad, when compared with the perfect state; secondly, whether it is or is not consistent with the idea and character which the lawgiver has set before his citizens. That in a well-ordered state the citizens should have leisure and not have to provide for their 35

daily wants is generally acknowledged, but there is a difficulty in seeing how this leisure is to be attained. The Thessalian Penestae have often risen against their masters, and the Helots in like manner against the Lacedaemonians, for whose misfortunes they are always

40 lying in wait. Nothing, however, of this kind has as yet happened to

1269ᵇ1 the Cretans; the reason probably is that the neighbouring cities, even when at war with one another, never form an alliance with rebellious serfs, rebellions not being for their interest, since they themselves have a dependent population. Whereas all the neighbours of the Lacedaemonians, whether Argives, Messenians, or Arcadians, were

5 their enemies. In Thessaly, again, the original revolt of the slaves occurred because the Thessalians were still at war with the neighbouring Achaeans, Perrhaebians and Magnesians. Besides, if there were no other difficulty, the treatment or management of slaves is a troublesome affair; for, if not kept in hand, they are insolent, and

10 think that they are as good as their masters, and, if harshly treated, they hate and conspire against them. Now it is clear that when these are the results the citizens of a state have not found out the secret of managing their subject population.

Again, the licence of the Lacedaemonian women defeats the intention of the Spartan constitution, and is adverse to the happiness

15 of the state. For, a husband and a wife being each a part of every family, the state may be considered as about equally divided into men and women; and, therefore, in those states in which the condition of the women is bad, half the city may be regarded as having no laws.

20 And this is what has actually happened at Sparta; the legislator wanted to make the whole state hardy, and he has carried out his intention in the case of the men, but he has neglected the women, who live in every sort of intemperance and luxury. The consequence is that in such a state wealth is too highly valued, especially if the citizens

25 fall under the dominion of their wives, after the manner of most warlike races, except the Celts and a few others who openly approve of male homosexuality. The old mythologer would seem to have been right in uniting Ares and Aphrodite, for all warlike races are prone to

30 the love either of men or of women. This was exemplified among the Spartans in the days of their greatness; many things were managed by their women. But what difference does it make whether women rule, or the rulers are ruled by women? The result is the same. Even in

35 regard to boldness, which is of no use in daily life, and is needed only

in war, the influence of the Lacedaemonian women has been most mischievous. The evil showed itself in the Theban invasion, when, unlike the women in other cities, they were utterly useless and caused more confusion than the enemy. This licence of the Lacedaemonian 40 women existed from the earliest times, and was only what might be expected. For during the wars of the Lacedaemonians, first against 1270ᵃ1 the Argives, and afterwards against the Arcadians and Messenians, the men were long away from home, and, on the return of peace, they gave themselves into the legislator's hand, already prepared by the 5 discipline of a soldier's life (in which there are many elements of excellence), to receive his enactments. But, when Lycurgus, as tradition says, wanted to bring the women under his laws, they resisted, and he gave up the attempt. These then are the causes of what then happened, and this defect in the constitution is clearly to be attributed to them. We are not, however, considering what is or is not 10 to be excused, but what is right or wrong, and the disorder of the women, as I have already said, not only gives an air of indecorum to the constitution considered in itself, but tends in a measure to foster avarice.

The mention of avarice naturally suggests a criticism on the 15 inequality of property. While some of the Spartan citizens have quite small properties, others have very large ones: hence the land has passed into the hands of a few. And this is due also to faulty laws; for, although the legislator rightly holds up to shame the sale or purchase 20 of an inheritance, he allows anybody who likes to give or bequeath it. Yet both practices lead to the same result. And nearly two-fifths of the whole country are held by women; this is owing to the number of heiresses and to the large dowries which are customary. It would 25 surely have been better to have given no dowries at all, or, if any, but small or moderate ones. As the law now stands, a man may bestow his heiress on any one whom he pleases, and, if he die intestate, the privilege of giving her away descends to his heir. Hence, although the country is able to maintain 1500 cavalry and 30,000 hoplites, the 30 whole number of Spartan citizens fell below 1000. The result proves the faulty nature of their laws respecting property; for the city sank under a single defeat; the want of men was their ruin. There is a tradition that, in the days of their ancient kings, they were in the habit 35 of giving the rights of citizenship to strangers, and therefore, in spite of their long wars, no lack of population was experienced by them;

indeed, at one time Sparta is said to have numbered not less than
10,000 citizens. Whether this statement is true or not, it would
certainly have been better to have maintained their numbers by the
40 equalization of property. Again, the law which relates to the procre-
1270ᵇ1 ation of children is adverse to the correction of this inequality. For the
legislator, wanting to have as many Spartans as he could, encouraged
the citizens to have large families; and there is a law at Sparta that the
father of three sons shall be exempt from military service, and he who
5 has four from all the burdens of the state. Yet it is obvious that, if there
were many children, the land being distributed as it is, many of them
must necessarily fall into poverty.

The Lacedaemonian constitution is defective also in respect of the
Ephorate. This magistracy has authority in the highest matters, but
the Ephors are chosen from the whole people, and so the office is apt
10 to fall into the hands of very poor men, who, being badly off, are open
to bribes. There have been many examples at Sparta of this evil in
former times; and quite recently, in the matter of the Andrians,
certain of the Ephors who were bribed did their best to ruin the state.
15 And so great and tyrannical is their power, that even the kings have
been compelled to court them, so that, in this way as well, together
with the royal office the whole constitution has deteriorated, and from
being an aristocracy has turned into a democracy. The Ephorate
certainly does keep the state together; for the people are contented
when they have a share in the highest office, and the result, whether
20 due to the legislator or to chance, has been advantageous. For if a
constitution is to be permanent, all the parts of the state must wish
that it should exist and these arrangements be maintained. This is the
case at Sparta, where the kings desire its permanence because they
have due honour in their own persons; the nobles because they are
represented in the council of elders (for the office of elder is a reward
25 of excellence); and the people, because all are eligible for the
Ephorate. The election of Ephors out of the whole people is perfectly
right, but ought not to be carried on in the present fashion, which is
too childish. Again, they have the decision of great causes, although
they are quite ordinary men, and therefore they should not determine
30 them merely on their own judgement, but according to written rules,
and to the laws. Their way of life, too, is not in accordance with the
spirit of the constitution – they have a deal too much licence; whereas,
in the case of the other citizens, the excess of strictness is so

intolerable that they run away from the law into the secret indulgence 35
of sensual pleasures.

Again, the council of elders is not free from defect. It may be said
that the elders are good men and well trained in manly virtue; and
that, therefore, there is an advantage to the state in having them. But
that judges of important causes should hold office for life is a
disputable thing, for the mind grows old as well as the body. And 1271ª1
when men have been educated in such a manner that even the
legislator himself cannot trust them, there is real danger. Many of the
elders are well known to have taken bribes and to have been guilty of
partiality in public affairs. And therefore they ought not to be non- 5
accountable; yet at Sparta they are so. All magistracies are accountable to the Ephors. But this prerogative is too great for them, and we
maintain that the control should be exercised in some other manner.
Further, the mode in which the Spartans elect their elders is childish; 10
and it is improper that the person to be elected should canvass for the
office; the worthiest should be appointed, whether he chooses or not.
And here the legislator clearly indicates the same intention which
appears in other parts of his constitution; he would have his citizens
ambitious, and he has reckoned upon this quality in the election of the 15
elders; for no one would ask to be elected if he were not. Yet ambition
and avarice, almost more than any other passions, are the motives of
voluntary injustices.

Whether kings are or are not an advantage to states, I will consider 20
at another time; they should at any rate be chosen, not as they are now,
but with regard to their personal life and conduct. The legislator
himself obviously did not suppose that he could make them really
good men; at least he shows a great distrust of their virtue. For this
reason the Spartans used to join enemies with them in the same 25
embassy, and the quarrels between the kings were held to preserve
the state.

Neither did the first introducer of the common meals, called
'phiditia', regulate them well. The entertainment ought to have been
provided at public cost, as in Crete; but among the Lacedaemonians
everyone is expected to contribute, and some of them are too poor to 30
afford the expense: thus the intention of the legislator is frustrated.
The common meals were meant to be a democratic institution, but
the existing manner of regulating them is the reverse of democratic.
For the very poor can scarcely take part in them; and, according to 35

ancient custom, those who cannot contribute are not allowed to retain their rights of citizenship.

The law about the Spartan admirals has often been censured, and
40 with justice; it is a source of dissension, for the kings are perpetual generals, and this office of admiral is but the setting up of another king.

1271ᵇ1   The charge which Plato brings, in the *Laws*, against the intention of the legislator, is likewise justified; the whole constitution has regard to one part of excellence only – the excellence of the soldier, which gives victory in war. So long as they were at war, therefore, their
5 power was preserved, but when they had attained empire they fell, for of the arts of peace they knew nothing, and have never engaged in any employment higher than war. There is another error, equally great, into which they have fallen. Although they truly think that the goods
10 for which men contend are to be acquired by excellence rather than by vice, they err in supposing that these goods are to be preferred to the excellence which gains them.

Again, the revenues of the state are ill-managed; there is no money in the treasury, although they are obliged to carry on great wars, and they are unwilling to pay taxes. The greater part of the land being in the hands of Spartans, they do not look closely into one another's
15 contributions. The result which the legislator has produced is the reverse of beneficial; for he has made his city poor, and his citizens greedy.

Enough respecting the Spartan constitution, of which these are the principal defects.

20 10 · The Cretan constitution nearly resembles the Spartan, and in some few points is quite as good; but for the most part less perfect in form. The older constitutions are generally less elaborate than the later, and the Lacedaemonian is said to be, and probably is, in a very great measure, a copy of the Cretan. According to tradition,
25 Lycurgus, when he ceased to be the guardian of King Charillus, went abroad and spent most of his time in Crete. For the two countries are nearly connected; the Lyctians are a colony of the Lacedaemonians, and the colonists, when they came to Crete, adopted the constitution
30 which they found existing among the inhabitants. Even to this day the Perioeci are governed by the original laws which Minos is supposed to have enacted. The island seems to be intended by nature for

dominion in Hellas, and to be well situated; it extends right across the sea, around which nearly all the Hellenes are settled; and while one 35 end is not far from the Peloponnese, the other almost reaches to the region of Asia about Triopium and Rhodes. Hence Minos acquired the empire of the sea, subduing some of the islands and colonizing others; at last he invaded Sicily, where he died near Camicus. 40

The Cretan institutions resemble the Lacedaemonian. The Helots are the husbandmen of the one, the Perioeci of the other, and both 1272ᵃ1 Cretans and Lacedaemonians have common meals, which were anciently called by the Lacedaemonians not 'phiditia' but 'andria'; and the Cretans have the same word, the use of which proves that the common meals originally came from Crete. Further, the two constitutions are similar; for the office of the Ephors is the same as that of 5 the Cretan Cosmi, the only difference being that whereas the Ephors are five, the Cosmi are ten in number. The elders, too, answer to the elders in Crete, who are termed by the Cretans the council. And the kingly office once existed in Crete, but was abolished, and the Cosmi 10 have now the duty of leading them in war. All classes share in the ecclesia, but it can only ratify the decrees of the elders and the Cosmi.

The common meals of Crete are certainly better managed than the Lacedaemonian; for in Lacedaemon every one pays so much per head, or, if he fails, the law, as I have already explained, forbids him to 15 exercise the rights of citizenship. But in Crete they are of a more popular character. There, of all the fruits of the earth, of the cattle raised on the public lands, and of the tribute which is paid by the Perioeci, one portion is assigned to the gods and to the service of the state, and another to the common meals, so that men, women, and children are all supported out of a common stock. The legislator has many ingenious ways of securing moderation in eating, which he conceives to be a gain; he likewise encourages the separation of men from women, lest they should have too many children, and the companionship of men with one another – whether this is a good or bad thing I shall have an opportunity of considering at another time. Thus that the Cretan common meals are better ordered than the Lacedaemonian there can be no doubt.

On the other hand, the Cosmi are even a worse institution than the Ephors, of which they have all the evils without the good. Like the Ephors, they are any chance persons, but in Crete this is not counter- 30 balanced by a corresponding political advantage. At Sparta everyone

is eligible, and the body of the people, having a share in the highest office, want the constitution to be permanent. But in Crete the Cosmi are elected out of certain families, and not out of the whole people,
35 and the elders out of those who have been Cosmi.

The same criticism may be made about the Cretan, which has been already made about the Lacedaemonian affairs. Their unaccountability and life tenure is too great a privilege, and their arbitrary power of acting upon their own judgement, and dispensing with
40 written law, is dangerous. It is no proof of the goodness of the institution that the people are not discontented at being excluded from it. For there is no profit to be made out of the office as out of the
1272^b1 Ephorate, since, unlike the Ephors the Cosmi, being in an island, are removed from temptation.

The remedy by which they correct the evil of this institution is an extraordinary one, suited rather to a dynasty than to a constitutional state. For the Cosmi are often expelled by a conspiracy of their own
5 colleagues, or of private individuals; and they are allowed also to resign before their term of office has expired. Surely all matters of this kind are better regulated by law than by the will of man, which is a very unsafe rule. Worst of all is the suspension of the office of Cosmi, a device to which the nobles often have recourse when they will not
10 submit to justice. This shows that the Cretan government, although possessing some of the characteristics of a constitutional state, is really a dynasty.

The nobles have a habit, too, of setting up a chief; they get together a party among the common people and their own friends and then quarrel and fight with one another. What is this but the temporary
15 destruction of the state and dissolution of society? A city is in a dangerous condition when those who are willing are also able to attack her. But, as I have already said, the island of Crete is saved by her situation; distance has the same effect as the prohibition of strangers. This is the reason why the Perioeci are contented in Crete,
20 whereas the Helots are perpetually revolting. For the Cretans have no foreign dominions and, when lately foreign invaders found their way into the island, the weakness of the Cretan constitution was revealed. Enough of the government of Crete.

11 · The Carthaginians are also considered to have an excellent
25 form of government, which differs from that of any other state in

several respects, though it is in some very like the Lacedaemonian.
Indeed, all three states – the Lacedaemonian, the Cretan, and the
Carthaginian – nearly resemble one another, and are very different
from any others. Many of the Carthaginian institutions are excellent. 30
The superiority of their constitution is proved by the fact that the
common people remains loyal to the constitution; the Carthaginians
have never had any rebellion worth speaking of, and have never been
under the rule of a tyrant.

Among the points in which the Carthaginian constitution
resembles the Lacedaemonian are the following: – The common
tables of the clubs answer to the Spartan phiditia, and their
magistracy of the 104 to the Ephors; but, whereas the Ephors are any 35
chance persons, the magistrates of the Carthaginians are elected
according to merit – this is an improvement. They have also their
kings and their council of elders, who correspond to the kings and
elders of Sparta. Their kings, unlike the Spartan, are not always of the
same family, nor that an ordinary one, but if there is some distinguished family they are selected out of it and not appointed by
seniority – this is far better. Such officers have great power, and
therefore, if they are persons of little worth, do a great deal of harm, 1273ᵃ1
and they have already done harm at Lacedaemon.

Most of the defects or deviations from the perfect state, for which
the Carthaginian constitution would be censured, apply equally to all
the forms of government which we have mentioned. But of the
deflections from aristocracy and constitutional government, some 5
incline more to democracy and some to oligarchy. The kings and
elders, if unanimous, may determine whether they will or will not
bring a matter before the people, but when they are not unanimous,
the people decide on such matters as well. And whatever the kings
and elders bring before the people is not only heard but also 10
determined by them, and anyone who likes may oppose it; now this is
not permitted in Sparta and Crete. That the magistracies of five who
have under them many important matters should be co-opted, that
they should choose the supreme council of 100, and should hold 15
office longer than other magistrates (for they are virtually rulers both
before and after they hold office) – these are oligarchical features;
their being without salary and not elected by lot, and any similar
points, such as the practice of having all suits tried by the magistrates,
and not some by one class and some by another, as at Lacedaemon, 20

are characteristic of aristocracy. The Carthaginian constitution devi-
ates from aristocracy and inclines to oligarchy, chiefly on a point
where popular opinion is on their side. For men in general think that
magistrates should be chosen not only for their merit, but for their
25 wealth: a man, they say, who is poor cannot rule well – he has not the
leisure. If, then, election of magistrates for their wealth be characteristic of oligarchy, and election for merit of aristocracy, there will be a
third form under which the constitution of Carthage is comprehended; for the Carthaginians choose their magistrates, and particu-
30 larly the highest of them – their kings and generals – with an eye both
to merit and to wealth.

But we must acknowledge that, in thus deviating from aristocracy,
the legislator has committed an error. Nothing is more absolutely
necessary than to provide that the highest class, not only when in
office, but when out of office, should have leisure and not disgrace
themselves in any way; and to this his attention should be first
35 directed. Even if you must have regard to wealth, in order to secure
leisure, yet it is surely a bad thing that the greatest offices, such as
those of kings and generals, should be bought. The law which allows
this abuse makes wealth of more account than excellence, and the
whole state becomes avaricious. For, whenever the chiefs of the state
40 deem anything honourable, the other citizens are sure to follow their
1273ᵇ1 example; and, where excellence has not the first place, there
aristocracy cannot be firmly established. Those who have been at the
expense of purchasing their places will be in the habit of repaying
themselves; and it is absurd to suppose that a poor and honest man
will be wanting to make gains, and that a lower stamp of man who has
5 incurred a great expense will not. That is why they should rule who
are able to rule best. And even if the legislator does not care to protect
the good from poverty, he should at any rate secure leisure for them
when in office.

It would seem also to be a bad principle that the same person
should hold many offices, which is a favourite practice among the
10 Carthaginians, for one business is better done by one man. The
legislator should see to this and should not appoint the same person to
be a flute-player and a shoemaker. Hence, where the state is large, it
is more in accordance both with constitutional and with democratic
principles that the offices of state should be distributed among many
persons. For, as I said, this arrangement is fairer to all, and any action

familiarized by repetition is better and sooner performed. We have a 15
proof in military and naval matters; the duties of command and of
obedience in both these services extend to all.

The government of the Carthaginians is oligarchical, but they
successfully escape the evils of oligarchy by being wealthy, sending
out one portion of the people after another to the cities. This is their
panacea and the means by which they give stability to the state. This is 20
the result of chance but it is the legislator who should be able to
provide against revolution. As things are, if any misfortune occurred,
and the bulk of the subjects revolted, there would be no way of
restoring peace by legal methods.

Such is the character of the Lacedaemonian, Cretan, and Cartha- 25
ginian constitutions, which are justly celebrated.

12 · Of those who have treated of governments, some have never
taken any part at all in public affairs, but have passed their lives in a
private station; about most of them, what was worth telling has been 30
already told. Others have been lawgivers, either in their own or in
foreign cities, whose affairs they have administered; and of these
some have only made laws, others have framed constitutions; for
example, Lycurgus and Solon did both. Of the Lacedaemonian 35
constitution I have already spoken. As to Solon, he is thought by some
to have been a good legislator, who put an end to the exclusiveness of
the oligarchy, emancipated the people, established the ancient
Athenian democracy, and harmonized the different elements of the
state. According to their view, the council of Areopagus was an 40
oligarchical element, the elected magistracy, aristocratic, and the
courts of law, democratic. The truth seems to be that the council and 1274ᵃ1
the elected magistracy existed before the time of Solon, and were
retained by him, but that he formed the courts of law out of all the
citizens, thus creating the democracy, which is the very reason why he
is sometimes blamed. For in giving the supreme power to the law
courts, which are elected by lot, he is thought to have destroyed the
non-democratic element. When the law courts grew powerful, to 5
please the people who were now playing the tyrant the old constitution was changed into the existing democracy. Ephialtes and Pericles
curtailed the power of the Areopagus; Pericles also instituted the
payment of the juries, and thus every demagogue in turn increased 10
the power of the democracy until it became what we now see. All this

seems, however, to be the result of circumstances, and not to have been intended by Solon. For the people, having been instrumental in gaining the empire of the sea in the Persian War, began to get a notion of itself, and followed worthless demagogues, whom the better class
15 opposed. Solon, himself, appears to have given the Athenians only that power of electing to offices and calling to account the magistrates which was absolutely necessary; for without it they would have been in a state of slavery and enmity to the government. All the magistrates he appointed from the notables and the men of wealth, that is to say,
20 from the pentacosiomedimni, or from the class called zeugitae, or from a third class of so-called knights. The fourth class were labourers who had no share in any magistracy.

Mere legislators were Zaleucus, who gave laws to the Epizephyrian Locrians, and Charondas, who legislated for his own city of Catana,
25 and for the other Chalcidian cities in Italy and Sicily. Some people attempt to make out that Onomacritus was the first person who had any special skill in legislation, and that he, although a Locrian by birth, was trained in Crete, where he lived in the exercise of his prophetic art; that Thales was his companion, and that Lycurgus and
30 Zaleucus were disciples of Thales, as Charondas was of Zaleucus. But their account is quite inconsistent with chronology.

There was also Philolaus, the Corinthian, who gave laws to the Thebans. This Philolaus was one of the family of the Bacchiadae, and a lover of Diocles, the Olympic victor, who left Corinth in horror of
35 the incestuous passion which his mother Halcyone had conceived for him, and retired to Thebes, where the two friends together ended their days. The inhabitants still point out their tombs, which are in full view of one another, but one is visible from the Corinthian territory, the other not. Tradition says the two friends arranged them thus,
40 Diocles out of horror at his misfortunes, so that the land of Corinth
1274ᵇ1 might not be visible from his tomb; Philolaus that it might. This is the reason why they settled at Thebes, and so Philolaus legislated for the Thebans, and, besides some other enactments, gave them laws about the procreation of children, which they call the 'Laws of Adoption'.
5 These laws were peculiar to him, and were intended to preserve the number of the lots.

In the legislation of Charondas there is nothing distinctive, except the suits against false witnesses. He is the first who instituted denunciation for perjury. His laws are more exact and more precisely expressed than even those of our modern legislators.

(Characteristic of Phaleas is the equalization of property; of Plato, 10 the community of women, children, and property, the common meals of women, and the law about drinking, that the sober shall be masters of the feast; also the training of soldiers to acquire by practice equal skill with both hands, so that one should be as useful as the other.)

Draco has left laws, but he adapted them to a constitution which 15 already existed, and there is no peculiarity in them which is worth mentioning, except the greatness and severity of the punishments.

Pittacus, too, was only a lawgiver, and not the author of a constitution; he has a law which is peculiar to him, that, if a drunken man do something wrong, he shall be more heavily punished than if he were 20 sober; he looked not to the excuse which might be offered for the drunkard, but only to expediency, for drunken more often than sober people commit acts of violence.

Androdamas of Rhegium gave laws to the Chalcidians of Thrace. Some of them relate to homicide, and to heiresses; but there is 25 nothing distinctive in them.

And here let us conclude our inquiry into the various constitutions which either actually exist, or have been devised by theorists.

BOOK III

1 · He who would inquire into the essence and attributes of various 32 kinds of government must first of all determine what a state is. At present this is a disputed question. Some say that the state has done a 35 certain act; others, not the state, but the oligarchy or the tyrant. And the legislator or statesman is concerned entirely with the state, a government being an arrangement of the inhabitants of a state. But a state is composite, like any other whole made up of many parts – these 40 are the citizens, who compose it. It is evident, therefore, that we must 1275^{a}1 begin by asking, Who is the citizen, and what is the meaning of the term? For here again there may be a difference of opinion. He who is a citizen in a democracy will often not be a citizen in an oligarchy. Leaving out of consideration those who have been made citizens, or 5

who have obtained the name of citizen in any other accidental manner, we may say, first, that a citizen is not a citizen because he lives in a certain place, for resident aliens and slaves share in the place; nor is he a citizen who has legal rights to the extent of suing and
10 being sued; for this right may be enjoyed under the provisions of a treaty. Resident aliens in many places do not possess even such rights completely, for they are obliged to have a patron, so that they do but imperfectly participate in the community, and we call them citizens only in a qualified sense, as we might apply the term to children who
15 are too young to be on the register, or to old men who have been relieved from state duties. Of these we do not say quite simply that they are citizens, but add in the one case that they are not of age, and in the other, that they are past the age, or something of that sort; the precise expression is immaterial, for our meaning is clear. Similar difficulties to those which I have mentioned may be raised and answered about disfranchised citizens and about exiles. But the citizen whom we are seeking to define is a citizen in the strictest sense,
20 against whom no such exception can be taken, and his special characteristic is that he shares in the administration of justice, and in offices. Now of offices some are discontinuous, and the same persons
25 are not allowed to hold them twice, or can only hold them after a fixed interval; others have no limit of time – for example, the office of juryman or member of the assembly. It may, indeed, be argued that these are not magistrates at all, and that their functions give them no share in the government. But surely it is ridiculous to say that those who have the supreme power do not govern. Let us not dwell further
30 upon this, which is a purely verbal question; what we want is a common term including both juryman and member of the assembly. Let us, for the sake of distinction, call it 'indefinite office', and we will assume that those who share in such office are citizens. This is the most comprehensive definition of a citizen, and best suits all those who are generally so called.
35 But we must not forget that things of which the underlying principles differ in kind, one of them being first, another second, another third, have, when regarded in this relation, nothing, or hardly anything, worth mentioning in common. Now we see that governments differ in kind, and that some of them are prior and that others
1275ᵇ1 are posterior; those which are faulty or perverted are necessarily posterior to those which are perfect. (What we mean by perversion

will be hereafter explained.) The citizen then of necessity differs under each form of government; and our definition is best adapted to the citizen of a democracy; but not necessarily to other states. For in some states the people are not acknowledged, nor have they any regular assembly, but only extraordinary ones; and law-suits are distributed by sections among the magistrates. At Lacedaemon, for instance, the Ephors determine suits about contracts, which they distribute among themselves, while the elders are judges of homicide, and other causes are decided by other magistrates. A similar principle prevails at Carthage; there certain magistrates decide all causes. We may, indeed, modify our definition of the citizen so as to include these states. In them it is the holder of a definite, not an indefinite office, who is juryman and member of the assembly, and to some or all such holders of definite offices is reserved the right of deliberating or judging about some things or about all things. The conception of the citizen now begins to clear up.

He who has the power to take part in the deliberative or judicial administration of any state is said by us to be a citizen of that state; and, speaking generally, a state is a body of citizens sufficing for the purposes of life.

2 · But in practice a citizen is defined to be one of whom both the parents are citizens (and not just one, i.e. father or mother); others insist on going further back; say to two or three or more ancestors. This is a short and practical definition; but there are some who raise the further question of how this third or fourth ancestor came to be a citizen. Gorgias of Leontini, partly because he was in a difficulty, partly in irony, said that mortars are what is made by the mortar-makers, and the citizens of Larissa are those who are made by the magistrates; for it is their trade to 'make Larissaeans'. Yet the question is really simple, for, if according to the definition just given they shared in the government, they were citizens. This is a better definition than the other. For the words, 'born of a father or mother who is a citizen', cannot possibly apply to the first inhabitants or founders of a state.

There is a greater difficulty in the case of those who have been made citizens after a revolution, as by Cleisthenes at Athens after the expulsion of the tyrants, for he enrolled in tribes many metics, both strangers and slaves. The doubt in these cases is, not who is, but

whether he who is ought to be a citizen; and there will still be a further
1276ᵃ1 doubt, whether he who ought not to be a citizen, is one in fact, for
what ought not to be is what is false. Now, there are some who hold
office, and yet ought not to hold office, whom we described as ruling,
but ruling unjustly. And the citizen was defined by the fact of his
5   holding some kind of rule or office – he who holds a certain sort of
office fulfils our definition of a citizen. It is evident, therefore, that the
citizens about whom the doubt has arisen must be called citizens.

3 · Whether they ought to be so or not is a question which is bound
up with the previous inquiry. For a parallel question is raised
respecting the state, whether a certain act is or is not an act of the
state; for example, in the transition from an oligarchy or a tyranny to a
10 democracy. In such cases persons refuse to fulfil their contracts or
any other obligations, on the ground that the tyrant, and not the state,
contracted them; they argue that some constitutions are established
by force, and not for the sake of the common good. But this would
15 apply equally to democracies, and then the acts of the democracy will
be neither more nor less acts of the state in question than those of an
oligarchy or of a tyranny. This question runs up into another: – on
what principle shall we ever say that the state is the same, or different?
20 It would be a very superficial view which considered only the place
and the inhabitants (for the soil and the population may be separated,
and some of the inhabitants may live in one place and some in
another). This, however, is not a very serious difficulty; we need only
remark that the word 'state' is ambiguous.
25   It is further asked: When are men, living in the same place, to be
regarded as a single city – what is the limit? Certainly not the wall of
the city, for you might surround all Peloponnesus with a wall.
Babylon, we may say, is like this, and every city that has the compass of
30 a nation rather than a city; Babylon, they say, had been taken for three
days before some part of the inhabitants became aware of the fact.
This difficulty may, however, with advantage be deferred to another
occasion; the statesman has to consider the size of the state, and
whether it should consist of more than one race or not.
35   Again, shall we say that while the race of inhabitants remains the
same, the city is also the same, although the citizens are always dying
and being born, as we call rivers and fountains the same, although the
40 water is always flowing away and more coming? Or shall we say that

the generations of men, like the rivers, are the same, but that the state changes? For, since the state is a partnership, and is a partnership of 1276ᵇ1 citizens in a constitution, when the form of the government changes, and becomes different, then it may be supposed that the state is no longer the same, just as a tragic differs from a comic chorus, although 5 the members of both may be identical. And in this manner we speak of every union or composition of elements as different when the form of their composition alters; for example, a scale containing the same sounds is said to be different, accordingly as the Dorian or the Phrygian mode is employed. And if this is true it is evident that the 10 sameness of the state consists chiefly in the sameness of the constitution, and it may be called or not called by the same name, whether the inhabitants are the same or entirely different. It is quite another question, whether a state ought or ought not to fulfil engagements when the form of government changes. 15

4 · There is a point nearly allied to the preceding: Whether the excellence of a good man and a good citizen is the same or not. But before entering on this discussion, we must certainly first obtain some general notion of the excellence of the citizen. Like the sailor, the 20 citizen is a member of a community. Now, sailors have different functions, for one of them is a rower, another a pilot, and a third a look-out man, a fourth is described by some similar term; and while the precise definition of each individual's excellence applies 25 exclusively to him, there is, at the same time, a common definition applicable to them all. For they have all of them a common object, which is safety in navigation. Similarly, one citizen differs from another, but the salvation of the community is the common business of them all. This community is the constitution; the excellence of the 30 citizen must therefore be relative to the constitution of which he is a member. If, then, there are many forms of government, it is evident that there is not one single excellence of the good citizen which is perfect excellence. But we say that the good man is he who has one single excellence which is perfect excellence. Hence it is evident that the good citizen need not of necessity possess the excellence which 35 makes a good man.

The same question may also be approached by another road, from a consideration of the best constitution. If the state cannot be entirely composed of good men, and yet each citizen is expected to do his own

40 business well, and must therefore have excellence, still, inasmuch as
1277ª1 all the citizens cannot be alike, the excellence of the citizen and of the
good man cannot coincide. All must have the excellence of the good
citizen – thus, and thus only, can the state be perfect; but they will not
have the excellence of a good man, unless we assume that in the good
state all the citizens must be good.

5 Again, the state, as composed of unlikes, may be compared to the
living being: as the first elements into which a living being is resolved
are soul and body, as soul is made up of rational principle and
appetite, the family of husband and wife, property of master and slave,
so of all these, as well as other dissimilar elements, the state is
10 composed; and therefore the excellence of all the citizens cannot
possibly be the same, any more than the excellence of the leader of a
chorus is the same as that of the performer who stands by his side. I
have said enough to show why the two kinds of excellence cannot be
absolutely the same.

But will there then be no case in which the excellence of the good
citizen and the excellence of the good man coincide? To this we
15 answer that the good *ruler* is a good and wise man, but the citizen need
not be wise. And some persons say that even the education of the ruler
should be of a special kind; for are not the children of kings instructed
in riding and military exercises? As Euripides says:

No subtle arts for me, but what the state requires.[1]

20 As though there were a special education needed for a ruler. If the
excellence of a good ruler is the same as that of a good man, and we
assume further that the subject is a citizen as well as the ruler, the
excellence of the good citizen and the excellence of the good man
cannot be absolutely the same, although in some cases they may; for
the excellence of a ruler differs from that of a citizen. It was the sense
of this difference which made Jason say that 'he felt hungry when he
25 was not a tyrant', meaning that he could not endure to live in a private
station. But, on the other hand, it may be argued that men are praised
for knowing both how to rule and how to obey, and he is said to be a
citizen of excellence who is able to do both well. Now if we suppose
the excellence of a good man to be that which rules, and the
excellence of the citizen to include ruling and obeying, it cannot be

---

[1] Fragment from the lost play, *Aeolus*.

said that they are equally worthy of praise. Since, then, it is sometimes thought that the ruler and the ruled must learn different things and not the same, but that the citizen must know and share in them both, the inference is obvious. There is, indeed, the rule of a master, which is concerned with menial offices – the master need not know how to perform these, but may employ others in the execution of them: the other would be degrading; and by the other I mean the power actually to do menial duties, which vary much in character and are executed by various classes of slaves, such, for example, as handicraftsmen, who, as their name signifies, live by the labour of their hands – under these the mechanic is included. Hence in ancient times, and among some nations, the working classes had no share in the government – a privilege which they only acquired under extreme democracy. Certainly the good man and the statesman and the good citizen ought not to learn the crafts of inferiors except for their own occasional use; if they habitually practise them, there will cease to be a distinction between master and slave.

But there is a rule of another kind, which is exercised over freemen and equals by birth – a constitutional rule, which the ruler must learn by obeying, as he would learn the duties of a general of cavalry by being under the orders of a general of cavalry, or the duties of a general of infantry by being under the orders of a general of infantry, and by having had the command of a regiment and of a company. It has been well said that he who has never learned to obey cannot be a good commander. The excellence of the two is not the same, but the good citizen ought to be capable of both; he should know how to govern like a freeman, and how to obey like a freeman – these are the excellences of a citizen. And, although the temperance and justice of a ruler are distinct from those of a subject, the excellence of a good man will include both; for the excellence of the good man who is free and also a subject, e.g. his justice, will not be one but will comprise distinct kinds, the one qualifying him to rule, the other to obey, and differing as the temperance and courage of men and women differ. For a man would be thought a coward if he had no more courage than a courageous woman, and a woman would be thought loquacious if she imposed no more restraint on her conversation than the good man; and indeed their part in the management of the household is different, for the duty of the one is to acquire, and of the other to preserve. Practical wisdom is the only excellence peculiar to the ruler:

it would seem that all other excellences must equally belong to ruler and subject. The excellence of the subject is certainly not wisdom, but only true opinion; he may be compared to the maker of the flute, while
30 his master is like the flute-player or user of the flute.

From these considerations may be gathered the answer to the question, whether the excellence of the good man is the same as that of the good citizen, or different, and how far the same, and how far different.

5 · There still remains one more question about the citizen: Is he
35 only a true citizen who has a share of office, or is the mechanic to be included? If they who hold no office are to be deemed citizens, not every citizen can have this excellence; for this man is a citizen. And if none of the lower class are citizens, in which part of the state are they to be placed? For they are not resident aliens, and they are not
1278ª1 foreigners. May we not reply, that as far as this objection goes there is no more absurdity in excluding them than in excluding slaves and freedmen from any of the above-mentioned classes? It must be admitted that we cannot consider all those to be citizens who are necessary to the existence of the state; for example, children are not citizens equally with grown-up men, who are citizens absolutely, but
5 children, not being grown up, are only citizens on a certain assumption. In ancient times, and among some nations, the artisan class *were* slaves or foreigners, and therefore the majority of them are so now. The best form of state will not admit them to citizenship; but if they are admitted, then our definition of the excellence of a citizen will not
10 apply to every citizen, nor to every free man as such, but only to those who are freed from necessary services. The necessary people are either slaves who minister to the wants of individuals, or mechanics and labourers who are the servants of the community. These reflections carried a little further will explain their position; and indeed what has been said already is of itself, when understood, explanation enough.
15 Since there are many forms of government there must be many varieties of citizens, and especially of citizens who are subjects; so that under some governments the mechanic and the labourer will be citizens, but not in others, as, for example, in so-called aristocracies,
20 if there are any, in which honours are given according to excellence

and merit; for no man can practise excellence who is living the life of a mechanic or labourer. In oligarchies the qualification for office is high, and therefore no labourer can ever be a citizen; but a mechanic may, for an actual majority of them are rich. At Thebes there was a 25 law that no man could hold office who had not retired from business for ten years. But in many states the law goes to the length of admitting aliens; for in some democracies a man is a citizen though his mother only be a citizen; and a similar principle is applied to illegitimate children among many. Nevertheless they make such people citizens because of the dearth of legitimate citizens (for they introduce this sort of legislation owing to lack of population); so when 30 the number of citizens increases, first the children of a male or a female slave are excluded; then those whose mothers only are citizens; and at last the right of citizenship is confined to those whose fathers and mothers are both citizens.

Hence, as is evident, there are different kinds of citizens; and he is 35 a citizen in the fullest sense who shares in the honours of the state. Compare Homer's words 'like some dishonoured stranger';[1] he who is excluded from the honours of the state is no better than an alien. But when this exclusion is concealed, then its object is to deceive their fellow inhabitants. 40

As to the question whether the excellence of the good man is the 1278^{b}1 same as that of the good citizen, the considerations already adduced prove that in some states the good man and the good citizen are the same, and in others different. When they are the same it is not every citizen who is a good man, but only the statesman and those who have or may have, alone or in conjunction with others, the conduct of public affairs. 5

6 · Having determined these questions, we have next to consider whether there is only one form of government or many, and if many, what they are, and how many, and what are the differences between them.

A constitution is the arrangement of magistracies in a state, especially of the highest of all. The government is everywhere 10 sovereign in the state, and the constitution is in fact the government.

---

[1] *Iliad*, IX 648.

For example, in democracies the people are supreme, but in oligarchies, the few; and, therefore, we say that these two constitutions also are different: and so in other cases.

First, let us consider what is the purpose of a state, and how many forms of rule there are by which human society is regulated. We have already said, in the first part of this treatise, when discussing household management and the rule of a master, that man is by nature a political animal. And therefore, men, even when they do not require one another's help, desire to live together; not but that they are also brought together by their common interests in so far as they each attain to any measure of well-being. This is certainly the chief end, both of individuals and of states. And mankind meet together and maintain the political community also for the sake of mere life (in which there is possibly some noble element so long as the evils of existence do not greatly overbalance the good). And we all see that men cling to life even at the cost of enduring great misfortune, seeming to find in life a natural sweetness and happiness.

There is no difficulty in distinguishing the various kinds of rule; they have been often defined already in our popular discussions. The rule of a master, although the slave by nature and the master by nature have in reality the same interests, is nevertheless exercised primarily with a view to the interest of the master, but accidentally considers the slave, since, if the slave perish, the rule of the master perishes with him. On the other hand, the government of a wife and children and of a household, which we have called household management, is exercised in the first instance for the good of the governed or for the common good of both parties, but essentially for the good of the governed, as we see to be the case in medicine, gymnastic, and the arts in general, which are only accidentally concerned with the good of the artists themselves. For there is no reason why the trainer may not sometimes practise gymnastics, and the helmsman is always one of the crew. The trainer or the helmsman considers the good of those committed to his care. But, when he is one of the persons taken care of, he accidentally participates in the advantage, for the helmsman is also a sailor, and the trainer becomes one of those in training. And so in politics: when the state is framed upon the principle of equality and likeness, the citizens think that they ought to hold office by turns. Formerly, as is natural, everyone would take his turn of service; and then again, somebody else would look after his interest, just as he, while in office, had looked after theirs. But nowadays, for the sake of the advantage which is to be gained from the public revenues and from office, men want to be always in office. One might imagine that the rulers, being sickly, were only kept in health while they continued 15 in office; in that case we may be sure that they would be hunting after places. The conclusion is evident: that governments which have a regard to the common interest are constituted in accordance with strict principles of justice, and are therefore true forms; but those which regard only the interest of the rulers are all defective and 20 perverted forms, for they are despotic, whereas a state is a community of freemen.

7 · Having determined these points, we have next to consider how many forms of government there are, and what they are; and in the first place what are the true forms, for when they are determined the perversions of them will at once be apparent. The words constitution 25 and government have the same meaning, and the government, which is the supreme authority in states, must be in the hands of one, or of a few, or of the many. The true forms of government, therefore, are those in which the one, or the few, or the many, govern with a view to 30 the common interest; but governments which rule with a view to the private interest, whether of the one, or of the few, or of the many, are perversions. For the members of a state, if they are truly citizens, ought to participate in its advantages. Of forms of government in which one rules, we call that which regards the common interest, kingship; that in which more than one, but not many, rule, 35 aristocracy; and it is so called, either because the rulers are the best men, or because they have at heart the best interests of the state and of the citizens. But when the many administer the state for the common interest, the government is called by the generic name – a constitution. And there is a reason for this use of language. One man or a few 40 may excel in excellence; but as the number increases it becomes more 1279ᵇ1 difficult for them to attain perfection in every kind of excellence, though they may in military excellence, for this is found in the masses. Hence in a constitutional government the fighting-men have the supreme power, and those who possess arms are the citizens.

Of the above-mentioned forms, the perversions are as follows: – of kingship, tyranny; of aristocracy, oligarchy; of constitutional govern- 5 ment, democracy. For tyranny is a kind of monarchy which has in view the interest of the monarch only; oligarchy has in view the interest of the wealthy; democracy, of the needy: none of them the common good of all.

8 · But there are difficulties about these forms of government, and it will therefore be necessary to state a little more at length the nature of each of them. For he who would make a philosophical study of the various sciences, and is not only concerned with practice, ought not to overlook or omit anything, but to set forth the truth in every particular. Tyranny, as I was saying, is monarchy exercising the rule of a master over the political society; oligarchy is when men of property have the government in their hands; democracy, the opposite, when the indigent, and not the men of property, are the rulers. And here arises the first of our difficulties, and it relates to the distinction just drawn. For democracy is said to be the government of the many. But what if the many are men of property and have the power in their hands? In like manner oligarchy is said to be the government of the few; but what if the poor are fewer than the rich, and have the power in their hands because they are stronger? In these cases the distinction which we have drawn between these different forms of government would no longer hold good.

Suppose, once more, that we add wealth to the few and poverty to the many, and name the governments accordingly – an oligarchy is said to be that in which the few and the wealthy, and a democracy that in which the many and the poor are the rulers – there will still be a difficulty. For, if the only forms of government are the ones already mentioned, how shall we describe those other governments also just mentioned by us, in which the rich are the more numerous and the poor are the fewer, and both govern in their respective states?

The argument seems to show that, whether in oligarchies or in democracies, the number of the governing body, whether the greater number, as in a democracy, or the smaller number, as in an oligarchy, is an accident due to the fact that the rich everywhere are few, and the poor numerous. But if so, there is a misapprehension of the causes of the difference between them. For the real difference between democracy and oligarchy is poverty and wealth. Wherever men rule by reason of their wealth, whether they be few or many, that is an oligarchy, and where the poor rule, that is a democracy. But in fact the rich are few and the poor many; for few are well-to-do, whereas

freedom is enjoyed by all, and wealth and freedom are the grounds on 5
which the two parties claim power in the state.

9 · Let us begin by considering the common definitions of oligarchy
and democracy, and what is oligarchical and democratic justice. For
all men cling to justice of some kind, but their conceptions are 10
imperfect and they do not express the whole idea. For example,
justice is thought by them to be, and is, equality – not, however, for all,
but only for equals. And inequality is thought to be, and is, justice;
neither is this for all, but only for unequals. When the persons are
omitted, then men judge erroneously. The reason is that they are
passing judgement on themselves, and most people are bad judges in 15
their own case. And whereas justice implies a relation to persons as
well as to things, and a just distribution, as I have already said in the
Ethics,[1] implies the same ratio between the persons and between the
things, they agree about the equality of the things, but dispute about
the equality of the persons, chiefly for the reason which I have just 20
given – because they are bad judges in their own affairs; and secondly,
because both the parties to the argument are speaking of a limited and
partial justice, but imagine themselves to be speaking of absolute
justice. For the one party, if they are unequal in one respect, for
example wealth, consider themselves to be unequal in all; and the
other party, if they are equal in one respect, for example free birth, 25
consider themselves to be equal in all. But they leave out the capital
point. For if men met and associated out of regard to wealth only,
their share in the state would be proportioned to their property, and
the oligarchical doctrine would then seem to carry the day. It would
not be just that he who paid one mina should have the same share of a 30
hundred minae, whether of the principal or of the profits, as he who
paid the remaining ninety-nine. But a state exists for the sake of a
good life, and not for the sake of life only: if life only were the object,
slaves and brute animals might form a state, but they cannot, for they
have no share in happiness or in a life based on choice. Nor does a
state exist for the sake of alliance and security from injustice, nor yet 35
for the sake of exchange and mutual intercourse; for then the
Tyrrhenians and the Carthaginians, and all who have commercial
treaties with one another, would be the citizens of one state. True,

[1] *NE*, v 3.

they have agreements about imports, and engagements that they will
40 do no wrong to one another, and written articles of alliance. But there
1280ᵇ1 are no magistracies common to the contracting parties; different
states have each their own magistracies. Nor does one state take care
that the citizens of the other are such as they ought to be, nor see that
those who come under the terms of the treaty do no wrong or
wickedness at all, but only that they do no injustice to one another.
5 Whereas, those who care for good government take into consideration political excellence and defect. Whence it may be further
inferred that excellence must be the care of a state which is truly so
called, and not merely enjoys the name: for without this end the
community becomes a mere alliance which differs only in place from
10 alliances of which the members live apart; and law is only a convention, 'a surety to one another of justice', as the sophist Lycophron
says, and has no real power to make the citizens good and just.

This is obvious; for suppose distinct places, such as Corinth and
15 Megara, to be brought together so that their walls touched, still they
would not be one city, not even if the citizens had the right to
intermarry, which is one of the rights peculiarly characteristic of
states. Again, if men dwelt at a distance from one another, but not so
far off as to have no intercourse, and there were laws among them that
they should not wrong each other in their exchanges, neither would
20 this be a state. Let us suppose that one man is a carpenter, another a
farmer, another a shoemaker, and so on, and that their number is ten
thousand: nevertheless if they have nothing in common but exchange,
alliance, and the like, that would not constitute a state. Why is this?
Surely not because they are at a distance from one another; for even
25 supposing that such a community were to meet in one place, but that
each man had a house of his own, which was in a manner his state, and
that they made alliance with one another, but only against evil-doers;
still an accurate thinker would not deem this to be a state, if their
intercourse with one another was of the same character after as before
30 their union. It is clear then that a state is not a mere society, having a
common place, established for the prevention of mutual crime and for
the sake of exchange. These are conditions without which a state
cannot exist; but all of them together do not constitute a state, which is
a community of families and aggregations of families in well-being,
35 for the sake of a perfect and self-sufficing life. Such a community can
only be established among those who live in the same place and

intermarry. Hence there arise in cities family connexions, brother-hoods, common sacrifices, amusements which draw men together. But these are created by friendship, for to choose to live together is friendship. The end of the state is the good life, and these are the means towards it. And the state is the union of families and villages in 40 a perfect and self-sufficing life, by which we mean a happy and 1281ª1 honourable life.

Our conclusion, then, is that political society exists for the sake of noble actions, and not of living together. Hence they who contribute most to such a society have a greater share in it than those who have 5 the same or a greater freedom or nobility of birth but are inferior to them in political excellence; or than those who exceed them in wealth but are surpassed by them in excellence.

From what has been said it will be clearly seen that all the partisans of different forms of government speak of a part of justice only. 10

10 · There is also a doubt as to what is to be the supreme power in the state: – Is it the multitude? Or the wealthy? Or the good? Or the one best man? Or a tyrant? Any of these alternatives seems to involve disagreeable consequences. If the poor, for example, because they are more in number, divide among themselves the property of the rich – is 15 not this unjust? No, by heaven (will be the reply), for the supreme authority justly willed it. But if this is not extreme injustice, what is? Again, when in the first division all has been taken, and the majority divide anew the property of the minority, is it not evident, if this goes on, that they will ruin the state? Yet surely, excellence is not the ruin of 20 those who possess it, nor is justice destructive of a state; and therefore this law of confiscation clearly cannot be just. If it were, all the acts of a tyrant must of necessity be just; for he only coerces other men by superior power, just as the multitude coerce the rich. But is it just 25 then that the few and the wealthy should be the rulers? And what if they, in like manner, rob and plunder the people – is this just? If so, the other case will likewise be just. But there can be no doubt that all these things are wrong and unjust.

Then ought the good to rule and have supreme power? But in that case everybody else, being excluded from power, will be dishonoured. 30 For the offices of a state are posts of honour; and if one set of men always hold them, the rest must be deprived of them. Then will it be well that the one best man should rule? That is still more oligarchical,

for the number of those who are dishonoured is thereby increased.
35 Someone may say that it is bad in any case for a man, subject as he is to all the accidents of human passion, to have the supreme power, rather than the law. But what if the law itself be democratic or oligarchical, how will that help us out of our difficulties? Not at all; the same consequences will follow.

11 · Most of these questions may be reserved for another occasion.
40 The principle that the multitude ought to be in power rather than the few best might seem to be solved and to contain some difficulty and perhaps even truth.[a] For the many, of whom each individual is not a
1281ᵇ1 good man, when they meet together may be better than the few good, if regarded not individually but collectively, just as a feast to which many contribute is better than a dinner provided out of a single purse. For each individual among the many has a share of excellence and
5 practical wisdom, and when they meet together, just as they become in a manner one man, who has many feet, and hands, and senses, so too with regard to their character and thought. Hence the many are better judges than a single man of music and poetry; for some understand one part, and some another, and among them they understand the whole. There is a similar combination of qualities in
10 good men, who differ from any individual of the many, as the beautiful are said to differ from those who are not beautiful, and works of art from realities, because in them the scattered elements are combined, although, if taken separately, the eye of one person or some other feature in another person would be fairer than in the
15 picture. Whether this principle can apply to every democracy, and to all bodies of men, is not clear. Or rather, by heaven, in some cases it is impossible to apply; for the argument would equally hold about
20 brutes; and wherein, it will be asked, do some men differ from brutes? But there may be bodies of men about whom our statement is nevertheless true. And if so, the difficulty which has been already raised, and also another which is akin to it – viz. what power should be
25 assigned to the mass of freemen and citizens, who are not rich and have no personal merit – are both solved. There is still a danger in allowing them to share the great offices of state, for their folly will lead them into error, and their dishonesty into crime. But there is a danger

---

[a] The text of this sentence is corrupt.

also in not letting them share, for a state in which many poor men are 30
excluded from office will necessarily be full of enemies. The only way
of escape is to assign to them some deliberative and judicial functions.
For this reason Solon and certain other legislators give them the
power of electing to offices, and of calling the magistrates to account,
but they do not allow them to hold office singly.[1] When they meet
together their perceptions are quite good enough, and combined with 35
the better class they are useful to the state (just as impure food when
mixed with what is pure sometimes makes the entire mass more
wholesome than a small quantity of the pure would be), but each
individual, left to himself, forms an imperfect judgement. On the
other hand the popular form of government involves certain difficulties. In the first place, it might be objected that he who can judge of
the healing of a sick man would be one who could himself heal his 40
disease, and make him whole – that is, in other words, the physician;
and so in all professions and arts. As, then, the physician ought to be 1282ª1
called to account by physicians, so ought men in general to be called
to account by their peers. But physicians are of three kinds: – there is
the ordinary practitioner, and there is the master physician, and
thirdly the man educated in the art: in all arts there is such a class; and 5
we attribute the power of judging to them quite as much as to
professors of the art. Secondly, does not the same principle apply to
elections? For a right election can only be made by those who have
knowledge; those who know geometry, for example, will choose a
geometrician rightly, and those who know how to steer, a pilot; and, 10
even if there be some occupations and arts in which private persons
share in the ability to choose, they certainly cannot choose better than
those who know. So that, according to this argument, neither the
election of magistrates, nor the calling of them to account, should be
entrusted to the many. Yet possibly these objections are to a great
extent met by our old answer, that if the people are not utterly 15
degraded, although individually they may be worse judges than those
who have special knowledge, as a body they are as good or better.
Moreover, there are some arts whose products are not judged of
solely, or best, by the artists themselves, namely those arts whose
products are recognized even by those who do not possess the art; for
example, the knowledge of the house is not limited to the builder only; 20

[1] Solon's laws are described in II 12.

the user, or, in other words, the master, of the house will actually be a better judge than the builder, just as the pilot will judge better of a rudder than the carpenter, and the guest will judge better of a feast than the cook.

This difficulty seems now to be sufficiently answered, but there is
25 another akin to it. That inferior persons should have authority in greater matters than the good would appear to be a strange thing, yet the election and calling to account of the magistrates is the greatest of all. And these, as I was saying, are functions which in some states are assigned to the people, for the assembly is supreme in all such matters. Yet persons of any age, and having but a small property
30 qualification, sit in the assembly and deliberate and judge, although for the great officers of state, such as treasurers and generals, a high qualification is required. This difficulty may be solved in the same manner as the preceding, and the present practice of democracies may be really defensible. For the power does not reside in the
35 juryman, or counsellor, or member of the assembly, but in the court, and the council, and the assembly, of which the aforesaid individuals – counsellor, assemblyman, juryman – are only parts or members. And for this reason the many may claim to have a higher authority than the few; for the people, and the council, and the courts consist of
40 many persons, and their property collectively is greater than the property of one or of a few individuals holding great offices. But enough of this.

1282^{b}1 The discussion of the first question shows nothing so clearly as that laws, when good, should be supreme; and that the magistrate or magistrates should regulate those matters only on which the laws are
5 unable to speak with precision owing to the difficulty of any general principle embracing all particulars. But what are good laws has not yet been clearly explained; the old difficulty remains. The goodness or badness, justice or injustice, of laws varies of necessity with the
10 constitutions of states. This, however, is clear, that the laws must be adapted to the constitutions. But, if so, true forms of government will of necessity have just laws, and perverted forms of government will have unjust laws.

15 12 · In all sciences and arts the end is a good, and the greatest good and in the highest degree a good in the most authoritative of all – this is the political science of which the good is justice, in other words, the

78

common interest. All men think justice to be a sort of equality; and to a certain extent they agree with what we have said in our philosophical works about ethics.[1] For they say that what is just is just *for* someone 20 and that it should be equal for equals. But there still remains a question: equality or inequality of what? Here is a difficulty which calls for political speculation. For very likely some persons will say that offices of state ought to be unequally distributed according to superior excellence, in whatever respect, of the citizen, although there is no other difference between him and the rest of the 25 community; for those who differ in any one respect have different rights and claims. But, surely, if this is true, the complexion or height of a man, or any other advantage, will be a reason for his obtaining a greater share of political rights. The error here lies upon the surface, 30 and may be illustrated from the other arts and sciences. When a number of flute-players are equal in their art, there is no reason why those of them who are better born should have better flutes given to them; for they will not play any better on the flute, and the superior instrument should be reserved for him who is the superior artist. If what I am saying is still obscure, it will be made clearer as we proceed. 35 For if there were a superior flute-player who was far inferior in birth and beauty, although either of these may be a greater good than the art of flute-playing and may excel flute-playing in a greater ratio than 40 he excels the others in his art, still he ought to have the best flutes given to him, unless the advantages of wealth and birth contribute to 1283ᵃ1 excellence in flute-playing, which they do not. Moreover, upon this principle any good may be compared with any other. For if a given height[a] may be measured against wealth and against freedom, height 5 in general may be so measured. Thus if A excels in height more than B in excellence, even if excellence in general excels height still more, all goods will be comparable; for if a certain amount is better than some other, it is clear that some other will be equal. But since no such comparison can be made, it is evident that there is good reason why in 10 politics men do not ground their claim to office on every sort of inequality. For if some be slow, and others swift, that is no reason why the one should have little and the others much; it is in gymnastic

[1] *NE*, v 3.

---

[a] Omitting συμβάλλοιτο

contests that such excellence is rewarded. Whereas the rival claims of
15 candidates for office can only be based on the possession of elements
which enter into the composition of a state. And therefore the well-
born, or free-born, or rich, may with good reason claim office; for
holders of offices must be freemen and tax-payers: a state can be no
more composed entirely of poor men than entirely of slaves. But if
20 wealth and freedom are necessary elements, justice and valour are
equally so; for without the former qualities a state cannot exist at all,
without the latter not well.

13 · If the existence of the state is alone to be considered, then it
would seem that all, or some at least, of these claims are just; but, if we
25 take into account a good life, then, as I have already said, education
and excellence have superior claims. As, however, those who are
equal in one thing ought not to have an equal share in all, nor those
who are unequal in one thing to have an unequal share in all, it is
certain that all forms of government which rest on either of these
30 principles are perversions. All men have a claim in a certain sense, as I
have already admitted, but not all have an absolute claim. The rich
claim because they have a greater share in the land, and land is the
common element of the state; also they are generally more trust-
worthy in contracts. The free claim under the same title as the well-
35 born; for they are nearly akin. For the well-born are citizens in a truer
sense than the low-born, and good birth is always valued in a man's
own home. Another reason is, that those who are sprung from better
ancestors are likely to be better men, for good birth is excellence of
race. Excellence, too, may be truly said to have a claim, for justice has
been acknowledged by us to be a social excellence, and it implies all
40 others. Again, the many may urge their claim against the few; for,
when taken collectively, and compared with the few, they are stronger
1283^b1 and richer and better. But, what if the good, the rich, the well-born,
and the other classes who make up a state, are all living together in the
same city, will there, or will there not, be any doubt who shall rule? –
5 No doubt at all in determining who ought to rule in each of the above-
mentioned forms of government. For states are characterized by
differences in their governing bodies – one of them has a government
of the rich, another of the good, and so on. But a difficulty arises when
all these elements coexist. How are we to decide? Suppose the good to
10 be very few in number: may we consider their numbers in relation to

their duties, and ask whether they are enough to administer the state, or so many as will make up a state? Objections may be urged against all the aspirants to political power. For those who found their claims 15 on wealth or family might be thought to have no basis of justice; on this principle, if any one person were richer than all the rest, it is clear that he ought to be ruler of them. In like manner he who is very distinguished by his birth ought to have the superiority over all those who claim on the ground that they are free-born. In an aristocracy a 20 like difficulty occurs about excellence; for if one citizen is better than the other members of the government, however good they may be, he too, upon the same principle of justice, should rule over them. And if the people are to be supreme because they are stronger than the few, then if one man, or more than one, but not a majority, is stronger than 25 the many, they ought to rule, and not the many.

All these considerations appear to show that none of the principles on which men claim to rule and to hold all other men in subjection to them are right. To those who claim to be masters of the government 30 on the ground of their excellence or their wealth, the many might fairly answer that they themselves are often better and richer than the few – I do not say individually, but collectively. And another problem which is sometimes put forward may be met in a similar manner. 35 Some persons doubt whether the legislator who desires to make the justest laws ought to legislate with a view to the good of the better or of the many, when the case which we have mentioned occurs. Now what is right must be construed as equally right, and what is equally right is 40 to be considered with reference to the advantage of the state, and the common good of the citizens. And a citizen is one who shares in governing and being governed. He differs under different forms of 1284ᵃ1 government, but in the best state he is one who is able and chooses to be governed and to govern with a view to the life of excellence.

If, however, there be some one person, or more than one, although not enough to make up the full complement of a state, whose 5 excellence is so pre-eminent that the excellence or the political capacity of all the rest admit of no comparison with his or theirs, he or they can be no longer regarded as part of a state; for justice will not be done to the superior, if he is reckoned only as the equal of those who are so far inferior to him in excellence and in political capacity. Such a 10 man may truly be deemed a God among men. Hence we see that legislation is necessarily concerned only with those who are equal in

birth and in capacity; and that for men of pre-eminent excellence there is no law – they are themselves a law. Anyone would be
15 ridiculous who attempted to make laws for them: they would probably retort what, in the fable of Antisthenes, the lions said to the hares, when in the council of the beasts the latter began haranguing and claiming equality for all. And for this reason democratic states have instituted ostracism; equality is above all things their aim, and
20 therefore they ostracized and banished from the city for a time those who seemed to predominate too much through their wealth, or the number of their friends, or through any other political influence. Mythology tells us that the Argonauts left Heracles behind for a similar reason; the ship Argo would not take him because she feared
25 that he would have been too much for the rest of the crew. That is why those who denounce tyranny and blame the counsel which Periander gave to Thrasybulus cannot be held altogether just in their censure. The story is that Periander, when the herald was sent to ask counsel of
30 him, said nothing, but only cut off the tallest ears of corn till he had brought the field to a level. The herald did not know the meaning of the action, but came and reported what he had seen to Thrasybulus, who understood that he was to cut off the principal men in the state; and this is a policy not only expedient for tyrants or in practice
35 confined to them, but equally necessary in oligarchies and democracies. Ostracism is a measure of the same kind, which acts by disabling and banishing the most prominent citizens. Great powers do the same to whole cities and nations, as the Athenians did to the Samians,
40 Chians, and Lesbians; no sooner had they obtained a firm grasp of the empire, than they humbled their allies contrary to treaty; and the
1284ʰ1 Persian king has repeatedly crushed the Medes, Babylonians, and other nations, when their spirit has been stirred by the recollection of their former greatness.

The problem is a universal one, and equally concerns all forms of government, true as well as false; for, although perverted forms with a
5 view to their own interests may adopt this policy, those which seek the common interest do so likewise. The same thing may be observed in the arts and sciences; for the painter will not allow the figure to have a
10 foot which, however beautiful, is not in proportion, nor will the shipbuilder allow the stern or any other part of the vessel to be unduly large, any more than the chorus-master will allow anyone who sings louder or better than all the rest to sing in the choir. Monarchs, too,

may practise compulsion and still live in harmony with their cities, if their own government is for the interest of the state. Hence where ₁₅ there is an acknowledged superiority the argument in favour of ostracism is based upon a kind of political justice. It would certainly be better that the legislator should from the first so order his state as to have no need of such a remedy. But if the need arises, the next best thing is that he should endeavour to correct the evil by this or some ₂₀ similar measure. The principle, however, has not been fairly applied in states; for, instead of looking to the good of their own constitution, they have used ostracism for factious purposes. It is true that under perverted forms of government, and from their special point of view, such a measure is just and expedient, but it is also clear that it is not absolutely just. In the perfect state there would be great doubts about ₂₅ the use of it, not when applied to excess in strength, wealth, popularity, or the like, but when used against someone who is pre-eminent in excellence – what is to be done with him? People will not say that such a man is to be expelled and exiled; on the other hand, he ₃₀ ought not to be a subject – that would be as if mankind should claim to rule over Zeus, dividing his offices among them. The only alternative is that all should happily obey such a ruler, according to what seems to be the order of nature, and that men like him should be kings in their state for life.

14 · The preceding discussion, by a natural transition, leads to the ₃₅ consideration of kingship, which we say is one of the true forms of government. Let us see whether in order to be well governed a state or country should be under the rule of a king or under some other form of government; and whether monarchy, although good for some, may ₄₀ not be bad for others. But first we must determine whether there is one species of kingship or many. It is easy to see that there are many, ₁₂₈₅ᵃ₁ and that the manner of government is not the same in all of them.

Of kingships according to law, the Lacedaemonian is thought to be the best example; but there the royal power is not absolute, except when the kings go on an expedition, and then they take the command. ₅ Matters of religion are likewise committed to them. The kingly office is in truth a kind of generalship, sovereign and perpetual. The king has not the power of life and death, except in certain cases, as for instance, in ancient times, he had it when upon a campaign, by right of force. This custom is described in Homer. For Agamemnon puts up ₁₀ with it when he is attacked in the assembly, but when the army goes out to battle he has the power even of life and death. Does he not say: 'When I find a man skulking apart from the battle, nothing shall save him from the dogs and vultures, for in my hands is death'?[1]

15 This, then, is one form of kingship – a generalship for life; and of such kingships some are hereditary and others elective.

There is another sort of monarchy not uncommon among foreigners, which nearly resembles tyranny. But this is both legal and
20 hereditary. For foreigners, being more servile in character than Hellenes, and Asiatics than Europeans, do not rebel against a despotic government. Such kingships have the nature of tyrannies because the people are by nature slaves; but there is no danger of their being overthrown, for they are hereditary and legal. For the same
25 reason, their guards are such as a king and not such as a tyrant would employ, that is to say, they are composed of citizens, whereas the guards of tyrants are mercenaries. For kings rule according to law over voluntary subjects, but tyrants over involuntary; and the one are guarded by their fellow-citizens, the others are guarded against them.

30 These are two forms of monarchy, and there was a third which existed in ancient Hellas, called an Aesymnetia. This may be defined generally as an elective tyranny, which, like foreign monarchy, is legal, but differs from it in not being hereditary. Sometimes the office was held for life, sometimes for a term of years, or until certain duties had
35 been performed. For example, the Mytilenaeans once elected Pittacus leader against the exiles, who were headed by Antimenides and Alcaeus the poet. And Alcaeus himself shows in one of his banquet odes that they chose Pittacus tyrant, for he reproaches his fellow-citizens for 'having made the low-born Pittacus tyrant of the spiritless
1285[b]1 and ill-fated city, with one voice shouting his praises'.

These forms of government have always had the character of tyrannies, because they possess despotic power; but inasmuch as they are elective and acquiesced in by their subjects, they are kingly.

There is a fourth species of kingly monarchy – that of the heroic
5 times – which was hereditary and legal, and was exercised over willing subjects. For the first chiefs were benefactors of the people in arts or arms; they either gathered them into a community, or procured land for them; and thus they became kings of voluntary subjects, and their
10 power was inherited by their descendants. They took the command in

[1] *Iliad*, II 391–3.

84

war and presided over the sacrifices except those which required a priest. They also decided law-suits either with or without an oath; and when they swore, the form of the oath was the stretching out of their sceptre. In ancient times their power extended continuously to all things in city and country and across the border; but at a later date 15 they relinquished several of these privileges, and others the people took from them, until in some states nothing was left to them but the sacrifices; and where they retained more of the reality they had only the right of leadership in war beyond the border.

These, then, are the four kinds of kingship. First the monarchy of 20 the heroic ages; this was exercised over voluntary subjects, but limited to certain functions; the king was a general and a judge, and had the control of religion. The second is that of foreigners, which is an hereditary despotic government in accordance with law. A third is the 25 power of the so-called Aesymnete; this is an elective tyranny. The fourth is the Lacedaemonian, which is in fact a generalship, hereditary and perpetual. These four forms differ from one another in the manner which I have described.

There is a fifth form of kingly rule in which one man has the disposal of all, just as each nation of each state has the disposal of 30 public matters; this form corresponds to the control of a household. For as household management is the kingly rule of a house, so kingly rule is the household management of a city, or of a nation, or of many nations.

15 · Of these forms we need only consider two, the Lacedaemonian and the absolute royalty; for most of the others lie in a region between 35 them, having less power than the last, and more than the first. Thus the inquiry is reduced to two points: first, is it advantageous to the state that there should be a perpetual general, and if so, should the office be confined to one family, or open to the citizens in turn? Secondly, is it well that a single man should have the supreme power 1286ᵃ1 in all things? The first question falls under the head of laws rather than of constitutions; for perpetual generalship might equally exist under any form of government, so that this matter may be dismissed 5 for the present. The other kind of kingship is a sort of constitution; this we have now to consider, and to run over the difficulties involved in it. We will begin by inquiring whether it is more advantageous to be ruled by the best man or by the best laws.

The advocates of kingship maintain that the laws speak only in 10 general terms, and cannot provide for circumstances; and that for any science to abide by written rules is absurd. In Egypt the physician is allowed to alter his treatment after the fourth day, but if sooner, he takes the risk. Hence it is clear that a government acting according to

15 written laws is plainly not the best. Yet surely the ruler cannot dispense with the general principle which exists in law; and that is a better ruler which is free from passion than that in which it is innate. Whereas the law is passionless, passion must always sway the heart of

20 man. Yes, it may be replied, but then on the other hand an individual will be better able to deliberate in particular cases.

The best man, then, must legislate, and laws must be passed, but these laws will have no authority when they miss the mark, though in all other cases retaining their authority. But when the law cannot

25 determine a point at all, or not well, should the one best man or should all decide? According to our present practice assemblies meet, sit in judgement, deliberate, and decide, and their judgements all relate to individual cases. Now any member of the assembly, taken separately, is certainly inferior to the wise man. But the state is made up of many individuals. And as a feast to which all the guests contribute is better

30 than a banquet furnished by a single man, so a multitude is a better judge of many things than any individual.

Again, the many are more incorruptible than the few; they are like the greater quantity of water which is less easily corrupted than a little. The individual is liable to be overcome by anger or by some other passion, and then his judgement is necessarily perverted; but it is hardly to be supposed that a great number of persons would all get

35 into a passion and go wrong at the same moment. Let us assume that they are the freemen, and that they never act in violation of the law, but fill up the gaps which the law is obliged to leave. Or, if such virtue is scarcely attainable by the multitude, we need only suppose that the majority are good men and good citizens, and ask which will be the

40 more incorruptible, the one good ruler, or the many who are all good?

1286ᵇ1 Will not the many? But, you will say, there may be factions among them, whereas the one man is not divided against himself. To which we may answer that their character is as good as his. If we call the rule

5 of many men, who are all of them good, aristocracy, and the rule of one man kingship, then aristocracy will be better for states than kingship, whether the government is supported by force or not, provided only that a number of men equal in excellence can be found.

The first governments were kingships, probably for this reason because of old, when cities were small, men of eminent excellence 10 were few. Further, they were made kings because they were benefactors, and benefits can only be bestowed by good men. But when many persons equal in merit arose, no longer enduring the pre-eminence of one, they desired to have a commonwealth, and set up a constitution. The ruling class soon deteriorated and enriched themselves out of the public treasury; riches became the path to honour, and so oligarchies 15 naturally grew up. These passed into tyrannies and tyrannies into democracies; for love of gain in the ruling classes was always tending to diminish their number, and so to strengthen the masses who in the end set upon their masters and established democracies. Since cities 20 have increased in size, no other form of government appears to be any longer even easy to establish.

Even supposing the principle to be maintained that kingly power is the best thing for states, how about the family of the king? Are his children to succeed him? If they are no better than anybody else, that will be mischievous. But perhaps the king, though he might, will not 25 hand on his power to his children? That, however, is hardly to be expected, and is too much to ask of human nature. There is also a difficulty about the force which he is to employ; should a king have guards about him by whose aid he may be able to coerce the 30 refractory? If not, how will he administer his kingdom? Even if he is the lawful sovereign who does nothing arbitrarily or contrary to law, still he must have some force wherewith to maintain the law. In the case of a limited monarchy there is not much difficulty in answering this question; the king must have such force as will be more than a 35 match for one or more individuals, but not so great as that of the people. The ancients observed this principle when they gave guards to anyone whom they appointed Aesymnete or tyrant. Thus, when Dionysius asked the Syracusans to allow him guards, somebody advised that they should give him only such a number. 40

16 · At this place in the discussion there impends the inquiry 1287ª1 respecting the king who acts solely according to his own will; he has now to be considered. The so-called kingship according to law, as I have already remarked, is not a form of government, for under all governments, as, for example, in a democracy or aristocracy, there 5 may be a general holding office for life, and one person is often made

supreme over the administration of a state. A magistracy of this kind exists at Epidamnus, and also at Opus, but in the latter city has a more limited power. Now, absolute monarchy, or the arbitrary rule of a
10 sovereign over all the citizens, in a city which consists of equals, is thought by some to be quite contrary to nature; it is argued that those who are by nature equals must have the same natural right and worth, and that for unequals to have an equal share, or for equals to have an unequal share, in the offices of state, is as bad as for different bodily
15 constitutions to have the same food and clothing. That is why it is thought to be just that among equals everyone be ruled as well as rule, and therefore that all should have their turn. We thus arrive at law; for an order of succession implies law. And the rule of the law, it is
20 argued, is preferable to that of any individual. On the same principle, even if it be better for certain individuals to govern, they should be made only guardians and ministers of the law. For magistrates there must be – this is admitted; but then men say that to give authority to any one man when all are equal is unjust. There may indeed be cases
25 which the law seems unable to determine, but such cases a man could not determine either. But the law trains officers for this express purpose, and appoints them to determine matters which are left undecided by it, to the best of their judgement. Further, it permits them to make any amendment of the existing laws which experience suggests. Therefore he who bids the law rule may be deemed to bid
30 God and Reason alone rule, but he who bids man rule adds an element of the beast; for desire is a wild beast, and passion perverts the minds of rulers, even when they are the best of men. The law is reason unaffected by desire. We are told that a patient should call in a physician; he will not get better if he is doctored out of a book. But the
35 parallel of the arts is clearly not in point; for the physician does nothing contrary to rule from motives of friendship; he only cures a patient and takes a fee; whereas magistrates do many things from spite and partiality. And, indeed, if a man suspected the physician of
40 being in league with his enemies to destroy him for a bribe, he would
1287ᵇ1 rather have recourse to the book. But certainly physicians, when they are sick, call in other physicians, and training-masters, when they are in training, other training-masters, as if they could not judge truly about their own case and might be influenced by their feelings. Hence it is evident that in seeking for justice men seek for the mean, for the
5 law is the mean. Again, customary laws have more weight, and relate

to more important matters, than written laws, and a man may be a safer ruler than the written law, but not safer than the customary law.

Again, it is by no means easy for one man to superintend many things; he will have to appoint a number of subordinates, and what difference does it make whether these subordinates always existed or were appointed by him because he needed them? If, as I said before, the good man has a right to rule because he is better, still two good men are better than one: this is the old saying.

> two going together,[1]

and the prayer of Agamemnon,

> would that I had ten such counsellors![2]

And even now there are magistrates, for example judges, who have authority to decide some matters which the law is unable to determine, since no one doubts that the law would command and decide in the best manner whatever it could. But some things can, and other things cannot, be comprehended under the law, and this is the origin of the vexed question whether the best law or the best man should rule. For matters of detail about which men deliberate cannot be included in legislation. Nor does anyone deny that the decision of such matters must be left to man, but it is argued that there should be many judges, and not one only. For every ruler who has been trained by the law judges well; and it would surely seem strange that a person should see better with two eyes, or hear better with two ears, or act better with two hands or feet, than many with many; indeed, it is already the practice of kings to make to themselves many eyes and ears and hands and feet. For they make colleagues of those who are the friends of themselves and their governments. They must be friends of the monarch and of his government; if not his friends, they will not do what he wants; but friendship implies likeness and equality; and, therefore, if he thinks that his friends ought to rule, he must think that those who are equal to himself and like himself ought to rule equally with himself. These are the principal controversies relating to monarchy.

17 · But may not all this be true in some cases and not in others? for

---

[1] Homer, *Iliad*, x 224.   [2] Homer, *Iliad*, ii 372.

there is by nature both a justice and an advantage appropriate to the rule of a master, another to kingly rule, another to constitutional rule; 40 but there is none naturally appropriate to tyranny, or to any other perverted form of government; for these come into being contrary to 1288ᵃ1 nature. Now, to judge at least from what has been said, it is manifest that, where men are alike and equal, it is neither expedient nor just that one man should be lord of all, whether there are laws, or whether there are no laws, but he himself is in the place of law. Neither should a good man be lord over good men, nor a bad man over bad; nor, even 5 if he excels in excellence, should he have a right to rule, unless in a particular case, at which I have already hinted, and to which I will once more recur. But first of all, I must determine what natures are suited for government by a king, and what for an aristocracy, and what for a constitutional government.

A people who are by nature capable of producing a race superior in the excellence needed for political rule are fitted for kingly govern-10 ment; and a people submitting to be ruled as freemen by men whose excellence renders them capable of political command are adapted for an aristocracy: while the people who are suited for constitutional freedom are those among whom there naturally exists a warlike multitude. In the former case the multitude is capable of being ruled by men whose excellence is appropriate to political command; in the latter case the multitude is able to rule and to obey in turn by a law 15 which gives office to the well-to-do according to their desert. But when a whole family, or some individual, happens to be so pre-eminent in excellence as to surpass all others, then it is just that they should be the royal family and supreme over all, or that this one 20 citizen should be king. For, as I said before, to give them authority is not only agreeable to that notion of justice which the founders of all states, whether aristocratic, or oligarchical, or again democratic, are accustomed to put forward (for these all recognize the claim of superiority, although not the same superiority), but accords with the principle already laid down. For surely it would not be right to kill, or 25 ostracize, or exile such a person, or require that he should take his turn in being governed. The whole is naturally superior to the part, and he who has this pre-eminence is in the relation of a whole to a part. But if so, the only alternative is that he should have the supreme power, and that mankind should obey him, not in turn, but always. 30 These are the conclusions at which we arrive respecting kingship and

its various forms, and this is the answer to the question, whether it is
or is not advantageous to states, and to which, and how.

18 · We maintain that the true forms of government are three, and
that the best must be that which is administered by the best, and in
which there is one man, or a whole family, or many persons, excelling ₃₅
all the others together in excellence, and both rulers and subjects are
fitted, the one to rule, the others to be ruled, in such a manner as to
attain the most desirable life. We showed at the commencement of
our inquiry that the excellence of the good man is necessarily the
same as the excellence of the citizen of the perfect state. Clearly then
in the same manner, and by the same means through which a man ₄₀
becomes truly good, he will frame a state that is to be ruled by an
aristocracy or by a king, and the same education and the same habits 1288ᵇ1
will be found to make a good man and a man fit to be a statesman or
king.

Having arrived at these conclusions, we must proceed to speak of
the perfect state, and describe how it comes into being and is
established.

So if we are to inquire in the appropriate way about it, we must.... ₅

BOOK IV

1 · In all arts and sciences which embrace the whole of any subject, ₁₀
and do not come into being in a fragmentary way, it is the province of a
single art or science to consider all that appertains to a single subject.
For example, the art of gymnastics considers not only the suitableness
of different modes of training to different bodies, but what sort is the
best (for the best must suit that which is by nature best and best
furnished with the means of life), and also what common form of ₁₅
training is adapted to the great majority of men. And if a man does not
desire the best habit of body, or the greatest skill in gymnastics, which
might be attained by him, still the trainer or the teacher of gymnastics
should be able to impart any lower degree of either. The same
principle equally holds in medicine and ship-building, and the ₂₀
making of clothes, and in the arts generally.

Hence it is obvious that government too is the subject of a single

science, which has to consider what government is best and what sort
it must be, to be most in accordance with our aspirations, if there were
no external impediment, and also what kind of government is adapted
25 to particular states. For the best is often unattainable, and therefore
the true legislator and statesman ought to be acquainted, not only
with that which is best in the abstract, but also with that which is best
relatively to circumstances. We should be able further to say how a
state may be constituted under any given conditions; both how it is
30 originally formed and, when formed, how it may be longest preserved;
the supposed state neither having the best constitution nor being
provided even with the conditions necessary for the best, nor being
the best under the circumstances, but of an inferior type.

We ought, moreover, to know the form of government which is best
35 suited to states in general; for political writers, although they have
excellent ideas, are often unpractical. We should consider, not only
what form of government is best, but also what is possible and what is
easily attainable by all. There are some who would have none but the
40 most perfect; for this many natural advantages are required. Others,
again, speak of a more attainable form, and, although they reject the
constitution under which they are living, they extol some one in
1289ᵃ1 particular, for example the Lacedaemonian. Any change of government which has to be introduced should be one which men, starting
from their existing constitutions, will be both willing and able to
adopt, since there is quite as much trouble in the reformation of an
old constitution as in the establishment of a new one, just as to
5 unlearn is as hard as to learn. And therefore, in addition to the
qualifications of the statesman already mentioned, he should be able
to find remedies for the defects of existing constitutions, as has been
said before. This he cannot do unless he knows how many forms of
government there are. It is often supposed that there is only one kind
10 of democracy and one of oligarchy. But this is a mistake; and, in order
to avoid such mistakes, we must ascertain what differences there are
in the constitutions of states, and in how many ways they are
combined. The same political insight will enable a man to know which
laws are the best, and which are suited to different constitutions; for
the laws are, and ought to be, framed with a view to the constitution,
15 and not the constitution to the laws. A constitution is the organization
of offices in a state, and determines what is to be the governing body,
and what is the end of each community. But laws are not to be

confounded with the principles of the constitution; they are the rules according to which the magistrates should administer the state, and proceed against offenders. So that we must know the varieties, and 20 the number of varieties, of each form of government, if only with a view to making laws. For the same laws cannot be equally suited to all oligarchies or to all democracies, since there is certainly more than one form both of democracy and of oligarchy. 25

2 · In our original discussion about governments we divided them into three true forms: kingly rule, aristocracy, and constitutional government, and three corresponding perversions – tyranny, oligarchy, and democracy. Of kingly rule and of aristocracy we have 30 already spoken, for the inquiry into the perfect state is the same thing as the discussion of the two forms thus named, since both imply a principle of excellence provided with external means. We have already determined in what aristocracy and kingly rule differ from one another, and when the latter should be established. In what 35 follows we have to describe the so-called constitutional government, which bears the common name of all constitutions, and the other forms, tyranny, oligarchy, and democracy.

It is obvious which of the three perversions is the worst, and which is the next in badness. That which is the perversion of the first and 40 most divine is necessarily the worst. And just as a royal rule, if not a mere name, must exist by virtue of some great personal superiority in 1289^{b}1 the king, so tyranny, which is the worst of governments, is necessarily the farthest removed from a well-constituted form; oligarchy is little better, for it is a long way from aristocracy, and democracy is the most tolerable of the three. 5

A writer who preceded me has already made these distinctions, but his point of view is not the same as mine. For he lays down the principle that when all the constitutions are good (the oligarchy and the rest being virtuous), democracy is the worst, but the best when all are bad. Whereas we maintain that they are in any case defective, and that one oligarchy is not to be accounted better than another, but only 10 less bad.

Not to pursue this question further at present, let us begin by determining how many varieties of constitution there are (since of democracy and oligarchy there are several); what constitution is the most generally acceptable, and what is preferable in the next degree 15

after the perfect state; and besides this what other there is which is aristocratic and well-constituted, and at the same time adapted to states in general; and of the other forms of government we must ask to what people each is suited. For democracy may meet the needs of
20 some better than oligarchy, and conversely. In the next place we have to consider in what manner a man ought to proceed who desires to establish some one among these various forms, whether of democracy or of oligarchy; and lastly, having briefly discussed these subjects to the best of our power, we will endeavour to ascertain the modes of
25 ruin and preservation both of constitutions generally and of each separately, and to what causes they are to be attributed.

3 · The reason why there are many forms of government is that every state contains many elements. In the first place we see that all
30 states are made up of families, and in the multitude of citizens there must be some rich and some poor, and some in a middle condition; the rich possess heavy armour, and the poor not. Of the common people, some are farmers, and some traders, and some artisans. There are also among the notables differences of wealth and property
35 – for example, in the number of horses which they keep, for they cannot afford to keep them unless they are rich. And therefore in old times the cities whose strength lay in their cavalry were oligarchies, and they used cavalry in wars against their neighbours; as was the practice of the Eretrians and Chalcidians, and also of the Magnesians on the river Mæander, and of other peoples in Asia. Besides
1290ª1 differences of wealth there are differences of rank and merit, and there are some other elements which were mentioned by us when in treating of aristocracy we enumerated the essentials of a state. Of
5 these elements, sometimes all, sometimes the lesser, and sometimes the greater number, have a share in the government. It is evident then that there must be many forms of government, differing in kind, since the parts of which they are composed differ from each other in kind. For a constitution is an organization of offices, which all the citizens distribute among themselves, according to the power which different
10 classes possess (for example the rich or the poor), or according to some principle of equality which includes both. There must therefore be as many forms of government as there are modes of arranging the offices, according to the superiorities and the differences of the parts of the state.

94

There are generally thought to be two principal forms: as men say
of the winds that there are but two, north and south, and that the rest 15
of them are only variations of these, so of governments there are said
to be only two forms – democracy and oligarchy. For aristocracy is
considered to be a kind of oligarchy, as being the rule of a few, and the
so-called constitutional government to be really a democracy, just as
among the winds we make the west a variation of the north, and the
east of the south wind. Similarly of musical modes there are said to be 20
two kinds, the Dorian and the Phrygian; the other arrangements of
the scale are comprehended under one or other of these two. About
forms of government this is a very favourite notion. But in either case
the better and more exact way is to distinguish, as I have done, the one
or two which are true forms, and to regard the others as perversions, 25
whether of the most perfectly attempered or of the best form of
government: the more taut and more overpowering are oligarchical,
and the more relaxed and gentler are democratic.

4 · It must not be assumed, as some are fond of saying, that 30
democracy is simply that form of government in which the greater
number are sovereign, for in oligarchies, and indeed in every government, the majority rules; nor again is oligarchy that form of government in which a few are sovereign. Suppose the whole population of a
city to be 1300, and that of these 1000 are rich, and do not allow the 35
remaining 300 who are poor, but free, and in all other respects their
equals, a share of the government – no one will say that this is a
democracy. In like manner, if the poor were few and the masters of
the rich who outnumber them, no one would ever call such a
government, in which the rich majority have no share of office, an 40
oligarchy. Therefore we should rather say that democracy is the form 1290^b1
of government in which the free are rulers, and oligarchy in which the
rich; it is only an accident that the free are the many and the rich are
the few. Otherwise a government in which the offices were given
according to stature, as is said to be the case in Ethiopia, or according 5
to beauty, would be an oligarchy; for the number of tall or good-
looking men is small. And yet oligarchy and democracy are not
sufficiently distinguished merely by these two characteristics of
wealth and freedom. Both of them contain many other elements, and
therefore we must carry our analysis further, and say that the
government is not a democracy in which the freemen, being few in 10

number, rule over the many who are not free, as at Apollonia on the Ionian Gulf, and at Thera (for in each of these states the nobles, who were also the earliest settlers, held office, although they were but a few out of many). Neither is it a democracy when the rich have the
15 government because they exceed in number; as was the case formerly at Colophon, where the bulk of the inhabitants were possessed of large property before the Lydian War. But the form of government is a democracy when the free, who are also poor and the majority, govern, and an oligarchy when the rich and the noble govern, they
20 being at the same time few in number.

I have said that there are many forms of government, and have explained to what causes the variety is due. Why there are more than those already mentioned, and what they are, and whence they arise, I will now proceed to consider, starting from the principle already admitted, which is that every state consists, not of one, but of many
25 parts. If we were going to speak of the different species of animals, we should first of all determine the organs which are indispensable to every animal, as for example some organs of sense and the instruments of receiving and digesting food, such as the mouth and the stomach, besides organs of locomotion. Assuming now that there are
30 only so many kinds of organs, but that there may be differences in them – I mean different kinds of mouths, and stomachs, and perceptive and locomotive organs – the possible combinations of these differences will necessarily furnish many varieties of animals. (For animals cannot be the same which have different kinds of
35 mouths or of ears.) And when all the combinations are exhausted, there will be as many sorts of animals as there are combinations of the necessary organs. The same, then, is true of the forms of government which have been described; states, as I have repeatedly said, are
40 composed, not of one, but of many elements. One element is the
1291ª1 food-producing class, who are called farmers; a second, the class of artisans who practise the arts without which a city cannot exist – of these arts some are absolutely necessary, others contribute to luxury or to the grace of life. The third class is that of traders, and by traders I
5 mean those who are engaged in buying and selling, whether in commerce or in retail trade. A fourth class is that of labourers. The military make up the fifth class, and they are as necessary as any of the others, if the country is not to be the slave of every invader. For how can a state which has any title to the name be of a slavish nature? The

state is independent and self-sufficing, but a slave is the reverse of 10
independent. Hence we see that this subject, though ingeniously, has
not been satisfactorily treated in the *Republic*.[1] Socrates says that a
state is made up of four sorts of people who are absolutely necessary;
these are a weaver, a farmer, a shoemaker, and a builder; afterwards,
finding that they are not enough, he adds a smith, and again a 15
herdsman, to look after the necessary animals; then a merchant, and
then a retail trader. All these together form the complement of the
first state, as if a state were established merely to supply the
necessaries of life, rather than for the sake of the good, or stood
equally in need of shoemakers and of farmers. But he does not admit
into the state a military class until the country has increased in size, 20
and is beginning to encroach on its neighbour's land, whereupon they
go to war. Yet even amongst his four original citizens, or whatever be
the number of those whom he associates in the state, there must be
some one who will dispense justice and determine what is just. And as
the soul may be said to be more truly part of an animal than the body, 25
so the higher parts of states, that is to say, the warrior class, the class
engaged in the administration of justice, and that engaged in
deliberation, which is the special business of political understanding
– these are more essential to the state than the parts which minister to
the necessaries of life. Whether their several functions are the
functions of different citizens, or of the same – for it may often 30
happen that the same persons are both soldiers and farmers – is
immaterial to the argument. The higher as well as the lower elements
are to be equally considered parts of the state, and if so, the military
element at any rate must be included. There are also the wealthy who
minister to the state with their property; these form the seventh class.
The eighth class is that of public servants and of administrators; for 35
the state cannot exist without rulers. And therefore some must be able
to take office and to serve the state, either always or in turn. There
only remains the class of those who deliberate and who judge between
disputants; we were just now distinguishing them. If the presence of 40
all these elements, and their fair and equitable organization, is
necessary to states, then there must also be persons who have the 1291^{b}1
ability of statesmen. Different functions appear to be often combined
in the same individual; for example, the soldier may also be a farmer,

---

[1] Plato, *Rep.*, II 369B–371E.

5   or an artisan; or, again the counsellor a judge. And all claim to possess political ability, and think that they are quite competent to fill most offices. But the same persons cannot be rich and poor at the same time. For this reason the rich and the poor are especially regarded as parts of a state. Again, because the rich are generally few in number,

10   while the poor are many, they appear to be antagonistic, and as the one or the other prevails they form the government. Hence arises the common opinion that there are two kinds of government – democracy and oligarchy.

     I have already explained that there are many forms of constitution,

15   and to what causes the variety is due. Let me now show that there are different forms both of democracy and oligarchy, as will indeed be evident from what has preceded. For both in the common people and in the notables various classes are included; of the common people, one class are farmers, another artisans; another traders, who are

20   employed in buying and selling; another are the sea-faring class, whether engaged in war or in trade, as ferrymen or as fishermen. (In many places any one of these classes forms quite a large population; for example, fishermen at Tarentum and Byzantium, crews of triremes at Athens, merchant seamen at Aegina and Chios, ferrymen

25   at Tenedos.) To the classes already mentioned may be added day-labourers, and those who, owing to their needy circumstances, have no leisure, or those who are not of free birth on both sides; and there may be other classes as well. The notables again may be divided according to their wealth, birth, excellence, education, and similar

30   differences.

     Of forms of democracy first comes that which is said to be based strictly on equality. In such a democracy the law says that it is just for the poor to have no more advantage than the rich; and that neither should be masters, but both equal. For if liberty and equality, as is

35   thought by some, are chiefly to be found in democracy, they will be best attained when all persons alike share in the government to the utmost. And since the people are the majority, and the opinion of the majority is decisive, such a government must necessarily be a democracy. Here then is one sort of democracy. There is another, in which the magistrates are elected according to a certain property

40   qualification, but a low one; he who has the required amount of property has a share in the government, but he who loses his property

1292ᵃ1 loses his rights. Another kind is that in which all the citizens who are under no disqualification share in the government, but still the law is supreme. In another, everybody, if he be only a citizen, is admitted to the government, but the law is supreme as before. A fifth form of democracy, in other respects the same, is that in which not the law, 5 but the multitude, have the supreme power, and supersede the law by their decrees. This is a state of affairs brought about by the demagogues. For in democracies which are subject to the law the best citizens hold the first place, and there are no demagogues; but where the laws are not supreme, there demagogues spring up. For the 10 people becomes a monarch, and is many in one; and the many have the power in their hand, not as individuals, but collectively. Homer says that 'it is not good to have a rule of many',[1] but whether he means this corporate rule, or the rule of many individuals, is uncertain. At all events this sort of democracy, which is now a monarchy, and no 15 longer under the control of law, seeks to exercise monarchical sway, and grows into a despot; the flatterer is held in honour; this sort of democracy is to other democracies what tyranny is to other forms of monarchy. The spirit of both is the same, and they alike exercise a despotic rule over the better citizens. The decrees of the one 20 correspond to the edicts of the tyrant; and the demagogue is to the one what the flatterer is to the other. Both have great power – the flatterer with the tyrant, the demagogue with democracies of the kind which we are describing. The demagogues make the decrees of the people override the laws, by referring all things to the popular 25 assembly. And therefore they grow great, because the people have all things in their hands, and they hold in their hands the votes of the people, who obey them. Further, those who have any complaint to bring against the magistrates say, 'let the people be judges'; the people are happy to accept the invitation; and so the authority of every 30 office is undermined. Such a democracy is fairly open to the objection that it is not a constitution at all; for where the laws have no authority, there is no constitution. The law ought to be supreme over all, and the magistracies should judge of particulars, and only this[a] should be considered a constitution. So that if democracy be a real form of 35 government, the sort of system in which all things are regulated by

---

[1] *Iliad*, II 204.

---

[a] Reading ταύτην for τήν

decrees is clearly not even a democracy in the true sense of the word, for decrees relate only to particulars.

These then are the different kinds of democracy.

5 · Of oligarchies, too, there are different kinds: one where the property qualification for office is such that the poor, although they form the majority, have no share in the government, yet he who acquires a qualification may obtain a share. Another sort is when there is a qualification for office, but a high one, and the vacancies in the governing body are filled by co-optation. If the election is made out of all the qualified persons, a constitution of this kind inclines to an aristocracy, if out of a privileged class, to an oligarchy. Another sort of oligarchy is when the son succeeds the father. There is a fourth form, likewise hereditary, in which the magistrates are supreme and not the law. Among oligarchies this is what tyranny is among monarchies, and the last-mentioned form of democracy among democracies; and in fact this sort of oligarchy receives the name of a dynasty.

These are the different sorts of oligarchies and democracies. It should, however, be remembered that in many states the constitution which is established by law, although not democratic, owing to the education and habits of the people may be administered democratically, and conversely in other states the established constitution may incline to democracy, but may be administered in an oligarchical spirit. This most often happens after a revolution; for governments do not change at once; at first the dominant party are content with encroaching a little upon their opponents. The laws which existed previously continue in force, but the authors of the revolution have the power in their hands.

6 · From what has been already said we may safely infer that there are these many democracies and oligarchies. For it is necessary that either all the classes whom we mentioned must share in the government, or some only and not others. When the class of farmers and of those who possess moderate fortunes have the supreme power, the government is administered according to law. For the citizens being compelled to live by their labour have no leisure; and so they set up the authority of the law, and attend assemblies only when necessary. They all obtain a share in the government when they have acquired

the qualification which is fixed by the law; hence all who have acquired the property qualification are admitted to a share in the constitution. For the absolute exclusion of any class would be oligarchical; but leisure cannot be provided for them unless there are revenues to support them. This is one sort of democracy, and these are the causes which give birth to it. Another kind is based on the distinction which naturally comes next in order; in this, everyone to 35 whose birth there is no objection is eligible, but actually shares in the government only if he can find leisure. Hence in such a democracy the supreme power is vested in the laws, because the state has no means of paying the citizens. A third kind is when all freemen have a right to share in the government, but do not actually share, for the reason which has been already given; so that in this form again the law 40 must rule. A fourth kind of democracy is that which comes latest in 1293ᵃ1 the history of states. For when cities have far outgrown their original size, and their revenues have increased, all the citizens have a place in the government, through the great preponderance of the multitude; and they all, including the poor who receive pay, and therefore have 5 leisure to exercise their rights, share in the administration. Indeed, when they are paid, the common people have the most leisure, for they are not hindered by the care of their property, which often fetters the rich, who are thereby prevented from taking part in the assembly or in the courts, and so the state is governed by the poor, who are a 10 majority, and not by the laws. Such and so many are the kinds of democracy, and they grow out of these necessary causes.

Of oligarchies, one form is that in which the majority of the citizens have some property, but not very much; and this is the first form, which allows anyone who obtains the required amount the right of sharing in the government. The sharers in the government being a 15 numerous body, it follows that the law must govern, and not individuals. For in proportion as they are further removed from a monarchical form of government, and in respect of property have neither so much as to be able to live without attending to business, nor so little as to need state support, they must admit the rule of law and not claim to 20 rule themselves. But if the men of property in the state are fewer than in the former case, and own more property, there arises a second form of oligarchy. For the stronger they are, the more power they claim, and having this object in view, they themselves select those of the other classes who are to be admitted to the government; but, not being

25 as yet strong enough to rule without the law, they make the law represent their wishes. When this power is intensified by a further diminution of their numbers and increase of their property, there arises a third and further stage of oligarchy, in which the governing class keep the offices in their own hands, and the law ordains that the son shall succeed the father. When, again, the rulers have great
30 wealth and numerous friends, this sort of family despotism approaches a monarchy; individuals rule and not the law. This is the fourth sort of oligarchy, and is analogous to the last sort of democracy.

35 7 · There are still two forms besides democracy and oligarchy; one of them is universally recognized and included among the four principal forms of government, which are said to be monarchy, oligarchy, democracy, and the so-called aristocracy. But there is also
40 a fifth, which retains the generic name of constitutional government; this is not common, and therefore has not been noticed by writers who
1293ʰ1 attempt to enumerate the different kinds of government; like Plato, in their books about the state, they recognize four only. The term 'aristocracy' is rightly applied to the form of government which is described in the first part of our treatise; for that only can be rightly
5 called aristocracy which is a government formed of the best men absolutely, and not merely of men who are good relative to some hypothesis. In the perfect state the good man is absolutely the same as the good citizen; whereas in other states the good citizen is only good relatively to his own form of government. But there are some states differing from oligarchies and also differing from the so-called constitutional government; these are termed aristocracies, and in
10 them magistrates are certainly chosen both according to their wealth and according to their merit. Such a form of government differs from each of the two just now mentioned, and is termed an aristocracy. For indeed in states which do not make excellence the aim of the community, men of merit and reputation for excellence may be
15 found. And so where a government has regard to wealth, excellence, and the populace, as at Carthage, that is aristocracy; and also where it has regard only to two out of the three, as at Lacedaemon, to excellence and the populace, and the two principles of democracy and excellence temper each other. There are these two forms of
20 aristocracy in addition to the first and perfect state, and there is a third

form, viz. the constitutions which incline more than the so-called constitutional government towards oligarchy.

8 · I have yet to speak of the so-called polity and of tyranny. I put them in this order, not because a polity or constitutional government is to be regarded as a perversion any more than the above-mentioned aristocracies. The truth is, that they all fall short of the most perfect 25 form of government, and so they are reckoned among perversions, and the really perverted forms are perversions of these, as I said in the original discussion. Last of all I will speak of tyranny, which I place last in the series because I am inquiring into the constitutions of 30 states, and this is the very reverse of a constitution.

Having explained why I have adopted this order, I will proceed to consider constitutional government; of which the nature will be clearer now that oligarchy and democracy have been defined. For polity or constitutional government may be described generally as a fusion of oligarchy and democracy; but the term is usually applied to 35 those forms of government which incline towards democracy, and the term aristocracy to those which incline towards oligarchy, because birth and education are commonly the accompaniments of wealth. Moreover, the rich already possess the external advantages the want of which is a temptation to crime, and hence they are called noblemen and gentlemen. And inasmuch as aristocracy seeks to give pre- 40 dominance to the best of the citizens, people say also of oligarchies that they are composed of noblemen and gentlemen. Now it appears 1294ᵃ1 to be an impossible thing that the state which is governed not by the best citizens but by the worst should be well-governed, and equally impossible that the state which is ill-governed should be governed by the best. But we must remember that good laws, if they are not obeyed, do not constitute good government. Hence there are two parts of good government; one is the actual obedience of citizens to 5 the laws, the other part is the goodness of the laws which they obey; they may obey bad laws as well as good. And there may be a further subdivision; they may obey either the best laws which are attainable to them, or the best absolutely.

The distribution of offices according to excellence is a special 10 characteristic of aristocracy, for the principle of an aristocracy is excellence, as wealth is of an oligarchy, and freedom of a democracy.

In all of them there of course exists the right of the majority, and whatever seems good to the majority of those who share in the government has authority, whether in an oligarchy, or aristocracy or a

15 democracy. Now in most states the form called polity exists, for the fusion goes no further than the attempt to unite the freedom of the poor and the wealth of the rich, who commonly take the place of the noble. But as there are three grounds on which men claim an equal

20 share in the government, freedom, wealth, and excellence (for the fourth, what is called good birth, is the result of the two last, being only ancient wealth and excellence), it is clear that the admixture of the two elements, that is to say, of the rich and poor, is to be called a polity or constitutional government; and the union of the three is to be called aristocracy, and more than any other form of government,

25 except the true and ideal, has a right to this name.

Thus far I have shown the existence of forms of states other than monarchy, democracy, and oligarchy, and what they are, and in what aristocracies differ from one another, and polities from aristocracies – that the two latter are not very unlike is obvious.

30 9 · Next we have to consider how by the side of oligarchy and democracy the so-called polity or constitutional government springs up, and how it should be organized. The nature of it will be at once understood from a comparison of oligarchy and democracy; we must ascertain their different characteristics, and taking a portion from

35 each, fit the two together, like the parts of a tally-stick. Now there are three modes in which fusions of government may be effected. In the first mode we must combine the laws made by both governments, say concerning the administration of justice. In oligarchies they impose a fine on the rich if they do not serve as judges, and to the poor they give

40 no pay; but in democracies they give pay to the poor and do not fine the rich. Now the union of these two modes is a common or middle

1294^{b}1 term between them, and is therefore characteristic of a constitutional government, for it is a combination of both. This is one mode of uniting the two elements. Or a mean may be taken between the enactments of the two: thus democracies require no property qualification, or only a small one, from members of the assembly, oligarchies

5 a high one; here neither of these is the common term, but a mean between them. There is a third mode, in which something is borrowed from the oligarchical and something from the democratic

principle. For example, the appointment of magistrates by lot is thought to be democratic, and the election of them oligarchical; democratic again when there is no property qualification, oligarchical 10 when there is. In the aristocratic or constitutional state, one element will be taken from each – from oligarchy the principle of electing to offices, from democracy the disregard of qualification. Such are the various modes of combination.

There is a true union of oligarchy and democracy when the same state may be termed either a democracy or an oligarchy; those who 15 use both names evidently feel that the fusion is complete. Such a fusion there is also in the mean; for both extremes appear in it. The Lacedaemonian constitution, for example, is often described as a 20 democracy, because it has many democratic features. In the first place the youth receive a democratic education. For the sons of the poor are brought up with the sons of the rich, who are educated in such a manner as to make it possible for the sons of the poor to be educated like them. A similar equality prevails in the following period of life, and when the citizens are grown up to manhood the same rule is 25 observed; there is no distinction between the rich and poor. In like manner they all have the same food at their public tables, and the rich wear only such clothing as any poor man can afford. Again, the people elect to one of the two greatest offices of state, and in the other they 30 share; for they elect the Senators and share in the Ephoralty. By others the Spartan constitution is said to be an oligarchy, because it has many oligarchical elements. That all offices are filled by election and none by lot, is one of these oligarchical characteristics; that the power of inflicting death or banishment rests with a few persons is another; and there are others. In a well attempered polity there should 35 appear to be both elements and yet neither; also the government should rely on itself, and not on foreign aid, and on itself not through the good will of a majority[a] – they might be equally well-disposed when there is a vicious form of government – but through the general willingness of all classes in the state to maintain the constitution.

Enough of the manner in which a constitutional government, and 40 in which the so-called aristocracies, ought to be framed.

10 · Of the nature of tyranny I have still to speak, in order that it may 1295ᵃ1

---

[a] Omitting ἔξωθεν.

have its place in our inquiry (since even tyranny is reckoned by us to be a form of government), although there is not much to be said about it. I have already in the former part of this treatise discussed royalty or kingship according to the most usual meaning of the term, and considered whether it is or is not advantageous to states, and what kind of royalty should be established, and from what source, and how.

When speaking of royalty we also spoke of two forms of tyranny, which are both according to law, and therefore easily pass into royalty. Among Barbarians, there are elected monarchs who exercise a despotic power; despotic rulers were also elected in ancient Greece, called Aesymnetes. These monarchies, when compared with one another, exhibit certain differences. And they are, as I said before, royal, in so far as the monarch rules according to law over willing subjects; but they are tyrannical in so far as he is despotic and rules according to his own fancy. There is also a third kind of tyranny, which is the most typical form, and is the counterpart of the perfect monarchy. This tyranny is just that arbitrary power of an individual which is responsible to no one, and governs all alike, whether equals or betters, with a view to its own advantage; not to that of its subjects, and therefore against their will. No freeman willingly endures such a government.

The kinds of tyranny are such and so many, and for the reasons which I have given.

11 · We have now to inquire what is the best constitution for most states, and the best life for most men, neither assuming a standard of excellence which is above ordinary persons, nor an education which is exceptionally favoured by nature and circumstances, nor yet an ideal state which is an aspiration only, but having regard to the life in which the majority are able to share, and to the form of government which states in general can attain. As to those aristocracies, as they are called, of which we were just now speaking, they either lie beyond the possibilities of the greater number of states, or they approximate to the so-called constitutional government, and therefore need no separate discussion. And in fact the conclusion at which we arrive respecting all these forms rests upon the same grounds. For if what was said in the *Ethics* is true, that the happy life is the life according to excellence lived without impediment,[1] and that excellence is a mean,[2]

---

[1] cf. *NE*, I 10, VII 13. 　　[2] cf. *NE*, II 6–9.

then the life which is in a mean, and in a mean attainable by everyone, must be the best. And the same principles of excellence and badness are characteristic of cities and of constitutions; for the constitution is 40 so to speak the life of the city.

Now in all states there are three elements: one class is very rich, 1295^{b}1 another very poor, and a third in a mean. It is admitted that moderation and the mean are best, and therefore it will clearly be best to possess the gifts of fortune in moderation; for in that condition of 5 life men are most ready to follow rational principle. But he who greatly excels in beauty, strength, birth, or wealth, or on the other hand who is very poor, or very weak, or of very low status, finds it difficult to follow rational principle. Of these two the one sort grow into violent and great criminals, the others into rogues and petty 10 rascals. And two sorts of offences correspond to them, the one committed from violence, the other from roguery [Again, the middle class is least likely to shrink from rule, or to be over-ambitious for it],^{a} both of which are injuries to the state. Again, those who have too much of the goods of fortune, strength, wealth, friends, and the like, 15 are neither willing nor able to submit to authority. The evil begins at home; for when they are boys, by reason of the luxury in which they are brought up, they never learn, even at school, the habit of obedience. On the other hand, the very poor, who are in the opposite extreme, are too degraded. So that the one class cannot obey, and can 20 only rule despotically; the other knows not how to command and must be ruled like slaves. Thus arises a city, not of freemen, but of masters and slaves, the one despising, the other envying; and nothing can be more fatal to friendship and good fellowship in states than this: for good fellowship springs from friendship; when men are at enmity with one another, they would rather not even share the same path. But a city ought to be composed, as far as possible, of equals and similars; 25 and these are generally the middle classes. Wherefore the city which is composed of middle-class citizens is necessarily best constituted in respect of the elements of which we say the fabric of the state naturally consists. And this is the class of citizens which is most secure in a state, for they do not, like the poor, covet other men's goods; nor do 30 others covet theirs, as the poor covet the goods of the rich; and as they neither plot against others, nor are themselves plotted against, they

---

^{a} Excised by Dreizehnter.

pass through life safely. Wisely then did Phocylides pray – 'Many things are best in the mean; I desire to be of a middle condition in my city.'

35 Thus it is manifest that the best political community is formed by citizens of the middle class, and that those states are likely to be well-administered in which the middle class is large, and stronger if possible than both the other classes, or at any rate than either singly; for the addition of the middle class turns the scale, and prevents either of the extremes from being dominant. Great then is the good
40 fortune of a state in which the citizens have a moderate and sufficient
1296ᵃ1 property; for where some possess much, and the others nothing, there may arise an extreme democracy, or a pure oligarchy; or a tyranny may grow of either extreme – either out of the most rampant democracy, or out of an oligarchy; but it is not so likely to arise out of the middle
5 constitutions and those akin to them. I will explain the reason for this hereafter, when I speak of the revolutions of states. The mean condition of states is clearly best, for no other is free from faction; and where the middle class is large, there are least likely to be factions and dissensions. For a similar reason large states are less liable to faction
10 than small ones, because in them the middle class is large; whereas in small states it is easy to divide all the citizens into two classes who are either rich or poor, and to leave nothing in the middle. And democracies are safer and more permanent than oligarchies, because
15 they have a middle class which is more numerous and has a greater share in the government; for when there is no middle class, and the poor are excessive in number, troubles arise, and the state soon comes to an end. A proof of the superiority of the middle class is that the best legislators have been of a middle condition; for example, Solon, as his
20 own verses testify; and Lycurgus, for he was not a king; and Charondas, and almost all legislators.

These considerations will help us to understand why most governments are either democratic or oligarchical. The reason is that the middle class is seldom numerous in them, and whichever party,
25 whether the rich or the common people, transgresses the mean and predominates, draws the constitution its own way, and thus arises either oligarchy or democracy. There is another reason – the poor and the rich quarrel with one another, and whichever side gets the
30 better, instead of establishing a just or popular government, regards political supremacy as the prize of victory, and the one party sets up a

democracy and the other an oligarchy. Further, both the parties which had the supremacy in Greece looked only to the interest of their own form of government, and established in states, the one, democracies, and the other, oligarchies; they thought of their own 35 advantage, and of the advantage of the other states not at all. For these reasons the middle form of government has rarely, if ever, existed, and among a very few only. One man alone of all who ever ruled in Greece was induced to give this middle constitution to states. But it 40 has now become a habit among the citizens of states not even to care 1296ᵇ1 about equality; all men are seeking for dominion, or, if conquered, are willing to submit.

What then is the best form of government, and what makes it the best, is evident; and of other constitutions, since we say that there are many kinds of democracy and many of oligarchy, it is not difficult to 5 see which has the first and which the second or any other place in the order of excellence, now that we have determined which is the best. For that which is nearest to the best must of necessity be better, and that which is further from the mean worse, if we are judging absolutely and not relatively to given conditions: I say 'relatively to 10 given conditions', since a particular government may be preferable, but another form may be better for some people.

12 · We have now to consider what and what kind of government is suitable to what and what kind of men. I may begin by assuming, as a general principle common to all governments, that the portion of the 15 state which desires the permanence of the constitution ought to be stronger than that which desires the reverse. Now every city is composed of quality and quantity. By quality I mean freedom, wealth, education, good birth, and by quantity, superiority of numbers. Quality may exist in one of the classes which make up the state, and 20 quantity in the other. For example, the meanly-born may be more in number than the well-born, or the poor than the rich, yet they may not so much exceed in quantity as they fall short in quality; and therefore there must be a comparison of quantity and quality. Where the number of the poor exceeds a given proportion, there will naturally be 25 a democracy, varying in form with the sort of people who compose it in each case. If, for example, the farmers exceed in number, the first form of democracy will then arise; if the artisans and labouring class, the last; and so with the intermediate forms. But where the rich and 30

the notables exceed in quality more than they fall short in quantity, there oligarchy arises, similarly assuming various forms according to the kind of superiority possessed by the oligarchs.

35   The legislator should always include the middle class in his government; if he makes his laws oligarchical, let him look to the middle class; if he makes them democratic, he should equally by his laws try to attach this class to the state. There only can the government ever be stable where the middle class exceeds one or both of the
40   others, and in that case there will be no fear that the rich will unite
1297ª1 with the poor against the rulers. For neither of them will ever be willing to serve the other, and if they look for some form of government more suitable to both, they will find none better than this, for the rich and the poor will never consent to rule in turn, because
5   they mistrust one another. The arbiter is always the one most trusted, and he who is in the middle is an arbiter. The more perfect the admixture of the political elements, the more lasting will be the constitution. Many even of those who desire to form aristocratic governments make a mistake, not only in giving too much power to
10   the rich, but in attempting to cheat the people. There comes a time when out of a false good there arises a true evil, since the encroachments of the rich are more destructive to the constitution than those of the people.

13 · The devices by which oligarchies deceive the people are five in
15   number; they relate to the assembly; the magistracies; the courts of law; the use of arms; and gymnastic exercises. The assemblies are thrown open to all, but either the rich only are fined for non-attendance, or a much larger fine is inflicted upon them. As to the
20   magistracies, those who are qualified by property cannot decline office upon oath, but the poor may. In the law-courts the rich, and the rich only, are fined if they do not serve, the poor are let off with impunity, or, as in the laws of Charondas, a larger fine is inflicted on the rich, and a smaller one on the poor. In some states all citizens who
25   have registered themselves are allowed to attend the assembly and to try causes; but if after registration they do not attend either in the assembly or at the courts, heavy fines are imposed upon them. The intention is that through fear of the fines they may avoid registering themselves, and then they cannot sit in the law-courts or in the
30   assembly. Concerning the possession of arms, and gymnastic

exercises, they legislate in a similar spirit. For the poor are not obliged to have arms, but the rich are fined for not having them; and in like manner no penalty is inflicted on the poor for non-attendance at the gymnasium, and consequently, having nothing to fear, they do not attend, whereas the rich are liable to a fine, and therefore they take care to attend.

These are the devices of oligarchical legislators, and in democracies they have counter-devices. They pay the poor for attending the assemblies and the law-courts, and they inflict no penalty on the rich for non-attendance. It is obvious that he who would duly mix the two principles should combine the practice of both, and provide that the poor should be paid to attend, and the rich fined if they do not attend, for then all will take part; if there is no such combination, power will be in the hands of one party only. The government should be confined to those who carry arms. As to the property qualification, no absolute rule can be laid down, but we must see what is the highest qualification sufficiently comprehensive to secure that the number of those who have the rights of citizens exceeds the number of those excluded. Even if they have no share in office, the poor, provided only that they are not outraged or deprived of their property, will be quiet enough.

But to secure gentle treatment for the poor is not an easy thing, since a ruling class is not always humane. And in time of war the poor are apt to hesitate unless they are fed; when fed, they are willing enough to fight. In some states the government is vested, not only in those who are actually serving, but also in those who have served; among the Malians, for example, the governing body consisted of the latter, while the magistrates were chosen from those actually on service. And the earliest government which existed among the Greeks, after the overthrow of the kingly power, grew up out of the warrior class, and was originally taken from the knights (for strength and superiority in war at that time depended on cavalry; indeed, without discipline, infantry are useless, and in ancient times there was no military knowledge or tactics, and therefore the strength of armies lay in their cavalry). But when cities increased and the heavy-armed grew in strength, more had a share in the government; and this is the reason why the states which we call constitutional governments have been hitherto called democracies. Ancient constitutions, as might be expected, were oligarchical and royal; their population being small,

35

40

1297ᵇ1

5

10

15

20

25

they had no considerable middle class; the people were weak in numbers and organization, and were therefore more content to be governed.

I have explained why there are various forms of government, and
30 why there are more than is generally supposed; for democracy, as well as other constitutions, has more than one form: also what their differences are, and whence they arise, and what is the best form of government, speaking generally, and to whom the various forms of government are best suited; all this has now been explained.

35 **14** · Having thus gained an appropriate basis of discussion we will proceed to speak of the points which follow next in order. We will consider the subject not only in general but with reference to particular constitutions. All constitutions have three elements, concerning which the good lawgiver has to regard what is expedient for each constitution. When they are well-ordered, the constitution is
40 well-ordered, and as they differ from one another, constitutions differ. There is one element which deliberates about public affairs;
1298ª1 secondly that concerned with the magistracies – the questions being, what they should be, over what they should exercise authority, and what should be the mode of electing to them; and thirdly that which has judicial power.

The deliberative element has authority in matters of war and peace,
5 in making and unmaking alliances; it passes laws, inflicts death, exile, confiscation, elects magistrates and audits their accounts. These powers must be assigned either all to all the citizens or all to some of them (for example, to one or more magistracies, or different causes to different magistracies), or some of them to all, and others of them
10 only to some. That all things should be decided by all is characteristic of democracy; this is the sort of equality which the people desire. But there are various ways in which all may share in the government; they may deliberate, not all in one body, but by turns, as in the constitution of Telecles the Milesian. There are other constitutions in which the
15 boards of magistrates meet and deliberate, but come into office by turns, and are elected out of the tribes and the very smallest divisions of the state, until every one has obtained office in his turn. The citizens, on the other hand, are assembled only for the purposes of legislation, and to consult about the constitution, and to hear the
20 edicts of the magistrates. In another variety of democracy the citizens

form one assembly, but meet only to elect magistrates, to pass laws, to advise about war and peace, and to make scrutinies. Other matters are referred severally to special magistrates, who are elected by vote or by lot out of all the citizens. Or again, the citizens meet about election to offices and about scrutinies, and deliberate concerning war or alliances while other matters are administered by the magistrates, who, as far as is possible, are elected by vote. I am speaking of those magistracies in which special knowledge is required. A fourth form of democracy is when all the citizens meet to deliberate about everything, and the magistrates decide nothing, but only make the preliminary inquiries; and that is the way in which the last form of democracy, corresponding, as we maintain, to the close family oligarchy and to tyranny, is at present administered. All these modes are democratic.

On the other hand, that some should deliberate about all is oligarchical. This again is a mode which, like the democratic, has many forms. When the deliberative class being elected out of those who have a moderate qualification are numerous and they respect and obey the prohibitions of the law without altering it, and anyone who has the required qualification shares in the government, then, just because of this moderation, the oligarchy inclines towards polity. But when only selected individuals and not the whole people share in the deliberations of the state, then, although, as in the former case, they observe the law, the government is a pure oligarchy. Or, again, when those who have the power of deliberation are self-elected, and son succeeds father, and they and not the laws are supreme – the government is of necessity oligarchical. Where, again, particular persons have authority in particular matters – for example, when the whole people decide about peace and war and hold scrutinies, but the magistrates regulate everything else, and they are elected by vote or by lot – there the government is an aristocracy or a constitutional government. And if some questions are decided by magistrates elected by vote, and others by magistrates elected by lot, either absolutely or out of select candidates, or elected partly by vote, partly by lot – these practices are partly characteristic of an aristocratic government, and partly of a pure constitutional government.

These are the various forms of the deliberative body; they correspond to the various forms of government. And the government of each state is administered according to one or other of the principles

which have been laid down. Now it is for the interest of democracy, according to the most prevalent notion of it (I am speaking of that
15 extreme form of democracy in which the people are supreme even over the laws), with a view to better deliberation to adopt the custom of oligarchies respecting courts of law. For in oligarchies the rich who are wanted to be judges are compelled to attend under pain of a fine, whereas in democracies the poor are paid to attend. And this practice of oligarchies should be adopted by democracies in their public
20 assemblies, for they will advise better if they all deliberate together, the people with the notables and the notables with the people. It is also a good plan that those who deliberate should be elected by vote or by lot in equal numbers out of the different classes; and that if the people greatly exceed in numbers those who have political training,
25 pay should not be given to all, but only to as many as would balance the number of the notables, or that the number in excess should be eliminated by lot. But in oligarchies either certain persons should be co-opted from the mass, or a class of officers should be appointed such as exist in some states, who are termed Probuli and guardians of the law; and the citizens should occupy themselves exclusively with
30 matters on which they have previously deliberated; for in that way the people will have a share in the deliberations of the state, but will not be able to disturb the principles of the constitution. Again, in oligarchies either the people ought to accept the measures of the government, or not to pass anything contrary to them; or, if all are allowed to share in counsel, the decision should rest with the magistrates. The opposite
35 of what is done in constitutional governments should be the rule in oligarchies; the veto of the majority should be final, their assent not final, but the proposal should be referred back to the magistrates. Whereas in constitutional governments they take the contrary course; the few have the negative, not the affirmative power; the affirmation
40 of everything rests with the multitude.
1299ᵃ1   These, then, are our conclusions respecting the deliberative, that is, the supreme element in states.

15 · Next we will proceed to consider the distribution of offices; this, too, being a part of politics concerning which many questions
5 arise: – What shall their number be? Over what shall they preside, and what shall be their duration? Sometimes they last for six months, sometimes for less; sometimes they are annual, whilst in other cases

offices are held for still longer periods. Shall they be for life or for a long term of years; or, if for a short term only, shall the same persons hold them over and over again, or once only? Also about the appointment to them – from whom are they to be chosen, by whom, and how? We should first be in a position to say what are the possible varieties of them, and then we may proceed to determine which are suited to different forms of government. But what are to be included under the term 'offices'? That is a question not quite so easily answered. For a political community requires many officers; and not every one who is chosen by vote or by lot is to be regarded as a ruler. In the first place there are the priests, who must be distinguished from political officers; masters of choruses and heralds, even ambassadors, are elected by vote. Some duties of superintendence again are political, extending either to all the citizens in a single sphere of action, like the office of the general who superintends them when they are in the field, or to a section of them only, like the inspectorships of women or of youth. Other offices are concerned with household management, like that of the corn measurers who exist in many states and are elected officers. There are also menial offices which the rich have executed by their slaves. Speaking generally, those are to be called offices to which the duties are assigned of deliberating about certain measures and of judging and commanding, especially the last; for to command is the especial duty of a magistrate. But the question is not of any importance in practice; no one has ever brought into court the meaning of the word, although such problems have a speculative interest.

What kinds of offices, and how many, are necessary to the existence of a state, and which, if not necessary, yet conduce to its well-being, are much more important considerations, affecting all constitutions, but more especially small states. For in great states it is possible, and indeed necessary, that every office should have a special function; where the citizens are numerous, many may hold office. And so it happens that some offices a man holds a second time only after a long interval, and others he holds once only; and certainly every work is better done which receives the sole and not the divided attention of the worker. But in small states it is necessary to combine many offices in a few hands, since the small number of citizens does not admit of many holding office – for who will there be to succeed them? And yet small states at times require the same offices and laws as large ones;

the difference is that the one want them often, the others only after long intervals. Hence there is no reason why the care of many offices should not be imposed on the same person, for they will not interfere with each other. When the population is small, offices should be like the spits which also serve to hold a lamp. We must first ascertain how many magistrates are necessary in every state, and also how many are not exactly necessary, but are nevertheless useful, and then there will be no difficulty in seeing what offices can be combined in one. We should also know over which matters several local tribunals are to have jurisdiction, and in which cases authority should be centralized: for example, should one person keep order in the market and another in some other place, or should the same person be responsible everywhere? Again, should offices be divided according to the subjects with which they deal, or according to the persons with whom they deal: I mean to say, should one person see to good order in general, or one look after the boys, another after the women, and so on? Further, under different constitutions, should the magistrates be the same or different? For example, in democracy, oligarchy, aristocracy, monarchy, should there be the same magistrates, although they are elected not out of equal or similar classes of citizens, but differently under different constitutions – in aristocracies, for example, they are chosen from the educated, in oligarchies from the wealthy, and in democracies from the free – or are there certain differences in the offices answering to them as well, and may the same be suitable to some, but different offices to others? For in some states it may be convenient that the same office should have a more extensive, in other states a narrower sphere. Special offices are peculiar to certain forms of government – for example that of Probuli, which is not a democratic office, although a council is democratic. There must be some body of men whose duty is to prepare measures for the people in order that they may not be diverted from their business; when these are few in number, the state inclines to an oligarchy: or rather the Probuli must always be few, and are therefore an oligarchical element. But when both institutions exist in a state, the Probuli are a check on the council; for the counsellor is a democratic element, but the Probuli are oligarchical. Even the power of the council disappears when democracy has taken that extreme form in which the people themselves are always meeting and deliberating about everything. This is the case when the members of the assembly receive abundant pay; for they have nothing to do and are always holding assemblies and deciding everything for themselves. A magistracy which controls the boys or the women, or any similar 5 office, is suited to an aristocracy rather than to a democracy; for how can the magistrates prevent the wives of the poor from going out of doors? Neither is it an oligarchical office; for the wives of the oligarchs are too grand.

Enough of these matters. I will now inquire into appointments to offices. The varieties depend on three terms, and the combinations of 10 these give all possible modes: first, who appoints? secondly, from whom? and thirdly, how? Each of these three admits of two varieties. For either all the citizens, or only some, appoint. Either the 15 magistrates are chosen out of all or out of some who are distinguished either by a property qualification, or by birth, or excellence, or for some special reason, as at Megara only those were eligible who had returned from exile and fought together against the democracy. They may be appointed either by vote or by lot. Again, these several varieties may be coupled, I mean that some officers may be elected by 20 some, others by all, and some again out of some, and others out of all, and some by vote and others by lot. Each variety of these terms admits of four modes.

For either all may appoint from all by vote, or all from all by lot, or all from some by vote, or all from some by lot. Again, if it is only some who appoint, they may do so from all by vote or from all by lot or from some by vote or from some by lot. And if from all, either by sections, as, for example, by tribes, and wards, and phratries, until all the 25 citizens have been gone through; or the citizens may be in all cases eligible indiscriminately; or sometimes in one way, sometimes in the other – I mean, from all by vote in some cases, by lot in others. Thus 30 the modes that arise, apart from the two couplings, number twelve. Of these systems two are popular, that all should appoint from all by vote or by lot – or by both, some of the offices by lot, others by vote. That all should not appoint at once, but should appoint from all or from some either by lot or by vote or by both, or appoint to some offices from all 35 and to others from some ('by both' meaning to some offices by lot, to others by vote), is characteristic of a polity. [And that some should appoint from all, to some offices by vote, to others by lot or by both – some by lot, others by vote – is oligarchical; and it is more oligarchical 40 to appoint by both. And to appoint to some offices from all, to others

from some, is characteristic of a polity with a leaning towards
1300ᵇ1 aristocracy – or to appoint some by vote, others by lot.]ᵃ That some
should appoint from some is oligarchical – even that some should
appoint from some by lot (and if this does not actually occur, it is none
the less oligarchical in character), or that some should appoint from
some by both. That some should appoint from all, and that sometimes
all should appoint from some, by vote, is aristocratic.

5   These are the different modes of constituting magistrates, and
these correspond to different forms of government: – which are
proper to which, or how they ought to be established, will be evident
when we determine the nature of their powers. By powers I mean
10   such powers as a magistrate exercises over the revenue or in defence
of the country; for there are various kinds of power: the power of the
general, for example, is not the same as that which regulates contracts
in the market.

16 · Of the three parts of government the judicial remains to be
considered, and this we shall divide on the same principle. There are
15   three points on which the varieties of law-courts depend: the persons
from whom they are appointed, the matters with which they are
concerned, and the manner of their appointment. I mean, are the
judges taken from all, or from some only? how many kinds of law-
courts are there? are the judges chosen by vote or by lot?

First, let me determine how many kinds of law-courts there are.
20   They are eight in number: one is the court of audits or scrutinies; a
second takes cognizance of ordinary offences against the state; a third
is concerned with treason against the constitution; the fourth
determines disputes respecting penalties, whether raised by
magistrates or by private persons; the fifth decides the more import-
25   ant civil cases; the sixth tries cases of homicide, which are of various
kinds, premeditated, involuntary, and cases in which the guilt is
confessed but the justice is disputed; and there may be a fourth court
in which murderers who have fled from justice are tried after their
return, such as the Court of Phreatto is said to be at Athens. But cases
30   of this sort rarely happen at all even in large cities. The different kinds
of homicide may be tried either by the same or by different courts.
There are courts for strangers: – of these there are two subdivisions,
one for the settlement of their disputes with one another, the other for

---

ᵃExcised by Dreizehnter. The text is uncertain throughout this paragraph.

the settlement of disputes between them and the citizens. And besides all these there must be courts for small suits about sums of a drachma up to five drachmas, or a little more, which have to be determined, but do not require many judges.   35

Nothing more need be said of these small suits, nor of the courts for homicide and for strangers – I would rather speak of political cases, which, when mismanaged, create division and disturbances in constitutions.

Now if all the citizens judge, in all the different cases which I have distinguished, they may be appointed by vote or by lot, or sometimes   40 by lot and sometimes by vote. Or when a single class of causes are tried, the judges who decide them may be appointed, some by vote,   1301ᵃ1 and some by lot. These then are the four modes of appointing judges from the whole people, and there will be likewise four modes, if they are elected from a part only; for they may be appointed from some by vote and judge in all causes; or they may be appointed from some by lot and judge in all causes; or they may be elected in some cases by vote, and in some cases taken by lot, or some courts, even when judging the same causes, may be composed of members some   5 appointed by vote and some by lot. These modes, then, as was said, answer to those previously mentioned.

Once more, the modes of appointment may be combined; I mean, that some may be chosen out of the whole people, others out of some, some out of both; for example, the same tribunal may be composed of some who were elected out of all, and of others who were elected out of some, either by vote or by lot or by both.

In how many forms law-courts can be established has now been   10 considered. The first form, viz. that in which the judges are taken from all the citizens, and in which all causes are tried, is democratic; the second, which is composed of a few only who try all causes, oligarchical; the third, in which some courts are taken from all classes, and some from certain classes only, aristocratic and constitutional.   15

BOOK V

1 · The design which we proposed to ourselves is now nearly completed. Next in order follow the causes of revolution in states,   20 how many, and of what nature they are; what modes of destruction

apply to particular states, and out of what, and into what they mostly change; also what are the modes of preservation in states generally, or in a particular state, and by what means each state may be best
25 preserved: these questions remain to be considered.

In the first place we must assume as our starting-point that in the many forms of government which have sprung up there has always been an acknowledgement of justice and proportionate equality, although mankind fail in attaining them, as indeed I have already explained. Democracy, for example, arises out of the notion that those who are equal in any respect are equal in all respects; because
30 men are equally free, they claim to be absolutely equal. Oligarchy is based on the notion that those who are unequal in one respect are in all respects unequal; being unequal, that is, in property, they suppose themselves to be unequal absolutely. The democrats think that as they are equal they ought to be equal in all things; while the oligarchs,
35 under the idea that they are unequal, claim too much, which is one form of inequality. All these forms of government have a kind of justice, but, tried by an absolute standard, they are faulty; and, therefore, both parties, whenever their share in the government does not accord with their preconceived ideas, stir up revolution. Those
40 who excel in excellence have the best right of all to rebel (for they
1301^{b}1 alone can with reason be deemed absolutely unequal), but then they are of all men the least inclined to do so. There is also a superiority which is claimed by men of rank; for they are thought noble because they spring from wealthy and excellent ancestors. Here then, so to
5 speak, are opened the very springs and fountains of revolution; and hence arise two sorts of changes in governments; the one affecting the constitution, when men seek to change from an existing form into some other, for example, from democracy into oligarchy, and from
10 oligarchy into democracy, or from either of them into constitutional government or aristocracy, and conversely; the other not affecting the constitution, when, without disturbing the form of government, whether oligarchy, or monarchy, or any other, they try to get the administration into their own hands. Further, there is a question of
15 degree; an oligarchy, for example, may become more or less oligarchical, and a democracy more or less democratic; and in like manner the characteristics of the other forms of government may be more or less strictly maintained. Or the revolution may be directed against a portion of the constitution only, e.g. the establishment or overthrow

of a particular office: as at Sparta it is said that Lysander attempted to ₂₀ overthrow the monarchy, and king Pausanias, the ephoralty. At Epidamnus, too, the change was partial. For instead of phylarchs or heads of tribes, a council was appointed; but to this day the magistrates are the only members of the ruling class who are compelled to go to the Heliaea when an election takes place, and the office of the single archon was another oligarchical feature. ₂₅ Everywhere inequality is a cause of revolution, but an inequality in which there is no proportion – for instance, a perpetual monarchy among equals; and always it is the desire for equality which rises in rebellion.

Now equality is of two kinds, numerical and proportional; by the ₃₀ first I mean sameness or equality in number or size; by the second, equality of ratios. For example, the excess of three over two is numerically equal to the excess of two over one; whereas four exceeds two in the same ratio in which two exceeds one, for two is the same part of four that one is of two, namely, the half. As I was saying before, ₃₅ men agree that justice in the abstract is proportion, but they differ in that some think that if they are equal in any respect they are equal absolutely, others that if they are unequal in any respect they should be unequal in all. Hence there are two principal forms of government, ₄₀ democracy and oligarchy; for good birth and excellence are rare, but 1302ᵃ1 wealth and numbers are more common. In what city shall we find a hundred persons of good birth and of excellence? whereas the rich everywhere abound. That a state should be ordered, simply and wholly, according to either kind of equality, is not a good thing; the proof is the fact that such forms of government never last. They are ₅ originally based on a mistake, and, as they begin badly, cannot fail to end badly. The inference is that both kinds of equality should be employed; numerical in some cases, and proportionate in others.

Still democracy appears to be safer and less liable to revolution than oligarchy. For in oligarchies there is the double danger of the ₁₀ oligarchs falling out among themselves and also with the people; but in democracies there is only the danger of a quarrel with the oligarchs. No dissension worth mentioning arises among the people themselves. And we may further remark that a government which is composed of the middle class more nearly approximates to democracy than to oligarchy, and is the safest of the imperfect forms of government. ₁₅

2 · In considering how dissensions and political revolutions arise, we must first of all ascertain the beginnings and causes of them which affect constitutions generally. They may be said to be three in
20 number; and we have now to give an outline of each. We want to know what is the state of mind and what are the motives of those who make them and whence arise political disturbances and quarrels. The universal and chief cause of this revolutionary feeling has been already mentioned; viz. the desire for equality, when men think that
25 they are equal to others who have more than themselves; or, again, the desire for inequality and superiority, when conceiving themselves to be superior they think that they have not more but the same or less than their inferiors; pretensions which may or may not be just.
30 Inferiors revolt in order that they may be equal, and equals that they may be superior. Such is the state of mind which creates revolutions. The motives for making them are the desire for gain and honour, or the fear of dishonour and loss; the authors of them want to divert punishment or dishonour from themselves or their friends. The
35 causes and reasons of revolutions, whereby men are themselves affected in the way described, and about the things which I have mentioned, viewed in one way may be regarded as seven, and in another as more than seven. Two of them have been already noticed; but they act in a different manner, for men are excited against one another by the love of gain and honour – not, as in the case which I have just supposed, in order to obtain them for themselves, but at
1302ᵇ1 seeing others, justly or unjustly, monopolising them. Other causes are insolence, fear, excessive predominance, contempt, disproportionate increase in some part of the state; causes of another sort are election intrigues, carelessness, neglect about trifles, dissimilarity of elements.

5 3 · What share insolence and avarice have in creating revolutions, and how they work, is plain enough. When the magistrates are insolent and grasping they conspire against one another and also against the constitution from which they derive their power, making
10 their gains either at the expense of individuals or of the public. It is evident, again, what an influence honour exerts and how it is a cause of revolution. Men who are themselves dishonoured and who see others obtaining honours rise in rebellion; the honour or dishonour when undeserved is unjust; and just when awarded according to

merit. Again, superiority is a cause of revolution when one or more 15
persons have a power which is too much for the state and the power of
the government; this is a condition of affairs out of which there tends
to arise a monarchy, or a family oligarchy. And therefore, in some
places, as at Athens and Argos, they have recourse to ostracism. But
how much better to provide from the first that there should be no such
pre-eminent individuals instead of letting them come into existence 20
and then finding a remedy.

Another cause of revolution is fear. Either men have committed
wrong, and are afraid of punishment, or they are expecting to suffer
wrong and are desirous of anticipating their enemy. Thus at Rhodes
the notables conspired against the people through fear of the suits
that were brought against them. Contempt is also a cause of insurrec- 25
tion and revolution; for example, in oligarchies – when those who
have no share in the state are the majority, they revolt, because they
think that they are the stronger. Or, again, in democracies, the rich
despise the disorder and anarchy of the state; at Thebes, for example,
where, after the battle of Oenophyta, the bad administration of the 30
democracy led to its ruin. At Megara the fall of the democracy was
due to a defeat occasioned by disorder and anarchy. And at Syracuse
the democracy aroused contempt before the tyranny of Gelo arose; at
Rhodes, before the insurrection.

Political revolutions also spring from a disproportionate increase in
any part of the state. For as a body is made up of many members, and 35
every member ought to grow in proportion so that symmetry may be
preserved, but it loses its nature if the foot is four cubits long and the
rest of the body two spans; and, should the abnormal increase be one
of quality as well as of quantity, it may even take the form of another 40
animal: even so a state has many parts, of which some one may often 1303ᵃ1
grow imperceptibly; for example, the number of poor in democracies
and in constitutional states. And this disproportion may sometimes
happen by an accident, as at Tarentum, from a defeat in which many
of the notables were slain in a battle with the Iapygians just after the 5
Persian War, the constitutional government in consequence becoming a democracy; or as was the case at Argos, where the Argives, after
their army had been cut to pieces on the seventh day of the month by
Cleomenes the Lacedaemonian, were compelled to admit to citizenship some of their serfs; and at Athens, when, after frequent defeats
of their infantry at the time of the Peloponnesian War, the notables 10

were reduced in number, because the soldiers had to be taken from the roll of citizens. Revolutions arise from this cause as well, in democracies as in other forms of government, but not to so great an extent. When the rich grow numerous or properties increase, the form of government changes into an oligarchy or a government of families. Forms of government also change – sometimes even without
15 revolution, owing to election contests, as at Heraea (where, instead of electing their magistrates, they took them by lot, because the electors were in the habit of choosing their own partisans); or owing to carelessness, when disloyal persons are allowed to find their way into the highest offices, as at Oreum, where, upon the accession of
20 Heracleodorus to office, the oligarchy was overthrown, and changed by him into a constitutional and democratic government.

Again, the revolution may be facilitated by the slightness of the change; I mean that a great change may sometimes slip into the constitution through neglect of a small matter; at Ambracia, for instance, the qualification for office, small at first, was eventually reduced to nothing. For the Ambraciots thought that a small qualifi-
25 cation was much the same as none at all.

Another cause of revolution is difference of races which do not at once acquire a common spirit; for a state is not the growth of a day, any more than it grows out of a multitude brought together by accident. Hence the reception of strangers in colonies, either at the time of their foundation or afterwards, has generally produced
30 revolution; for example, the Achaeans who joined the Troezenians in the foundation of Sybaris, becoming later the more numerous, expelled them; hence the curse fell upon Sybaris. At Thurii the Sybarites quarrelled with their fellow-colonists; thinking that the land belonged to them, they wanted too much of it and were driven out. At Byzantium the new colonists were detected in a conspiracy, and were expelled by force of arms; the people of Antissa, who had
35 received the Chian exiles, fought with them, and drove them out; and the Zancleans, after having received the Samians, were driven by them out of their own city. The citizens of Apollonia of the Euxine, after the introduction of a fresh body of colonists, had a revolution; the Syracusans, after the expulsion of their tyrants, having admitted
1303^{b}1 strangers and mercenaries to the rights of citizenship, quarrelled and came to blows; the people of Amphipolis, having received Chalcidian colonists, were nearly all expelled by them.

Now, in oligarchies the masses make revolution under the idea that they are unjustly treated, because, as I said before, they are equals, 5 and have not an equal share, and in democracies the notables revolt, because they are not equals, and yet have only an equal share.

Again, the situation of cities is a cause of revolution when the country is not naturally adapted to preserve the unity of the state. For example, the Chytians at Clazomenae did not agree with the people of the island; and the people of Colophon quarrelled with the Notians; 10 at Athens, too, the inhabitants of the Peiraeus are more democratic than those who live in the city. For just as in war the impediment of a ditch, however small, may break a regiment, so every cause of difference makes a breach in a city. The greatest opposition is 15 confessedly that of excellence and badness; next comes that of wealth and poverty; and there are other antagonistic elements, greater or less, of which one is this difference of place.

4 · In revolutions the occasions may be trifling, but great interests are at stake. Even trifles are most important when they concern the rulers, as was the case of old at Syracuse; for the Syracusan 20 constitution was once changed by a love-quarrel of two young men, who were in the government. The story is that while one of them was away from home his beloved was gained over by his companion, and he to revenge himself seduced the other's wife. They then drew the 25 members of the ruling class into their quarrel and so split all the people into portions. We learn from this story that we should be on our guard against the beginnings of such evils, and should put an end to the quarrels of chiefs and mighty men. The mistake lies in the beginning – as the proverb says – 'Well begun is half done'; so an error at the beginning, though quite small, bears the same ratio to the 30 errors in the other parts. In general, when the notables quarrel, the whole city is involved, as happened in Hestiaea after the Persian War. The occasion was the division of an inheritance; one of two brothers refused to give an account of their father's property and the treasure 35 which he had found: so the poorer of the two quarrelled with him and enlisted in his cause the popular party, the other, who was very rich, the wealthy classes.

At Delphi, again, a quarrel about a marriage was the beginning of all the troubles which followed. In this case the bridegroom, fancying 1304ª1 some occurrence to be of evil omen, came to the bride, and went away

without taking her. Whereupon her relations, thinking that they were insulted by him, put some of the sacred treasure among his offerings while he was sacrificing, and then slew him, pretending that he had been robbing the temple. At Mytilene, too, a dispute about heiresses
5 was the beginning of many misfortunes, and led to the war with the Athenians in which Paches took their city. A wealthy citizen, named Timophanes, left two daughters; Dexander, another citizen, wanted to obtain them for his sons; but he was rejected in his suit, whereupon he stirred up a revolution, and instigated the Athenians (of whom he
10 was representative) to interfere. A similar quarrel about an heiress arose at Phocis between Mnaseas the father of Mnason, and Euthycrates the father of Onomarchus; this was the beginning of the Sacred War. A marriage-quarrel was also the cause of a change in the
15 government of Epidamnus. A certain man betrothed his daughter to a person whose father, having been made a magistrate, fined the father of the girl, and the latter, stung by the insult, conspired with the unenfranchised classes to overthrow the state.

Governments also change into oligarchy or into democracy or into a constitutional government because the magistrates, or some other section of the state, increase in power or renown. Thus at Athens the
20 reputation gained by the court of the Areopagus, in the Persian War, seemed to tighten the reins of government. On the other hand, the victory of Salamis, which was gained by the common people who served in the fleet, and won for the Athenians the empire due to command of the sea, strengthened the democracy. At Argos, the
25 notables, having distinguished themselves against the Lacedaemonians in the battle of Mantinea, attempted to put down the democracy. At Syracuse, the people, having been the chief authors of the victory in the war with the Athenians, changed the constitutional government into democracy. At Chalcis, the people, uniting with the
30 notables, killed Phoxus the tyrant, and then seized the government. At Ambracia, the people, in like manner, having joined with the conspirators in expelling the tyrant Periander, transferred the government to themselves. And generally, it should be remembered that those who have secured power to the state, whether private
35 citizens, or magistrates, or tribes, or any other part or section of the state, are apt to cause revolutions. For either envy of their greatness draws others into rebellion, or they themselves, in their pride of superiority, are unwilling to remain on a level with others.

Revolutions also break out when opposite parties, e.g. the rich and 1304^b1
the people, are equally balanced, and there is little or no middle class;
for, if either party were manifestly superior, the other would not risk
an attack upon them. And for this reason, those who are eminent in
excellence usually do not stir up insurrections, being always a
minority. Such in general are the beginnings and causes of the 5
disturbances and revolutions to which every form of government is
liable.

Revolutions are effected in two ways, by force and by fraud. Force
may be applied either at the time of making the revolution or
afterwards. Fraud, again, is of two kinds; for sometimes the citizens 10
are deceived into acquiescing in a change of government, and
afterwards they are held in subjection against their will. This was
what happened in the case of the Four Hundred, who deceived the
people by telling them that the king would provide money for the war
against the Lacedaemonians, and, having cheated the people, still 15
endeavoured to retain the government. In other cases the people are
persuaded at first, and afterwards, by a repetition of the persuasion,
their goodwill and allegiance are retained. The revolutions which
affect constitutions generally spring from the above-mentioned
causes.

5 · And now, taking each constitution separately, we must see what
follows from the principles already laid down. 20

Revolutions in democracies are generally caused by the intemperance of demagogues, who either in their private capacity lay
information against rich men until they compel them to combine (for
a common danger unites even the bitterest enemies), or coming
forward in public stir up the people against them. The truth of this 25
remark is proved by a variety of examples. At Cos the democracy was
overthrown because wicked demagogues arose, and the notables
combined. At Rhodes the demagogues not only provided pay for the
multitude, but prevented them from making good to the trierarchs the
sums which had been expended by them; and they, in consequence of
the suits which were brought against them, were compelled to 30
combine and put down the democracy. The democracy at Heraclea
was overthrown shortly after the foundation of the colony by the
injustice of the demagogues, which drove out the notables, who came
back in a body and put an end to the democracy. Much in the same

35 manner the democracy at Megara was overturned; there the demagogues drove out many of the notables in order that they might be able
to confiscate their property. At length the exiles, becoming
numerous, returned, and, engaging and defeating the people,
established the oligarchy. The same thing happened with the
1305ᵃ1 democracy of Cyme, which was overthrown by Thrasymachus. And
we may observe that in most states the changes have been of this
character. For sometimes the demagogues, in order to curry favour
with the people, wrong the notables and so force them to combine –
5 either they make a division of their property, or diminish their
incomes by the imposition of public services, and sometimes they
bring accusations against the rich so that they may have their wealth to
confiscate.

   Of old, the demagogue was also a general, and then democracies
changed into tyrannies. Most of the ancient tyrants were originally
10 demagogues. They are not so now, but they were then; and the reason
is that they were generals and not orators, for oratory had not yet
come into fashion. Whereas in our day, when the art of rhetoric has
made such progress, the orators lead the people, but their ignorance
of military matters prevents them from usurping power; at any rate
15 instances to the contrary are few and slight. Tyrannies were more
common formerly than now, for this reason also, that great power was
placed in the hands of individuals; thus a tyranny arose at Miletus out
of the office of the Prytanis, who had supreme authority in many
important matters. Moreover, in those days, when cities were not
20 large, the people dwelt in the fields, busy at their work; and their
chiefs, if they possessed any military talent, seized the opportunity,
and winning the confidence of the masses by professing their hatred
of the wealthy, they succeeded in obtaining the tyranny. Thus at
Athens Peisistratus led a faction against the men of the plain, and
25 Theagenes at Megara slaughtered the cattle of the wealthy, which he
found by the river side, where they had put them to graze. Dionysius,
again, was thought worthy of the tyranny because he denounced
Daphnaeus and the rich; his enmity to the notables won for him the
confidence of the people. Changes also take place from the ancient to
the latest form of democracy; for where there is a popular election of
30 the magistrates and no property qualification, the aspirants for office
get hold of the people, and contrive at last even to set them above the

laws. A more or less complete cure for this state of things is for the separate tribes, and not the whole people, to elect the magistrates.

These are the principal causes of revolutions in democracies.   35

6 · There are two patent causes of revolutions in oligarchies: first, when the oligarchs oppress the people, for then anybody is good enough to be their champion, especially if he be himself a member of the oligarchy, as Lygdamis at Naxos, who afterwards came to be tyrant. But revolutions which commence outside the governing class 1305ᵇ1 may be further subdivided. Sometimes, when the government is very exclusive, the revolution is brought about by persons of the wealthy class who are excluded, as happened at Massalia and Istros and 5 Heraclea, and other cities. Those who had no share in the government created a disturbance, until first the elder brothers, and then the younger, were admitted; for in some places father and son, in others, elder and younger brothers, do not hold office together. At Massalia the oligarchy became more like a constitutional government, but at 10 Istros ended in a democracy, and at Heraclea was enlarged to 600. At Cnidos, again, the oligarchy underwent a considerable change. For the notables fell out among themselves, because only a few shared in the government; there existed among them the rule already mentioned, that father and son could not hold office together, and, if there 15 were several brothers, only the eldest was admitted. The people took advantage of the quarrel, and choosing one of the notables to be their leader, attacked and conquered the oligarchs, who were divided, and division is always a source of weakness. The city of Erythrae, too, in old times was ruled, and ruled well, by the Basilidae, but the people 20 took offence at the narrowness of the oligarchy and changed the constitution.

Of internal causes of revolutions in oligarchies one is the personal rivalry of the oligarchs, which leads them to play the demagogue. Now, the oligarchical demagogue is of two sorts: either he practises upon the oligarchs themselves (for, although the oligarchy are quite a small number, there may be a demagogue among them, as at Athens 25 Charicles' party won power by courting the Thirty, that of Phrynichus by courting the Four Hundred); or the oligarchs may play the demagogue with the people. This was the case at Larissa, where the guardians of the citizens endeavoured to gain over the people because

30 they were elected by them; and such is the fate of all oligarchies in which the magistrates are elected, as at Abydos, not by the class in which they belong, but by the heavy-armed or by the people, although they may be required to have a high qualification, or to be members of a political club; or, again, where the law-courts are composed of persons outside the government, the oligarchs flatter the people in
35 order to obtain a decision in their own favour, and so they change the constitution; this happened at Heraclea in Pontus. Again, oligarchies change whenever any attempt is made to narrow them; for then those who desire equal rights are compelled to call in the people. Changes in the oligarchy also occur when the oligarchs waste their private
40 property by extravagant living; for then they want to innovate, and either try to make themselves tyrants, or install some one else in the
1306ª1 tyranny, as Hipparinus did Dionysius at Syracuse, and as at Amphipolis a man named Cleotimus introduced Chalcidian colonists, and when they arrived, stirred them up against the rich. For a like reason in Aegina the person who carried on the negotiation with
5 Chares endeavoured to revolutionize the state. Sometimes a party among the oligarchs try directly to create a political change; sometimes they rob the treasury, and then either the thieves or, as happened at Apollonia in Pontus, those who resist them in their thieving quarrel with the rulers. But an oligarchy which is at unity
10 with itself is not easily destroyed from within; of this we may see an example at Pharsalus, for there, although the rulers are few in number, they govern a large city, because they have a good understanding among themselves.

Oligarchies, again, are overthrown when another oligarchy is created within the original one, that is to say, when the whole
15 governing body is small and yet they do not all share in the highest offices. Thus at Elis the governing body was a small senate; and very few ever found their way into it, because the senators were only ninety in number, and were elected for life and out of certain families in a
20 manner similar to the Lacedaemonian elders. Oligarchy is liable to revolutions alike in war and in peace; in war because, not being able to trust the people, the oligarchs are compelled to hire mercenaries, and the general who is in command of them often ends in becoming a tyrant, as Timophanes did at Corinth; or if there are more generals
25 than one they make themselves into a junta. Sometimes the oligarchs, fearing this danger, give the people a share in the government

because their services are necessary to them. And in time of peace, from mutual distrust, the two parties hand over the defence of the state to the army and to an arbiter between the two factions, who often ends the master of both. This happened at Larissa when Simos the 30 Aleuad had the government, and at Abydos in the days of Iphiades and the political clubs. Revolutions also arise out of marriages or lawsuits which lead to the overthrow of one party among the oligarchs by another. Of quarrels about marriages I have already mentioned some instances; another occurred at Eretria, where Diagoras overturned the oligarchy of the knights because he had been wronged about a marriage. A revolution at Heraclea, and another at Thebes, both arose out of decisions of law-courts upon a charge of adultery; in both cases the punishment was just, but executed in the spirit of party, at Heraclea upon Eurytion, and at Thebes upon Archias; for their 1306ᵇ1 enemies were jealous of them and so had them pilloried in the agora. Many oligarchies have been destroyed by some members of the ruling class taking offence at their excessive despotism; for example, the oligarchy at Cnidus and at Chios. 5

Changes of constitutional governments, and also of oligarchies which limit the office of counsellor, judge, or other magistrate to persons having a certain money qualification, often occur by accident. The qualification may have been originally fixed according to the circumstances of the time, in such a manner as to include in an 10 oligarchy a few only, or in a constitutional government the middle class. But after a time of prosperity, whether arising from peace or some other good fortune, the same property becomes many times as valuable, and then everybody participates in every office; this happens sometimes gradually and insensibly, and sometimes quickly. These 15 are the causes of changes and revolutions in oligarchies.

We must remark generally, both of democracies and oligarchies, that they sometimes change, not into the opposite forms of government, but only into another variety of the same class; I mean to say, from those forms of democracy and oligarchy which are regulated by 20 law into those which are arbitrary, and conversely.

7 · In aristocracies revolutions are stirred up when a few only share in the honours of the state; a cause which has been already shown to affect oligarchies; for an aristocracy is a sort of oligarchy, and, like an oligarchy, is the government of a few, although few not for the same 25

reason; hence the two are often confused. And revolutions will be most likely to happen, and must happen, when the mass of the people are of the high-spirited kind, and have a notion that they are as good as their rulers. Thus at Lacedaemon the so-called Partheniae, who

30 were the sons of the Spartan peers, attempted a revolution, and, being detected, were sent away to colonize Tarentum. Again, revolutions occur when great men who are at least of equal excellence are denied honours by those higher in office, as Lysander was by the kings of Sparta; or, when a brave man is excluded from the honours of the

35 state, like Cinadon, who conspired against the Spartans in the reign of Agesilaus; or, again, when some are very poor and others very rich, a state of society which is most often the result of war, as at Lacedaemon in the days of the Messenian War; this is proved from

1307ᵃ1 the poem of Tyrtaeus, entitled 'Good Order'; for he speaks of certain citizens who were ruined by the war and wanted to have a redistribution of the land. Again, revolutions arise when an individual who is great, and might be greater, wants to rule alone, as, at Lacedaemon, Pausanias, who was general in the Persian War, or like Hanno at

5 Carthage.

Constitutional governments and aristocracies are commonly overthrown owing to some deviation from justice in the constitution itself; the cause of the downfall is, in the former, the ill-mingling of the two elements democracy and oligarchy; in the latter, of the three

10 elements, democracy, oligarchy, and excellence, but especially democracy and oligarchy. For to combine these is the endeavour of constitutional governments; and most of the so-called aristocracies have a like aim, but differ from polities in the mode of combination; hence some of them are more and some less permanent. Those which

15 incline more to oligarchy are called aristocracies, and those which incline to democracy constitutional governments. And therefore the latter are the safer of the two; for the greater the number, the greater the strength, and when men are equal they are contented. But the rich, if the constitution gives them power, are apt to be insolent and

20 avaricious; and, in general, whichever way the constitution inclines, in that direction it changes as either party gains strength, a constitutional government becoming a democracy, an aristocracy an oligarchy. But the process may be reversed, and aristocracy may change into democracy. This happens when the poor, under the idea that they are

25 being wronged, force the constitution to take an opposite form. In like

manner constitutional governments change into oligarchies. The only stable principle of government is equality according to merit, and for every man to enjoy his own.

What I have just mentioned actually happened at Thurii, where the qualification for office, at first high, was therefore reduced, and the magistrates increased in number. The notables had previously acquired the whole of the land contrary to law; for the government 30 tended to oligarchy, and they were able to encroach. . . .*ᵃ* But the people, who had been trained by war, soon got the better of the guards kept by the oligarchs, until those who had too much gave up their land.

Again, since all aristocratic governments incline to oligarchy, the notables are apt to be grasping; thus at Lacedaemon, where property 35 tends to pass into few hands, the notables can do too much as they like, and are allowed to marry whom they please. The city of Locri was ruined by a marriage connexion with Dionysius, but such a thing could never have happened in a democracy, or in a well-balanced 40 aristocracy.

I have already remarked that in all states revolutions are occasioned by trifles. In aristocracies, above all, they are of a gradual and 1307ᵇ1 imperceptible nature. The citizens begin by giving up some part of the constitution, and so with greater ease the government change something else which is a little more important, until they have 5 undermined the whole fabric of the state. At Thurii there was a law that generals should only be re-elected after an interval of five years, and some young men who were popular with the soldiers of the guard for their military prowess, despising the magistrates and thinking that 10 they would easily gain their purpose, wanted to abolish this law and allow their generals to hold perpetual commands; for they well knew that the people would be glad enough to elect them. Whereupon the magistrates who had charge of these matters, and who are called councillors, at first determined to resist, but they afterwards consented, thinking that, if only this one law was changed, no further inroad 15 would be made on the constitution. But other changes soon followed which they in vain attempted to oppose; and the state passed into the hands of the revolutionists, who established a dynastic oligarchy.

All constitutions are overthrown either from within or from 20

ᵃ Dreizehnter marks a lacuna.

without; the latter, when there is some government close at hand having an opposite interest, or at a distance, but powerful. This was exemplified by the Athenians and the Lacedaemonians; the Athenians everywhere put down the oligarchies, and the Lacedaemonians the democracies.

25   I have now explained what are the chief causes of revolutions and dissensions in states.

8 · We have next to consider what means there are of preserving constitutions in general, and in particular cases. In the first place it is evident that if we know the causes which destroy constitutions, we also know the causes which preserve them; for opposites produce
30 opposites, and destruction is the opposite of preservation.

In all well-balanced governments there is nothing which should be more jealously maintained than the spirit of obedience to law, more especially in small matters; for transgression creeps in unperceived and at last ruins the state, just as the constant recurrence of small expenses in time eats up a fortune. The expense does not take place
35 all at once, and therefore is not observed; the mind is deceived, as in the fallacy which says that 'if each part is little, then the whole is little'. And this is true in one way, but not in another, for the whole and the all are not little, although they are made up of littles.

In the first place, then, men should guard against the beginning to
40 change, and in the second place they should not rely upon the political
1308ª1 devices of which I have already spoken, invented only to deceive the people, for they are proved by experience to be useless. Further, we note that oligarchies as well as aristocracies may last, not from any inherent stability in such forms of government, but because the rulers
5 are on good terms both with the unenfranchised and with the governing classes, not maltreating any who are excluded from the government, but introducing into it the leading spirits among them. They should never wrong the ambitious in a matter of honour, or the common people in a matter of money; and they should treat one
10 another and their fellow-citizens in a spirit of equality. The equality which the friends of democracy seek to establish for the multitude is not only just but likewise expedient among equals. Hence, if the governing class are numerous, many democratic institutions are
15 useful; for example, the restriction of the tenure of offices to six months, so that all those who are of equal rank may share in them.

Indeed, a group of equals is a kind of democracy, and therefore demagogues are very likely to arise among them, as I have already remarked. The short tenure of office prevents oligarchies and aristocracies from falling into the hands of families; it is not easy for a 20 person to do any great harm when his tenure of office is short, whereas long possession begets tyranny in oligarchies and democracies. For the aspirants to tyranny are either the principal men of the state, who in democracies are demagogues and in oligarchies members of ruling houses, or those who hold great offices, and have a long tenure of them.

Constitutions are preserved when their destroyers are at a distance, 25 and sometimes also because they are near, for the fear of them makes the government keep in hand the constitution. Wherefore the ruler who has a care of the constitution should invent terrors, and bring distant dangers near, in order that the citizens may be on their guard, and, like sentinels in a night-watch, never relax their attention. He 30 should endeavour too by help of the laws to control the contentions and quarrels of the notables, and to prevent those who have not hitherto taken part in them from catching the spirit of contention. No ordinary man can discern the beginning of evil, but only the true statesman.

As to the change produced in oligarchies and constitutional 35 governments by the alternation of the qualification, when this arises, not out of any variation in the qualification but only out of the increase of money, it is well to compare the new valuation of property with that of past years, annually in those cities in which the census is taken 40 annually, and in larger cities every third or fifth year. If the whole is 1308^{b}1 many times greater or many times less than when the ratings recognized by the constitution were fixed, there should be power given by law to raise or lower the qualification as the amount is greater 5 or less. Where this is not done a constitutional government passes into an oligarchy, and an oligarchy is narrowed to a rule of families; or in the opposite case constitutional government becomes democracy, and oligarchy either constitutional government or democracy. 10

It is a principle common to democracy, oligarchy, and every other form of government not to allow the disproportionate increase of any citizen, but to give moderate honour for a long time rather than great honour for a short time. For men are easily spoilt; not every one can bear prosperity. But if this rule is not observed, at any rate the

15 honours which are given all at once should be taken away by degrees
and not all at once. Especially should the laws provide against any one
having too much power, whether derived from friends or money; if he
has, he should be sent clean out of the country. And since innovations
20 creep in through the private life of individuals also, there ought to be a
magistracy which will have an eye to those whose life is not in
harmony with the government, whether oligarchy or democracy or
any other. And for a like reason an increase of prosperity in any part of
25 the state should be carefully watched. The proper remedy for this evil
is always to give the management of affairs and offices of state to
opposite elements; such opposites are the good and the many, or the
rich and the poor. Another way is to combine the poor and the rich in
30 one body, or to increase the middle class: thus an end will be put to the
revolutions which arise from inequality.

But above all every state should be so administered and so
regulated by law that its magistrates cannot possibly make money. In
oligarchies special precautions should be used against this evil. For
35 the people do not take any great offence at being kept out of the
government – indeed they are rather pleased than otherwise at having
leisure for their private business – but what irritates them is to think
that their rulers are stealing the public money; then they are doubly
annoyed; for they lose both honour and profit. If office brought no
40 profit, then and then only could democracy and aristocracy be
1309^{a}1 combined; for both notables and people might have their wishes
gratified. All would be able to hold office, which is the aim of
democracy, and the notables would be magistrates, which is the aim
of aristocracy. And this result may be accomplished when there is no
5 possibility of making money out of the offices; for the poor will not
want to have them when there is nothing to be gained from them –
they would rather be attending to their own concerns; and the rich,
who do not want money from the public treasury, will be able to take
them; and so the poor will keep to their work and grow rich, and the
10 notables will not be governed by the lower class. In order to avoid
peculation of the public money, the transfer of revenue should be
made at a general assembly of the citizens, and duplicates of the
accounts deposited with the different brotherhoods, companies, and
tribes. And honours should be given by law to magistrates who have
15 the reputation of ruling without gain. In democracies the rich should
be spared; not only should their property not be divided, but their

incomes also, which in some states are taken from them imperceptibly, should be protected. It is a good thing to prevent the wealthy citizens, even if they are willing, from undertaking expensive and useless public services, such as the giving of choruses, torch-races, and the like. In an oligarchy, on the other hand, great care should be 20 taken of the poor, and lucrative offices should go to them; if any of the wealthy classes insult them, the offender should be punished more severely than if he had wronged one of his own class. Provision should be made that estates pass by inheritance and not by gift, and no person should have more than one inheritance; for in this way properties will 25 be equalized, and more of the poor rise to wealth. It is also expedient both in a democracy and in an oligarchy to assign to those who have less share in the government (i.e. to the rich in a democracy and to the poor in an oligarchy) an equality or preference in all but the principal 30 offices of state. The latter should be entrusted chiefly or only to members of the governing class.

9 · There are three qualifications required in those who have to fill the highest offices – first of all, loyalty to the established constitution; then the greatest administrative capacity; and excellence and justice 35 of the kind proper to each form of government; for, if what is just is not the same in all governments, the quality of justice must also differ. There may be a doubt, however, when all these qualities do not meet 40 in the same person; suppose, for example, a good general is a bad man 1309^{b}1 and not a friend to the constitution, and another man is loyal and just, which should we choose? In making the election ought we not to consider two points? what qualities are common, and what are rare. Thus in the choice of a general, we should regard his experience 5 rather than his excellence; for few have military experience, but many have excellence. In any office of trust or stewardship, on the other hand, the opposite rule should be observed; for more excellence than ordinary is required in the holder of such an office, but the necessary knowledge is of a sort which all men possess.

It may, however, be asked what a man wants with excellence if he has political ability and is loyal, since these two qualities alone will make him do what is for the public interest. But may not men have both of them and yet be deficient in self control? – If, knowing and loving their own interests, they do not always attend to them, may they not be equally negligent of the interests of the public?

Speaking generally, we may say that whatever legal enactments are
15 held to be for the interest of various constitutions, all these preserve
them. And the great preserving principle is the one which has been
repeatedly mentioned – to have a care that the loyal citizens should be
stronger than the disloyal. Neither should we forget the mean, which
at the present day is lost sight of in perverted forms of government; for
20 many practices which appear to be democratic are the ruin of
democracies, and many which appear to be oligarchical are the ruin of
oligarchies. Those who think that all excellence is to be found in their
own party principles push matters to extremes; they do not consider
that disproportion destroys a state. A nose which varies from the ideal
25 of straightness to a hook or snub may still be of good shape and
agreeable to the eye; but if the excess is very great, all symmetry is lost,
and the nose at last ceases to be a nose at all on account of some excess
in one direction or defect in the other; and this is true of every other
30 part of the human body. The same law of proportion equally holds in
states. Oligarchy or democracy, although a departure from the most
perfect form, may yet be a good enough government, but if any one
attempts to push the principles of either to an extreme, he will begin
by spoiling the government and end by having none at all. Therefore
35 the legislator and the statesman ought to know what democratic
measures save and what destroy a democracy, and what oligarchical
measures save or destroy an oligarchy. For neither the one nor the
other can exist or continue to exist unless both rich and poor are
40 included in it. If equality of property is introduced, the state must of
1310ᵃ1 necessity take another form; for when by laws carried to excess one or
other element in the state is ruined, the constitution is ruined.

There is an error common both to oligarchies and to democracies:
– in the latter the demagogues, when the multitude are above the law,
5 are always cutting the city in two by quarrels with the rich, whereas
they should always profess to be maintaining their cause; just as in
oligarchies the oligarchs should profess to maintain the cause of the
people, and should take oaths the opposite of those which they now
take. For there are cities in which they swear – 'I will be an enemy to
10 the people, and will devise all the harm against them which I can'; but
they ought to exhibit and to entertain the very opposite feeling; in the
form of their oath there should be an express declaration – 'I will do
no wrong to the people.'

But of all the things which I have mentioned that which most contributes to the permanence of constitutions is the adaptation of education to the form of government, and yet in our own day this principle is universally neglected. The best laws, though sanctioned 15 by every citizen of the state, will be of no avail unless the young are trained by habit and education in the spirit of the constitution, if the laws are democratic, democratically, or oligarchically, if the laws are oligarchical. For there may be a want of self-discipline in states as well as in individuals. Now, to have been educated in the spirit of the 20 constitution is not to perform the actions in which oligarchs or democrats delight, but those by which the existence of an oligarchy or of a democracy is made possible. Whereas among ourselves the sons of the ruling class in an oligarchy live in luxury, but the sons of the poor are hardened by exercise and toil, and hence they are both more 25 inclined and better able to make a revolution. And in democracies of the more extreme type there has arisen a false idea of freedom which is contradictory to the true interests of the state. For two principles are characteristic of democracy, the government of the majority and freedom. Men think that what is just is equal; and that equality is the 30 supremacy of the popular will; and that freedom means doing what one likes. In such democracies every one lives as he pleases, or in the words of Euripides, 'according to his fancy'. But this is all wrong; men should not think it slavery to live according to the rule of the 35 constitution; for it is their salvation.

I have now discussed generally the cause of the revolution and destruction of states, and the means of their preservation and continuance.

10 · I have still to speak of monarchy, and the causes of its 40 destruction and preservation. What I have said already respecting forms of constitutional government applies almost equally to royal 1310^{b}1 and tyrannical rule. For royal rule is of the nature of an aristocracy, and a tyranny is a compound of oligarchy and democracy in their most extreme forms; it is therefore most injurious to its subjects, being 5 made up of two evil forms of government, and having the perversions and errors of both. These two forms of monarchy are contrary in their very origin. The appointment of a king is the resource of the better classes against the people, and he is elected by them out of their own number, because either he himself or his family excel in excellence 10 and excellent actions; whereas a tyrant is chosen from the people to be

their protector against the notables, and in order to prevent them from being injured. History shows that almost all tyrants have been
15 demagogues who gained the favour of the people by their accusation of the notables. At any rate this was the manner in which the tyrannies arose in the days when cities had increased in power. Others which were older originated in the ambition of kings wanting to overstep the limits of their hereditary power and become despots. Others again
20 grew out of the class which were chosen to be chief magistrates; for in ancient times the people who elected them gave the magistrates, whether civil or religious, a long tenure. Others arose out of the custom which oligarchies had of making some individual supreme over the highest offices. In any of these ways an ambitious man had no
25 difficulty, if he desired, in creating a tyranny, since he had the power in his hands already, either as king or as one of the officers of state. Thus Pheidon at Argos and several others were originally kings, and ended by becoming tyrants; Phalaris, on the other hand, and the Ionian tyrants, acquired the tyranny by holding great offices. Whereas
30 Panaetius at Leontini, Cypselus at Corinth, Peisistratus at Athens, Dionysius at Syracuse, and several others who afterwards became tyrants, were at first demagogues.

And so, as I was saying, royalty ranks with aristocracy, for it is based upon merit, whether of the individual or of his family, or on benefits conferred, or on these claims with power added to them. For all who
35 have obtained this honour have benefited, or had in their power to benefit, states and nations; some, like Codrus, have prevented the state from being enslaved in war; others, like Cyrus, have given their country freedom, or have settled or gained a territory, like the
40 Lacedaemonian, Macedonian, and Molossian kings. The idea of a
1311ᵃ1 king is to be a protector of the rich against unjust treatment, of the people against insult and oppression. Whereas a tyrant, as has often been repeated, has no regard to any public interest, except as
5 conducive to his private ends; his aim is pleasure, the aim of a king, honour. Therefore they differ also in their excesses; the tyrant accumulates riches, the king seeks what brings honour. And the guards of a king are citizens, but of a tyrant mercenaries.

That tyranny has all the vices both of democracy and oligarchy is
10 evident. As of oligarchy so of tyranny, the end is wealth (for by wealth only can the tyrant maintain his guard and his luxury). Both mistrust the people, and therefore deprive them of their arms. Both agree too

in injuring the people and driving them out of the city and dispersing them. From democracy tyrants have borrowed the art of making war upon the notables and destroying them secretly or openly, or of exiling them because they are rivals and stand in the way of their power; and also because plots against them are contrived by men of this class, who either want to rule or to escape subjection. Hence Periander advised Thrasybulus by cutting off the tops of the tallest ears of corn, meaning that he must always put out of the way the citizens who overtop the rest. And so, as I have already intimated, the beginnings of change are the same in monarchies as in forms of constitutional government; subjects attack their sovereigns out of fear or contempt, or because they have been unjustly treated by them. And of injustice the most common form is insult, another is confiscation of property.

The ends sought by conspiracies against monarchies, whether tyrannies or royalties, are the same as the ends sought by conspiracies against other forms of government. Monarchs have great wealth and honour, which are objects of desire to all mankind. The attacks are made sometimes against their lives, sometimes against the office; where the sense of insult is the motive, against their lives. Any sort of insult (and there are many) may stir up anger, and when men are angry, they commonly act out of revenge, and not from ambition. For example, the attempt made upon the Peisistratidae arose out of the public dishonour offered to the sister of Harmodius and the insult tc himself. He attacked the tyrant for his sister's sake, and Aristogeiton joined in the attack for the sake of Harmodius. A conspiracy was also formed against Periander, the tyrant of Ambracia, because, when drinking with a favourite youth, he asked him whether by this time he was not with child by him. Philip, too, was attacked by Pausanias because he permitted him to be insulted by Attalus and his friends, and Amyntas the Little, by Derdas, because he boasted of having enjoyed his youth. Evagoras of Cyprus, again, was slain by the eunuch to revenge an insult; for his wife had been carried off by Evagoras's son. Many conspiracies have originated in shameful attempts made by sovereigns on the persons of their subjects. Such was the attack of Crataeas upon Archelaus; he had always hated his intercourse with the king, and so, when Archelaus, having promised him one of his two daughters in marriage, did not give him either of them, but broke his word and married the elder to the king of Elymeia, when he was hard

pressed in a war against Sirrhas and Arrhabaeus, and the younger to his own son Amyntas, under the idea that Amyntas would then be less
15 likely to quarrel with his son by Cleopatra – Crataeas made this slight a pretext for attacking Archelaus, though even a less reason would have sufficed, for the real cause of the estrangement was the disgust which he felt at his sexual subjection. And from a like motive Hellanocrates of Larissa conspired with him; for when Archelaus, who was his lover, did not fulfil his promise of restoring him to his
20 country, he thought that the intercourse between them had originated, not in sexual desire, but in the wish to insult him. Pytho, too, and Heracleides of Aenos, slew Cotys in order to avenge their father, and Adamas revolted from Cotys in revenge for the wanton outrage which he had committed in castrating him when a child.

Many, too, enraged by blows inflicted on the person which they
25 deemed an insult, have either killed or attempted to kill officers of state and royal princes by whom they have been injured. Thus, at Mytilene, Megacles and his friends attacked and slew the Penthilidae, as they were going about and striking people with clubs. At a later date Smerdis, who had been beaten and torn away from his wife
30 by Penthilus, slew him. In the conspiracy against Archelaus, Decamnichus stimulated the fury of the assassins and led the attack; he was enraged because Archelaus had delivered him to Euripides to be scourged; for the poet had been irritated at some remark made by Decamnichus on the foulness of his breath. Many other examples
35 might be cited of murders and conspiracies which have arisen from similar causes.

Fear is another motive which, as we have said, has caused conspiracies as well in monarchies as in more popular forms of government. Thus Artapanes conspired against Xerxes and slew him, fearing that he would be accused of hanging Darius against his orders – he having been under the impression that Xerxes would forget what
40 he had said in the middle of a meal, and that the offence would be forgiven.

1312ªI   Another motive is contempt, as in the case of Sardanapalus, whom someone saw carding wool with his women, if the story-tellers say truly; and the tale may be true, if not of him, of someone else. Dion attacked the younger Dionysius because he despised him, and saw
5 that he was equally despised by his own subjects, and that he was always drunk. Even the friends of a tyrant will sometimes attack him

out of contempt; for the confidence which he reposes in them breeds contempt, and they think that they will not be found out. The expectation of success is likewise a sort of contempt; the assailants are ready to strike, and think nothing of the danger, because they seem to 10 have the power in their hands. Thus generals of armies attack monarchs; as, for example, Cyrus attacked Astyages, despising the effeminacy of his life, and believing that his power was worn out. Thus again, Seuthes the Thracian conspired against Amadocus, whose general he was.

And sometimes men are actuated by more than one motive, like 15 Mithridates, who conspired against Ariobarzanes, partly out of contempt and partly from the love of gain.

Bold natures, placed by their sovereigns in a high military position, are most likely to make the attempt in the expectation of success; for courage is emboldened by power, and the union of the two inspires 20 them with the hope of an easy victory.

Attempts of which the motive is ambition arise in a different way as well as in those already mentioned. There are men who will not risk their lives in the hope of gains and honours however great, but who 25 nevertheless regard the killing of a tyrant simply as an extraordinary action which will make them famous and notable in the world; they wish to acquire, not a kingdom, but a name. It is rare, however, to find 30 such men; he who would kill a tyrant must be prepared to lose his life if he fails. He must have the resolution of Dion, who, when he made war upon Dionysius, took with him very few troops, saying 'that 35 whatever measure of success he might attain would be enough for him, even if he were to die the moment he landed; such a death would be welcome to him'. But this is a temper to which few can attain.

Once more, tyrannies, like all other governments, are destroyed 40 from without by some opposite and more powerful form of government. That such a government will have the will to attack them is 1312ᵇ1 clear; for the two are opposed in principle; and all men, if they can, do what they want to. Democracy is antagonistic to tyranny, on the principle of Hesiod, 'Potter hates potter',[1] because they are nearly 5 akin, for the extreme form of democracy is tyranny; and royalty and aristocracy are both alike opposed to tyranny, because they are constitutions of a different type. And therefore the Lacedaemonians

---

[1] Hesiod, *Works and Days*, 25.

put down most of the tyrannies, and so did the Syracusans during the time when they were well governed.

Again, tyrannies are destroyed from within, when the reigning
10 family are divided among themselves, as that of Gelo was, and more recently that of Dionysius; in the case of Gelo because Thrasybulus, the brother of Hiero, flattered the son of Gelo and led him into excesses in order that he might rule in his name. Whereupon the family got together a party to get rid of Thrasybulus and save the
15 tyranny; but those of the people who conspired with them seized the opportunity and drove them all out. In the case of Dionysius, Dion, his own relative, attacked and expelled him with the assistance of the people; he afterwards perished himself.

There are two chief motives which induce men to attack tyrannies –
20 hatred and contempt. Hatred of tyrants is inevitable, and contempt is also a frequent cause of their destruction. Thus we see that most of those who have acquired, have retained their power, but those who have inherited, have lost it, almost at once; for, living in luxurious
25 ease, they have become contemptible, and offer many opportunities to their assailants. Anger, too, must be included under hatred, and produces the same effects. It is often even more ready to strike – the angry are more impetuous in making an attack, for they do not follow
30 rational principle. And men are very apt to give way to their passions when they are insulted. To this cause is to be attributed the fall of the Peisistratidae and of many others. Hatred is more reasonable, for anger is accompanied by pain, which is an impediment to reason, whereas hatred is painless.

In a word, all the causes which I have mentioned as destroying the
35 last and most unmixed form of oligarchy, and the extreme form of democracy, may be assumed to affect tyranny; indeed the extreme forms of both are only tyrannies distributed among several persons. Kingly rule is little affected by external causes and is therefore lasting; it is generally destroyed from within. And there are two ways in which
1313ª1 the destruction may come about; when the members of the royal family quarrel among themselves, and when the kings attempt to administer the state too much after the fashion of a tyranny, and to extend their authority contrary to the law. Royalties do not now come into existence; where such forms of government arise, they are rather
5 monarchies or tyrannies. For the rule of a king is over voluntary subjects, and he is supreme in all important matters; but in our own

day men are more upon an equality, and no one is so immeasurably superior to others as to represent adequately the greatness and dignity of the office. Hence mankind will not, willingly, endure it, and any one who obtains power by force or fraud is at once thought to be a tyrant. In hereditary monarchies a further cause of destruction is the fact that kings often fall into contempt, and, although possessing not tyrannical power, but only royal dignity, are apt to outrage others. Their overthrow is then readily effected; for there is an end to the king when his subjects do not want to have him, but the tyrant lasts, whether they like him or not.

The destruction of monarchies is to be attributed to these and the like causes.

11 · And they are preserved, to speak generally, by the opposite causes; or, if we consider them separately, royalty is preserved by the limitation of its powers. The more restricted the functions of kings, the longer their power will last unimpaired; for then they are more moderate and not so despotic in their ways; and they are less envied by their subjects. This is the reason why the kingly office has lasted so long among the Molossians. And for a similar reason it has continued among the Lacedaemonians, because there it was always divided between two, and afterwards further limited by Theopompus in various respects, more particularly by the establishment of the Ephoralty. He diminished the power of the kings, but established on a more lasting basis the kingly office, which was thus made in a certain sense not less, but greater. There is a story that when his wife once asked him whether he was not ashamed to leave to his sons a royal power which was less than he had inherited from his father, 'No indeed', he replied, 'for the power which I leave to them will be more lasting'.

As to tyrannies, they are preserved in two quite opposite ways. One of them is the old traditional method in which most tyrants administer their government. Of such arts Periander of Corinth is said to have been the great master, and many similar devices may be gathered from the Persians in the administration of their government. There are firstly the prescriptions mentioned some distance back, for the preservation of a tyranny, in so far as this is possible; viz. that the tyrant should lop off those who are too high; he must put to death men of spirit; he must not allow common meals, clubs, education and the

like; he must be upon his guard against anything which is likely to
inspire either courage or confidence among his subjects; he must
prohibit schools or other meetings for discussion, and he must take
5 every means to prevent people from knowing one another (for
acquaintance begets mutual confidence). Further, he must compel all
persons staying in the city to appear in public and live at his gates; then
he will know what they are doing: if they are always kept under, they
will learn to be humble. In short, he should practise these and the like
10 Persian and barbaric arts, which all have the same object. A tyrant
should also endeavour to know what each of his subjects says or does,
and should employ spies, like the 'female detectives' at Syracuse, and
the eavesdroppers whom Hiero was in the habit of sending to any
15 place of resort or meeting; for the fear of informers prevents people
from speaking their minds, and if they do, they are more easily found
out. Another art of the tyrant is to sow quarrels among the citizens;
friends should be embroiled with friends, the people with the
notables, and the rich with one another. Also he should impoverish
his subjects; he thus provides against the maintenance of a guard by
20 the citizens, and the people, having to keep hard at work, are
prevented from conspiring. The Pyramids of Egypt afford an example
of this policy; also the offerings of the family of Cypselus, and the
building of the temple of Olympian Zeus by the Peisistratidae, and
the great Polycratean monuments at Samos; all these works were
25 alike intended to occupy the people and keep them poor. Another
practice of tyrants is to multiply taxes, after the manner of Dionysius
at Syracuse, who contrived that within five years his subjects should
bring into the treasury their whole property. The tyrant is also fond of
making war in order that his subjects may have something to do and
30 be always in want of a leader. And whereas the power of a king is
preserved by his friends, the characteristic of a tyrant is to distrust his
friends, because he knows that all men want to overthrow him, and
they above all have the power to do so.

Again, the practices of the last and worst form of democracy are all
found in tyrannies. Such are the power given to women in their
35 families in the hope that they will inform against their husbands, and
the licence which is allowed to slaves in order that they may betray
their masters; for slaves and women do not conspire against tyrants;
and they are of course friendly to tyrannies and also to democracies,
since under them they have a good time. For the people too would

146

fain be a monarch, and therefore by them, as well as by the tyrant, the
flatterer is held in honour; in democracies he is the demagogue; and 40
the tyrant also has those who associate with him in a humble spirit,
which is a work of flattery. 1314ᵃ1

Hence tyrants are always fond of bad men, because they love to be
flattered, but no man who has the spirit of a freeman in him will lower
himself by flattery; good men love others, or at any rate do not flatter
them. Moreover, the bad are useful for bad purposes; 'nail knocks out 5
nail', as the proverb says. It is characteristic of a tyrant to dislike every
one who has dignity or independence; he wants to be alone in his glory
but anyone who claims a like dignity or asserts his independence
encroaches upon his prerogative and is hated by him as an enemy to
his power. Another mark of a tyrant is that he likes foreigners better 10
than citizens, and lives with them and invites them to his table; for the
one are enemies, but the others enter into no rivalry with him.

Such are the marks of the tyrant and the arts by which he preserves
his power; there is no wickedness too great for him. All that we have
said may be summed up under three heads, which answer to the three 15
aims of the tyrant. These are, the humiliation of his subjects, for he
knows that a mean-spirited man will not conspire against anybody:
the creation of mistrust among them; for a tyrant is not overthrown
until men begin to have confidence in one another; and this is the
reason why tyrants are at war with the good; they are under the idea
that their power is endangered by them, not only because they will not 20
be ruled despotically, but also because they are loyal to one another,
and to other men, and do not inform against one another or against
other men: the tyrant desires that his subjects shall be incapable of
action, for no one attempts what is impossible, and they will not
attempt to overthrow a tyranny if they are powerless. Under these 25
three heads the whole policy of a tyrant may be summed up, and to
one or other of them all his ideas may be referred: he sows distrust
among his subjects; he takes away their power; and he humbles them.

This then is one of the two methods by which tyrannies are 30
preserved; and there is another which proceeds upon an almost
opposite principle of action. The nature of this latter method may be
gathered from a comparison of the causes which destroy kingdoms,
for as one mode of destroying kingly power is to make the office of
king more tyrannical, so the salvation of a tyranny is to make it more 35
like the rule of a king. But of one thing the tyrant must be careful; he

must keep power enough to rule over his subjects, whether they like him or not, for if he once gives this up he gives up his tyranny. But though power must be retained as the foundation, in all else the tyrant
40 should act or appear to act in the character of a king. In the first place
1314^b1 he should pretend concern for the public revenues, and not waste money in making presents of a sort at which the common people get excited when they see their hard-won earnings snatched from them and lavished on courtesans and foreigners and artists. He should give
5 an account of what he receives and of what he spends (a practice which has been adopted by some tyrants); for then he will seem to be a steward of the public rather than a tyrant; nor need he fear that, while he is the lord of the city, he will ever be in want of money. Such a
10 policy is at all events much more advantageous for the tyrant when he goes from home, than to leave behind him a hoard, for then the garrison who remain in the city will be less likely to attack his power; and a tyrant, when he is absent from home, has more reason to fear the guardians of his treasure than the citizens, for the one accompany him, but the others remain behind. In the second place, he should be
15 seen to collect taxes and to require public services only for state purposes, and so as to form a fund in case of war, and generally he ought to make himself the guardian and treasurer of them, as if they belonged, not to him, but to the public. He should appear, not harsh, but dignified, and when men meet him they should look upon him
20 with reverence, and not with fear. Yet it is hard for him to be respected if he inspires no respect, and therefore whatever virtues he may neglect, at least he should maintain the character of a great soldier, and produce the impression that he is one. Neither he nor any
25 of his associates should ever assault the young of either sex who are his subjects, and the women of his family should observe a like self-control towards other women; the insolence of women has ruined many tyrannies. In the indulgence of pleasures he should be the
30 opposite of our modern tyrants, who not only begin at dawn and pass whole days in sensuality but want other men to see them, so that they may admire their happy and blessed lot. In these things a tyrant should if possible be moderate, or at any rate should not parade his
35 vices to the world; for a drunken and drowsy tyrant is soon despised and attacked; not so he who is temperate and wide awake. His conduct should be the very reverse of nearly everything which has been said before about tyrants. He ought to adorn and improve his

city, as though he were not a tyrant, but the guardian of the state. Also
he should appear to be particularly earnest in the service of the gods; 40
for if men think that a ruler is religious and has a reverence for the
gods, they are less afraid of suffering injustice at his hands, and they 1315ᵃ1
are less disposed to conspire against him, because they believe him to
have the very gods fighting on his side. At the same time his religion
must not be thought foolish. And he should honour men of merit, and
make them think that they would not be held in more honour by the 5
citizens if they had a free government. The honour he should
distribute himself, but the punishment should be inflicted by officers
and courts of law. It is a precaution which is taken by all monarchs not
to make one person great; but if one, then two or more should be
raised, that they may keep an eye on one another. If after all some one 10
has to be made great, he should not be a man of bold spirit; for such
dispositions are ever most inclined to strike. And if any one is to be
deprived of his power, let it be diminished gradually, not taken from
him all at once. The tyrant should abstain from all outrage; in 15
particular from personal violence and from wanton conduct towards
the young. He should be especially careful of his behaviour to men
who are lovers of honour; for as the lovers of money are offended
when their property is touched, so are the lovers of honour and the
good when their honour is affected. Therefore a tyrant ought either 20
not to commit such acts at all; or he should be thought only to employ
fatherly correction, and not to trample upon others – and his
acquaintance with youth should be supposed to arise from desire, and
not from the insolence of power, and in general he should compen-
sate the appearance of dishonour by the increase of honour.

Of those who attempt assassination they are the most dangerous, 25
and require to be most carefully watched, who do not care to survive,
if they effect their purpose. Therefore special precaution should be
taken about any who think that either they or those for whom they care
have been insulted; for when men are led away by passion to assault
others they are regardless of themselves. As Heracleitus says, 'It is 30
difficult to fight against anger; for a man will buy revenge with his
soul.'

And whereas states consist of two classes, of poor men and of rich,
the tyrant should lead both to imagine that they are preserved and
prevented from harming one another by his rule, and whichever of the 35
two is stronger he should attach to his government; for, having this

advantage, he has no need either to emancipate slaves or to disarm the citizens; either party added to the force which he already has will make him stronger than his assailants.

40 But enough of these details – what should be the general policy of
1315ᵇ1 the tyrant is obvious. He ought to show himself to his subjects in the light, not of a tyrant, but of a steward and a king. He should not appropriate what is theirs, but should be their guardian; he should be moderate, not extravagant in his way of life; he should win the notables by companionship, and the multitude by flattery. For then
5 his rule will of necessity be nobler and happier, because he will rule over better men whose spirits are not crushed, and who do not hate and fear him. His power too will be more lasting. His disposition will be virtuous, or at least half virtuous; and he will not be wicked, but
10 half wicked only.

12 · Yet no forms of government are so short-lived as oligarchy and tyranny. The tyranny which lasted longest was that of Orthagoras and his sons at Sicyon; this continued for a hundred years. The reason
15 was that they treated their subjects with moderation, and to a great extent observed the laws; and in various ways gained the favour of the people by the care which they took of them. Cleisthenes, in particular, was respected for his military ability. If report may be believed, he crowned the judge who decided against him in the games; and, as
20 some say, the sitting statue in the Agora of Sicyon is the likeness of this person. (A similar story is told of Peisistratus, who is said on one occasion to have allowed himself to be summoned and tried before the Areopagus.)

Next in duration to the tyranny of Orthagoras was that of the
25 Cypselidae at Corinth, which lasted seventy-three years and six months: Cypselus reigned thirty years, Periander forty and a half, and Psammetichus the son of Gorgus three. Their continuance was due to similar causes: Cypselus was a popular man, who during the whole time of his rule never had a body-guard; and Periander, although he was a tyrant, was a great soldier. Third in duration was the rule of the
30 Peisistratidae at Athens, but it was interrupted; for Peisistratus was twice driven out, so that out of thirty-three years he reigned only seventeen; and his sons reigned eighteen – altogether thirty-five years. Of other tyrannies, that of Hiero and Gelo at Syracuse was the
35 most lasting. Even this, however, was short, not more than eighteen

years in all; for Gelo continued tyrant for seven years, and died in the eighth; Hiero reigned for ten years, and Thrasybulus was driven out in the eleventh month. In fact, tyrannies generally have been of quite short duration.

I have now gone through almost all the causes by which constitu- 40 tional governments and monarchies are either destroyed or preserved.

In the *Republic* of Plato, Socrates treats of revolutions, but not well, 1316ª1 for he mentions no cause of change which peculiarly affects the first or perfect state. He only says that the cause is that nothing is abiding, but all things change in a certain cycle; and that the origin of the 5 change consists in those numbers 'of which 4 and 3, married with 5, furnish two harmonies' (he means when the number of this figure becomes solid);[1] he conceives that nature at certain times produces bad men who will not submit to education; in which latter particular he may very likely be not far wrong, for there may well be some men 10 who cannot be educated and made virtuous. But why is such a cause of change peculiar to his ideal state, and not rather common to all states, or indeed, to everything which comes into being at all? And is it by the agency of time, which, as he declares, makes all things change, 15 that things which did not begin together, change together? For example, if something has come into being the day before the completion of the cycle, will it change with things that came into being before? Further, why should the perfect state change into the Spartan? For governments more often take an opposite form than one akin to them. The same remark is applicable to the other changes; he 20 says that the Spartan constitution changes into an oligarchy, and this into a democracy, and this again into a tyranny. And yet the contrary happens quite as often; for a democracy is even more likely to change into an oligarchy than into a monarchy. Further, he never says 25 whether tyranny is, or is not, liable to revolutions, and if it is, what is the cause of them, or into what form it changes. And the reason is, that he could not very well have told: for there is no rule; according to him it should revert to the first and best, and then there would be a complete cycle. But in point of fact a tyranny often changes into a tyranny, as that at Sicyon changed from the tyranny of Myron into that 30 of Cleisthenes; into oligarchy, as the tyranny of Antileon did at

---

[1] Plato, *Rep.*, VIII 546c.

Chalcis; into democracy, as that of Gelo's family did at Syracuse; into aristocracy, as at Carthage, and the tyranny of Charilaus in
35 Lacedaemon. Often an oligarchy changes into a tyranny, like most of the ancient oligarchies in Sicily; for example, the oligarchy at Leontini changed into the tyranny of Panaetius; that at Gela into the tyranny of Cleander; that at Rhegium into the tyranny of Anaxilaus; the same thing has happened in many other states. And it is absurd to suppose that the state changes into oligarchy merely because the
1316ᵇ1 ruling class are lovers and makers of money, and not because the very rich think it unfair that the very poor should have an equal share in the government with themselves. Moreover, in many oligarchies there
5 are laws against making money in trade. But at Carthage, which is a democracy, there is no such prohibition; and yet to this day the Carthaginians have never had a revolution. It is absurd too for him to say that an oligarchy is two cities, one of the rich, and the other of the poor.[1] Is not this just as much the case in the Spartan constitution, or in any other in which either all do not possess equal property, or all are
10 not equally good men? Nobody need be any poorer than he was before, and yet the oligarchy may change all the same into a democracy, if the poor form the majority; and a democracy may change into an oligarchy, if the wealthy class are stronger than the people, and the one are energetic, the other indifferent. Once more,
15 although the causes of the change are very numerous, he mentions only one, which is, that the citizens become poor through dissipation and debt, as though he thought that all, or the majority of them, were originally rich. This is not true: though it is true that when any of the leaders lose their property they are ripe for revolution; but, when
20 anybody else does, it is no great matter, and an oligarchy does not even then more often pass into a democracy than into any other form of government. Again, if men are deprived of the honours of state, and are wronged, and insulted, they make revolutions, and change forms of government, even although they have not wasted their substance because they might do what they like – of which extravagance he declares excessive freedom to be the cause.
25 Finally, although there are many forms of oligarchies and democracies, Socrates speaks of their revolutions as though there were only one form of either of them.

[1] *Rep.*, VIII 551D.

BOOK VI

1 · We have now considered the varieties of the deliberative or 30
supreme power in states, and the various arrangements of law-courts
and state offices, and which of them are adapted to different forms of
governments. We have also spoken of the destruction and preservation of constitutions, how and from what causes they arise.   35

Of democracy and all other forms of government there are many
kinds; and it will be well to assign to them severally the modes of
organization which are proper and advantageous to each, adding what
remains to be said about them. Moreover, we ought to consider the 40
various combinations of these modes themselves; for such combina- 1317ᵃ1
tions make constitutions overlap one another, so that aristocracies
have an oligarchical character, and constitutional governments
incline to democracies.

When I speak of the combinations which remain to be considered,
and thus far have not been considered by us, I mean such as these: –
when the deliberative part of the government and the election of 5
officers is constituted oligarchically, and the law-courts aristocrati-
cally, or when the courts and the deliberative part of the state are
oligarchical, and the election of offices aristocratic, or when in any
other way there is a want of harmony in the composition of a state.

I have shown already what forms of democracy are suited to 10
particular cities, and what forms of oligarchy to particular peoples,
and to whom each of the other forms of government is suited.
Further, we must not only show which of these governments is the
best for each state, but also briefly proceed to consider how these and
other forms of government are to be established.   15

First of all let us speak of democracy, which will also bring to light
the opposite form of government commonly called oligarchy. For the
purposes of this inquiry we need to ascertain all the elements and
characteristics of democracy, since from the combinations of these
the varieties of democratic government arise. There are several of 20
these differing from each other, and the difference is due to two
causes. One has been already mentioned – differences of population;
for the popular element may consist of farmers, or of artisans, or of 25
labourers, and if the first of these is added to the second, or the third
to the two others, not only does the democracy become better or

worse, but its very nature is changed. A second cause remains to be
30 mentioned: the various properties and characteristics of democracy,
when variously combined, make a difference. For one democracy will
have less and another will have more, and another will have all of
these characteristics. There is an advantage in knowing them all,
whether a man wishes to establish some new form of democracy, or
35 only to remodel an existing one. Founders of states try to bring
together all the elements which accord with the ideas of the several
constitutions; but this is a mistake of theirs, as I have already
remarked when speaking of the destruction and preservation of
states. We will now set forth the principles, characteristics, and aims
of such states.

40 2 · The basis of a democratic state is liberty; which, according to the
common opinion of men, can only be enjoyed in such a state – this
1317^b1 they affirm to be the great end of every democracy. One principle of
liberty is for all to rule and be ruled in turn, and indeed democratic
justice is the application of numerical not proportionate equality;
5 whence it follows that the majority must be supreme, and that
whatever the majority approve must be the end and the just. Every
citizen, it is said, must have equality, and therefore in a democracy the
poor have more power than the rich, because there are more of them,
10 and the will of the majority is supreme. This, then, is one note of
liberty which all democrats affirm to be the principle of their state.
Another is that a man should live as he likes. This, they say, is the
mark of liberty, since, on the other hand, not to live as a man likes is
the mark of a slave. This is the second characteristic of democracy,
15 whence has arisen the claim of men to be ruled by none, if possible,
or, if this is impossible, to rule and be ruled in turns; and so it
contributes to the freedom based upon equality.

Such being our foundation and such the principle from which we
start, the characteristics of democracy are as follows: – the election of
officers by all out of all; and that all should rule over each, and each in
20 his turn over all; that the appointment to all offices, or to all but those
which require experience and skill, should be made by lot; that no
property qualification should be required for offices, or only a very
low one; that a man should not hold the same office twice, or not
often, or in the case of few except military offices; that the tenure of all
25 offices, or of as many as possible, should be brief; that all men should

sit in judgement, or that judges selected out of all should judge, in all matters, or in most and in the greatest and most important – such as the scrutiny of accounts, the constitution, and private contracts; that the assembly should be supreme over all causes, or at any rate over the most important, and the magistrates over none or only over a very few. 30 Of all magistracies, a council is the most democratic when there is not the means of paying all the citizens, but when they are paid even this is robbed of its power; for the people then draw all cases to themselves, as I said in the previous discussion. The next characteristic of 35 democracy is payment for services; assembly, law-courts, magistrates, everybody receives pay, when it is to be had; or when it is not to be had for all, then it is given to the law-courts and to the stated assemblies, to the council and to the magistrates, or at least to any of them who are compelled to have their meals together. [And whereas oligarchy is characterized by birth, wealth, and education, the marks of democracy appear to be the opposite of these – low birth, poverty, 40 mean employment.]*a* Another characteristic is that no magistracy is perpetual, but if any such have survived some ancient change in the 1318ª1 constitution it should be stripped of its power, and the holders should be elected by lot and no longer by vote. These are the points common to all democracies; but democracy and demos in their truest form are based upon the recognized principle of democratic justice, that all 5 should count equally; for equality implies that the poor should have no more share in the government than the rich, and should not be the only rulers, but that all should rule equally according to their numbers. And in this way men think that they will secure equality and freedom in their state.   10

3 · Next comes the question, how is this equality to be obtained? Are we to assign to a thousand poor men the property qualifications of five hundred rich men? and shall we give the thousand a power equal to that of the five hundred? or, if this is not to be the mode, ought we, still 15 retaining the same ratio, to take equal numbers from each and give them the control of the elections and of the courts? – Which, according to the democratic notion, is the juster form of the constitution – this or one based on numbers only? Democrats say that justice is that to which the majority agree, oligarchs that to which the 20

---

a Excised by Dreizehnter.

wealthier class agree; in their opinion the decision should be given according to the amount of property. In both principles there is some inequality and injustice. For if justice is the will of the few, any one person who has more wealth than all the rest of the rich put together, ought, upon the oligarchical principle, to have the sole power – but this would be tyranny; or if justice is the will of the majority, as I was
25 before saying,[1] they will unjustly confiscate the property of the wealthy minority. To find a principle of equality in which they both agree we must inquire into their respective ideas of justice.

Now they agree in saying that whatever is decided by the majority of
30 the citizens is to be deemed law. Granted, but not without some reserve; since there are two classes out of which a state is composed – the poor and the rich – that is to be deemed law, on which both or the greater part of both agree; and if they disagree, that which is approved by the greater number, and by those who have the higher qualification. For example, suppose that there are ten rich and twenty poor,
35 and some measure is approved by six of the rich and is disapproved by fifteen of the poor, and the remaining four of the rich join with the party of the poor, and the remaining five of the poor with that of the rich; in such a case the will of those whose qualifications, when both sides are added up, are the greatest, should prevail. If they turn out to
40 be equal, there is no greater difficulty than at present, when, if the
1318^b1 assembly or the courts are divided, recourse is had to the lot, or to some similar expedient. But, although it may be difficult in theory to know what is just and equal, the practical difficulty of inducing those to forbear who can, if they like, encroach, is far greater, for the weaker
5 are always asking for equality and justice, but the stronger care for none of these things.

4 · Of the four kinds of democracy, as was said in the previous discussion, the best is that which comes first in order; it is also the oldest of them all. I am speaking of them according to the natural classification of their inhabitants. For the best material of democracy
10 is an agricultural population; there is no difficulty in forming a democracy where the mass of the people live by agriculture or tending of cattle. Being poor, they have no leisure, and therefore do not often attend the assembly, and having the necessaries of life they are always

---

[1] III 10.

at work and do not covet the property of others. Indeed, they find their employment pleasanter than the cares of government or office where 15 no great gains can be made out of them, for the many are more desirous of gain than of honour. A proof is that even the ancient tyrannies were patiently endured by them, as they still endure oligarchies, if they are allowed to work and are not deprived of their 20 property; for some of them grow quickly rich and the others are well enough off. Moreover, they have the power of electing the magistrates and calling them to account; their ambition, if they have any, is thus satisfied; and in some democracies, although they do not all share in the appointment of offices, except through representatives elected in turn out of the whole people, as at Mantinea – yet, if they have the 25 power of deliberating, the many are contented. Even this form of government may be regarded as a democracy, and was such at Mantinea. Hence it is both expedient and customary in the afore-mentioned type of democracy that all should elect to offices, and conduct scrutinies, and sit in the law-courts, but that the great offices should be filled up by election and from persons having a qualifica-tion; the greater requiring a greater qualification, or, if there are no 30 offices for which a qualification is required, then those who are marked out by special ability should be appointed. Under such a form of government the citizens are sure to be governed well (for the offices will always be held by the best persons; the people are willing enough to elect them and are not jealous of the good). The good and the 35 notables will then be satisfied, for they will not be governed by men who are their inferiors, and the persons elected will rule justly, because others will call them to account. Every man should be responsible to others, nor should anyone be allowed to do just as he pleases; for where absolute freedom is allowed there is nothing to 40 restrain the evil which is inherent in every man. But the principle of 1319ᵃ1 responsibility secures that which is the greatest good in states; the right persons rule and are prevented from doing wrong, and the people have their due. It is evident that this is the best kind of democracy – and why? because the people are drawn from a certain 5 class. Some of the ancient laws of most states were useful with a view to making the people husbandmen. They provided either that no one should possess more than a certain quantity of land, or that, if he did, the land should not be within a certain distance from the town or the acropolis. Formerly in many states there was a law forbidding anyone 10

to sell his original allotment of land. There is a similar law attributed
to Oxylus, which is to the effect that there should be a certain portion
of every man's land on which he could not borrow money. A useful
corrective to the evil of which I am speaking would be the law of the
Aphytaeans, who, although they are numerous, and do not possess
much land, are all of them farmers. For their properties are reckoned
in the census, not entire, but only in such small portions that even the
poor may have more than the amount required.

Next best to an agricultural, and in many respects similar, are a
pastoral people, who live by their flocks; they are the best trained of
any for war, robust in body and able to camp out. The people of whom
other democracies consist are far inferior to them, for their life is
inferior; there is no room for excellence in any of their employments,
whether they be artisans or traders or labourers. Besides, people of
this class can readily come to the assembly, because they are con-
tinually moving about in the city and in the agora; whereas farmers are
scattered over the country and do not meet or feel the same need of
assembling together. Where the territory also happens to extend to a
distance from the city, there is no difficulty in making an excellent
democracy or constitutional government; for the people are compelled to settle in the country, and even if there is a town population
the assembly ought not to meet, in democracies, when the country
people cannot come. We have thus explained how the first and best
form of democracy should be constituted; it is clear that the other or
inferior sorts will deviate in a regular order, and the population which
is excluded will at each stage be of a lower kind.

The last form of democracy, that in which all share alike, is one
which cannot be borne by all states, and will not last long unless well
regulated by laws and customs. The more general causes which tend
to destroy this or other kinds of government have been pretty fully
considered. In order to constitute such a democracy and strengthen
the people, the leaders have been in the habit of including as many as
they can, and making citizens not only of those who are legitimate, but
even of the illegitimate, and of those who have only one parent a
citizen, whether father or mother; for nothing of this sort comes amiss
to such a democracy. This is the way in which demagogues proceed.
Whereas the right thing would be to make no more additions when
the number of the commonalty exceeds that of the notables and of the
middle class and not to go beyond this. When in excess of this point,

the constitution becomes disorderly, and the notables grow excited 15
and impatient of the democracy, as in the insurrection at Cyrene; for
no notice is taken of a little evil, but when it increases it strikes the eye.
Measures like those which Cleisthenes passed when he wanted to 20
increase the power of the democracy at Athens, or such as were taken
by the founders of popular government at Cyrene, are useful in the
extreme form of democracy. Fresh tribes and brotherhoods should be
established; the private rites of families should be restricted and
converted into public ones; in short, every contrivance should be 25
adopted which will mingle the citizens with one another and get rid of
old connexions. Again, the measures which are taken by tyrants
appear all of them to be democratic; such, for instance, as the licence
permitted to slaves (which may be to a certain extent advantageous)
and also to women and children, and the allowing everybody to live as 30
he likes. Such a government will have many supporters, for most
persons would rather live in a disorderly than in a sober manner.

5 · The mere establishment of a democracy is not the only or
principal business of the legislator, or of those who wish to create 35
such a state, for any state, however badly constituted, may last one,
two, or three days; a far greater difficulty is the preservation of it. The
legislator should therefore endeavour to have a firm foundation
according to the principles already laid down concerning the
preservation and destruction of states; he should guard against the
destructive elements, and should make laws, whether written or 40
unwritten, which will contain all the preservatives of states. He must 1320ᵃ1
not think the truly democratic or oligarchical measure to be that
which will give the greatest amount of democracy or oligarchy, but
that which will make them last longest. The demagogues of our own
day often get property confiscated in the law-courts in order to please 5
the people. Hence those who have the welfare of the state at heart
should counteract them, and make a law that the property of the
condemned should not be public and go into the treasury but be
sacred. Thus offenders will be as much afraid, for they will be
punished all the same, and the people, having nothing to gain, will not 10
be so ready to condemn the accused. Care should also be taken that
state trials are as few as possible, and heavy penalties should be
inflicted on those who bring groundless accusations; for it is the
practice to indict, not members of the popular party, but the notables,

15 although the citizens ought to be all attached to the constitution as
well, or at any rate should not regard their rulers as enemies.

Now, since in the last form of democracy the citizens are very
numerous, and can hardly be made to assemble unless they are paid,
and to pay them when there are no revenues presses hardly upon the
20 notables (for the money must be obtained by a property-tax and
confiscations and corrupt practices of the courts, things which have
before now overthrown many democracies); where, I say, there are no
revenues, the government should hold few assemblies, and the law-
courts should consist of many persons, but sit for a few days only.
This system has two advantages: first, the rich do not fear the
25 expense, even though they are unpaid themselves when the poor are
paid; and secondly, cases are better tried, for wealthy persons,
although they do not like to be long absent from their own affairs, do
not mind going for a few days to the law-courts. Where there are
30 revenues the demagogues should not be allowed after their manner to
distribute the surplus; the poor are always receiving and always
wanting more and more, for such help is like water poured into a leaky
cask. Yet the true friend of the people should see that they are not too
poor, for extreme poverty lowers the character of the democracy;
35 measures therefore should be taken which will give them lasting
prosperity; and as this is equally the interest of all classes, the
proceeds of the public revenues should be accumulated and distributed among its poor, if possible, in such quantities as may enable
them to purchase a little farm, or, at any rate, make a beginning in
1320ᵇ1 trade or farming. And if this benevolence cannot be extended to all,
money should be distributed in turn according to tribes or other
divisions, and in the meantime the rich should pay the fee for the
attendance of the poor at the necessary assemblies; and should in
return be excused from useless public services. By administering the
5 state in this spirit the Carthaginians retain the affections of the
people; their policy is from time to time to send some of them into
their dependent towns, where they grow rich. It is also worthy of a
generous and sensible nobility to divide the poor amongst them, and
give them the means of going to work. The example of the people of
10 Tarentum is also well deserving of imitation, for, by sharing the use of
their own property with the poor, they gain their good will. Moreover,
they divide all their offices into two classes, some of them being
elected by vote, the others by lot; the latter, so that the people may

participate in them, and the former, so that the state may be better administered. A like result may be gained by dividing the same offices, so as to have two classes of magistrates, one chosen by vote, the other by lot. 15

Enough has been said of the manner in which democracies ought to be constituted.

6 · From these considerations there will be no difficulty in seeing what should be the constitution of oligarchies. We have only to reason from opposites and compare each form of oligarchy with the cor- 20 responding form of democracy.

The first and best balanced of oligarchies is akin to a constitutional government. In this there ought to be two standards of qualification; the one high, the other low – the lower qualifying for the humbler yet indispensable offices and the higher for the superior ones. He who 25 acquires the prescribed qualification should have the rights of citizenship. The number of those admitted should be such as will make the entire governing body stronger than those who are excluded, and the new citizen should be always taken out of the better class of the people. The principle, narrowed a little, gives another 30 form of oligarchy; until at length we reach the most cliquish and tyrannical of them all, answering to the extreme democracy, which, being the worst, requires vigilance in proportion to its badness. For as healthy bodies and ships well provided with sailors may undergo many mishaps and survive them, whereas sickly constitutions and 35 rotten ill-manned ships are ruined by the very least mistake, so do the worst forms of government require the greatest care. The populousness of democracies generally preserves them (for number is to 1321ᵃ1 democracy in the place of justice based on merit); whereas the preservation of an oligarchy clearly depends on an opposite principle, viz. good order.

7 · As there are four chief divisions of the common people, farmers, 5 artisans, traders, labourers; so also there are four kinds of military forces – the cavalry, the heavy infantry, the light-armed troops, the navy. When the country is adapted for cavalry, then a strong oligarchy is likely to be established. For the security of the inhabitants depends 10 upon a force of this sort, and only rich men can afford to keep horses. The second form of oligarchy prevails when the country is adapted to

heavy infantry; for this service is better suited to the rich than to the poor. But the light-armed and the naval element are wholly
15 democratic; and nowadays, where they are numerous, if the two parties quarrel, the oligarchy are often worsted by them in the struggle. A remedy for this state of things may be found in the practice of generals who combine a proper contingent of light-armed troops with cavalry and heavy-armed. And this is the way in which the poor get the better of the rich in civil contests; being lightly armed, they
20 fight with advantage against cavalry and heavy infantry. An oligarchy which raises such a force out of the lower classes raises a power against itself. And therefore, since the ages of the citizens vary and some are older and some younger, the fathers should have their own sons, while they are still young, taught the agile movements of light-
25 armed troops; and these, when they have been taken out of the ranks of the youth, should become light-armed warriors in reality. The oligarchy should also yield a share in the government to the people, either, as I said before, to those who have a property qualification, or, as in the case of Thebes, to those who have abstained for a certain
30 number of years from mean employments, or, as at Massalia, to men of merit who are selected for their worthiness, whether previously citizens or not. The magistracies of the highest rank, which ought to be in the hands of the governing body, should have expensive duties attached to them, and then the people will not desire them and will take no offence at the privileges of their rulers when they see that they
35 pay a heavy fine for their dignity. It is fitting also that the magistrates on entering office should offer magnificent sacrifices or erect some public edifice, and then the people who participate in the entertain-ments, and see the city decorated with votive offerings and buildings, will not desire an alteration in the government, and the notables will
40 have memorials of their munificence. This, however, is anything but the fashion of our modern oligarchs, who are as covetous of gain as
1321^{b}1 they are of honour; oligarchies like theirs may be well described as petty democracies. Enough of the manner in which democracies and oligarchies should be organized.

8 · Next in order follows the right distribution of offices, their
5 number, their nature, their duties, of which indeed we have already spoken. No state can exist not having the necessary offices, and no state can be well administered not having the offices which tend to

preserve harmony and good order. In small states, as we have already remarked, there must not be many of them, but in larger states there 10 must be a larger number, and we should carefully consider which offices may properly be united and which separated.

First among necessary offices is that which has the care of the market; a magistrate should be appointed to inspect contracts and to maintain order. For in every state there must inevitably be buyers and 15 sellers who will supply one another's wants; this is the readiest way to make a state self-sufficient and so fulfil the purpose for which men come together into one state. A second office of a similar kind undertakes the supervision and embellishment of public and private buildings, the maintaining and repairing of houses and roads, the 20 prevention of disputes about boundaries, and other concerns of a like nature. This is commonly called the office of City-warden, and has various departments, which, in more populous towns, are shared 25 among different persons, one, for example, taking charge of the walls, another of the fountains, a third of harbours. There is another equally necessary office, and of a similar kind, having to do with the same matters outside the walls and in the country – the magistrates who hold this office are called Wardens of the country, or Inspectors of the 30 woods. Besides these three there is a fourth office of receivers of taxes, who have under their charge the revenue which is distributed among the various departments; these are called Receivers or Treasurers. Another officer registers all private contracts, and deci- 35 sions of the courts, all public indictments, and also all preliminary proceedings. This office again is sometimes subdivided; but in some places a single officer is responsible for all these matters. These officers are called Recorders or Sacred Recorders, Presidents, and the like.   40

Next to these comes an office of which the duties are the most necessary and also the most difficult, viz. that to which is committed the execution of punishments, or the exaction of fines from those who are posted up according to the registers; and also the custody of 1322ª1 prisoners. The difficulty of this office arises out of the odium which is attached to it; no one will undertake it unless great profits are to be made, and anyone who does is loath to execute the law. Still the office is necessary; for judicial decisions are useless if they take no effect; 5 and if society cannot exist without them, neither can it exist without the execution of them. It is an office which, being so unpopular,

should not be entrusted to one person, but divided among several taken from different courts. In like manner an effort should be made
10 to distribute among different persons the writing up of those who are on the register of public debtors. Some sentences should be executed by the magistrates also, and in particular penalties due to the outgoing magistrates should be exacted by the incoming ones; and as regards those due to magistrates already in office, when one court has given judgement, another should exact the penalty; for example, the wardens of the city should exact the fines imposed by the wardens of the agora, and others again should exact the fines imposed by them.
15 For penalties are more likely to be exacted when less odium attaches to the exaction of them; but a double odium is incurred when the judges who have passed also execute the sentence, and if they are always the executioners, they will be the enemies of all.

In many places, while one magistracy executes the sentence,
20 another has the custody of the prisoners, as, for example, 'the Eleven' at Athens. It is well to separate off the jailorship also, and try by some device to render the office less unpopular. For it is quite as necessary as that of the executioners; but good men do all they can to avoid it, and worthless persons cannot safely be trusted with it; for they
25 themselves require a guard, and are not fit to guard others. There ought not therefore to be a single or permanent officer set apart for this duty; but it should be entrusted to the young, wherever they are organized into a band or guard, and different magistrates acting in turn should take charge of it.
30 These are the indispensable officers, and should be ranked first – next in order follow others, equally necessary, but of higher rank, and requiring great experience and trustworthiness. Such are the offices to which are committed the guard of the city, and other military
35 functions. Not only in time of war but of peace their duty will be to defend the walls and gates, and to muster and marshal the citizens. In some states there are many such offices; in others there are a few only, while small states are content with one; these officers are called
1322b1 generals or commanders. Again, if a state has cavalry or light-armed troops or archers or a naval force, it will sometimes happen that each of these departments has separate officers who are called admirals, or generals of cavalry or of light-armed troops. And there are subordinate officers called naval captains, and captains of light-armed troops

and of horse, having others under them – all these are included in the 5 department of war. Thus much of military command.

But since some, not to say all, of these offices handle the public money, there must of necessity be another office which examines and audits them, and has no other functions. Such officers are called by 10 various names – Scrutineers, Auditors, Accountants, Controllers. Besides all these offices there is another which is supreme over them; for the same office often deals with rates and taxes, or presides, in a democracy, over the assembly. For there must be a body which 15 convenes the supreme authority in the state. In some places they are called 'probuli', because they hold previous deliberations, but in a democracy more commonly 'councillors'. These are the chief political offices.

Another set of officers is concerned with the maintenance of religion; priests and guardians see to the preservation and repair of the temples of the gods and to other matters of religion. One office of 20 this sort may be enough in small places, but in larger ones there are a great many besides the priesthood; for example superintendents of public worship, guardians of shrines, treasurers of the sacred 25 revenues. Nearly connected with these there are also the officers appointed for the performance of the public sacrifices, except any which the law assigns to the priests; such sacrifices derive their dignity from the public hearth of the city. They are sometimes called archons, sometimes kings, and sometimes prytanies.

These, then, are the necessary offices, which may be summed up as 30 follows: offices concerned with matters of religion, with war, with the revenue and expenditure, with the market, with the city, with the harbours, with the country; also with the courts of law, with the records of contracts, with execution of sentences, with custody of 35 prisoners, with audits and scrutinies and accounts of magistrates; lastly, there are those which preside over the public deliberations of the state. There are likewise magistracies characteristic of states which are peaceful and prosperous, and at the same time have a regard to good order: such as the offices of guardians of women, guardians of the laws, guardians of children, and directors of gymnastics; also superintendents of gymnastic and Dionysiac con- 1323^{a}1 tests, and of other similar spectacles. Some of these are clearly not democratic offices; for example, the guardianships of women and

5 children – the poor, not having any slaves, must employ both their women and children as servants.

Once more: there are three offices according to whose directions the highest magistrates are chosen in certain states – guardians of the law, probuli, councillors – of these, the guardians of the law are an aristocratic, the probuli an oligarchical, the council a democratic,
10 institution. Enough, in outline, of the different kinds of offices.

BOOK VII

1 · He who would duly inquire about the best form of a state ought
15 first to determine which is the most eligible life; while this remains uncertain the best form of the state must also be uncertain; for, in the natural order of things, those men may be expected to lead the best life who are governed in the best manner of which their circum-
20 stances admit. We ought therefore to ascertain, first of all, which is the most generally eligible life, and then whether the same life is or is not best for the state and for individuals.

Assuming that enough has been already said in discussions outside the school concerning the best life, we will now only repeat what is contained in them. Certainly no one will dispute the propriety of that
25 partition of goods which separates them into three classes, viz. external goods, goods of the body, and goods of the soul, or deny that the happy man must have all three. For no one would maintain that he is happy who has not in him a particle of courage or temperance or justice or practical wisdom, who is afraid of every insect which flutters
30 past him, and will commit any crime, however great, in order to gratify his lust for meat or drink, who will sacrifice his dearest friend for the sake of half a farthing, and is as feeble and false in mind as a child or a madman. These propositions are almost universally acknowledged as
35 soon as they are uttered, but men differ about the degree or relative superiority of this or that good. Some think that a very moderate amount of excellence is enough, but set no limit to their desires for wealth, property, power, reputation, and the like. To them we shall reply by an appeal to facts, which easily prove that mankind does not
40 acquire or preserve the excellences by the help of external goods, but
1323^{b}1 external goods by the help of the excellences, and that happiness,

whether consisting in pleasure or excellence, or both, is more often found with those who are most highly cultivated in their mind and in their character, and have only a moderate share of external goods, than among those who possess external goods to a useless extent but are deficient in higher qualities; and this is not only a matter of experience, but, if reflected upon, will easily appear to be in accordance with reason. For, whereas external goods have a limit, like any other instrument, and all things useful are useful for a purpose, and where there is too much of them they must either do harm, or at any rate be of no use, to their possessors, every good of the soul, the greater it is, is also of greater use, if the epithet useful as well as noble is appropriate to such subjects. No proof is required to show that the best state of one thing in relation to another corresponds in degree of excellence to the interval between the natures of which we say that these very states are states: so that, if the soul is more noble than our possessions or our bodies, both absolutely and in relation to us, it must be admitted that the best state of either has a similar ratio to the other. Again, it is for the sake of the soul that goods external and goods of the body are desirable at all, and all wise men ought to choose them for the sake of the soul, and not the soul for the sake of them.

Let us acknowledge then that each one has just so much of happiness as he has of excellence and wisdom, and of excellent and wise action. The gods are a witness to us of this truth, for they are happy and blessed, not by reason of any external good, but in themselves and by reason of their own nature. And herein of necessity lies the difference between good fortune and happiness; for external goods come of themselves, and chance is the author of them, but no one is just or temperate by or through chance. In like manner, and by a similar train of argument, the happy state may be shown to be that which is best and which acts rightly; and it cannot act rightly without doing right actions, and neither individual nor state can do right actions without excellence and wisdom. Thus, the courage, justice, and wisdom of a state have the same form and nature as the qualities which give the individual who possesses them the name of just, wise or temperate.

Thus much may suffice by way of preface: for I could not avoid touching upon these questions, neither could I go through all the arguments affecting them; these are the business of another science.

Let us assume then that the best life, both for individuals and
40 states, is the life of excellence, when excellence has external goods
1324ᵃ1 enough for the performance of good actions. If there are any who
dispute our assertion, we will in this treatise pass them over, and
consider their objections hereafter.

5 2 · There remains to be discussed the question, whether the happiness of the individual is the same as that of the state, or different.
Here again there can be no doubt – no one denies that they are the
same. For those who hold that the well-being of the individual
10 consists in his wealth, also think that riches make the happiness of the
whole state, and those who value most highly the life of a tyrant deem
that city the happiest which rules over the greatest number; while they
who approve an individual for his excellence say that the more
excellent a city is, the happier it is. Two points here present
15 themselves for consideration: first, which is the more desirable life,
that of a citizen who is a member of a state, or that of an alien who has
no political ties; and again, which is the best form of constitution or
the best condition of a state, either on the supposition that political
privileges are desirable for all, or for a majority only? Since the good
of the state and not of the individual is the proper subject of political
20 thought and speculation, and we are engaged in a political discussion,
while the first of these two points has a secondary interest for us, the
latter will be the main subject of our inquiry.

Now it is evident that that form of government is best in which
25 every man, whoever he is, can act best and live happily. But even those
who agree in thinking that the life of excellence is the most desirable
raise a question, whether the life of business and politics is or is not
more desirable than one which is wholly independent of external
goods, I mean than a contemplative life, which by some is maintained
to be the only one worthy of a philosopher. For these two lives – the
life of the philosopher and the life of the statesman – appear to have
30 been preferred by those who have been most keen in the pursuit of
excellence, both in our own and in other ages. Which is the better is a
question of no small amount; for the wise man, like the wise state, will
35 necessarily regulate his life according to the best end. There are some
who think that while a despotic rule over others is the greatest
injustice, to exercise a constitutional rule over them, even though not
unjust, is a great impediment to a man's individual well-being. Others

take an opposite view; they maintain that the true life of man is the practical and political, and that every excellence admits of being practised, quite as much by statesmen and rulers as by private individuals. Others, again, are of the opinion that arbitrary and tyrannical rule alone makes for happiness; indeed, in some states the entire aim both of the laws and of the constitution is to give men despotic power over their neighbours. And, therefore, although in most cities the laws may be said generally to be in a chaotic state, still, if they aim at anything, they aim at the maintenance of power: thus in Lacedaemon and Crete the system of education and the greater part of the laws are framed with a view to war. And in all nations which are able to gratify their ambition military power is held in esteem, for example among the Scythians and Persians and Thracians and Celts. In some nations there are even laws tending to stimulate the warlike virtues, as at Carthage, where we are told that men obtain the honour of wearing as many armlets as they have served campaigns. There was once a law in Macedonia that he who had not killed an enemy should wear a halter, and among the Scythians no one who had not slain his man was allowed to drink out of the cup which was handed round at a certain feast. Among the Iberians, a warlike nation, the number of enemies whom a man has slain is indicated by the number of obelisks which are fixed in the earth round his tomb; and there are numerous practices among other nations of a like kind, some of them established by law and others by custom. Yet to a reflecting mind it must appear very strange that the statesman should be always considering how he can dominate and tyrannize over others, whether they are willing or not. How can that which is not even lawful be the business of the statesman or the legislator? Unlawful it certainly is to rule without regard to justice, for there may be might where there is no right. The other arts and sciences offer no parallel; a physician is not expected to persuade or coerce his patients, nor a pilot the passengers in his ship. Yet most men appear to think that the art of despotic government is statesmanship, and what men affirm to be unjust and inexpedient in their own case they are not ashamed of practising towards others; they demand just rule for themselves, but where other men are concerned they care nothing about it. Such behaviour is irrational; unless the one party is, and the other is not, born to serve, in which case men have a right to command, not indeed all their fellows, but only those who are intended to be subjects; just as we ought not to hunt men, whether for

40 food or sacrifice, but only those animals which may be hunted for food
or sacrifice, that is to say, such wild animals as are eatable. And surely
1325ᵃ1 there may be a city happy in isolation, which we will assume to be
well-governed (for it is quite possible that a city thus isolated might be
well-administered and have good laws); but such a city would not be
constituted with any view to war or the conquest of enemies – all that
5 sort of thing must be excluded. Hence we see very plainly that warlike
pursuits, although generally to be deemed honourable, are not the
supreme end of all things, but only means. And the good lawgiver
should inquire how states and races of men and communities may
10 participate in a good life, and in the happiness which is attainable by
them. His enactments will not be always the same; and where there
are neighbours he will have to see what sort of studies should be
practised in relation to their several characters, or how the measures
appropriate in relation to each are to be adopted. The end at which
the best form of government should aim may be properly made a
15 matter of future consideration.

3 · Let us now address those who, while they agree that the life of
excellence is the most desirable, differ about the manner of practising
it. For some renounce political power, and think that the life of the
20 freeman is different from the life of the statesman and the best of all;
but others think the life of the statesman best. The argument of the
latter is that he who does nothing cannot do well, and that acting well
is identical with happiness. To both we say: 'you are partly right and
partly wrong'. The first class are right in affirming that the life of the
25 freeman is better than the life of the despot; for there is nothing noble
in having the use of a slave, in so far as he is a slave; or in issuing
commands about necessary things. But it is an error to suppose that
every sort of rule is despotic like that of a master over slaves, for there
is as great a difference between rule over freemen and rule over slaves
30 as there is between slavery by nature and freedom by nature, about
which I have said enough at the commencement of this treatise. And it
is equally a mistake to place inactivity above action, for happiness is
activity, and the actions of the just and wise are the realization of
much that is noble.

But perhaps someone, accepting these premises, may still maintain
35 that supreme power is the best of all things, because the possessors of
it are able to perform the greatest number of noble actions. If so, the

man who is able to rule, instead of giving up anything to his neighbour, ought rather to take away his power; and the father should care nothing for his son, nor the son for his father, nor friend for friend; they should not bestow a thought on one another in comparison with this higher object, for the best is the most desirable and 40 'acting well' is the best. There might be some truth in such a view if we assume that robbers and plunderers attain the chief good. But this 1325^{b}1 can never be; their hypothesis is false. For the actions of a ruler cannot really be honourable, unless he is as much superior to other men as a man is to a woman, or a father to his children, or a master to 5 his slaves. And therefore he who violates the law can never recover by any success, however great, what he has already lost in departing from excellence. For equals the honourable and the just consist in sharing alike, as is just and equal. But that the unequal should be given to equals, and the unlike to those who are like, is contrary to nature, and nothing which is contrary to nature is good. If, therefore, there is 10 anyone superior in excellence and in the power of performing the best actions, he is the man we ought to follow and obey, but he must have the capacity for action as well as excellence.

If we are right in our view, and happiness is assumed to be acting 15 well, the active life will be the best, both for every city collectively, and for individuals. Not that a life of action must necessarily have relation to others, as some persons think, nor are those ideas only to be regarded as practical which are pursued for the sake of practical results, but much more the thoughts and contemplations which are independent and complete in themselves; since acting well, and 20 therefore a certain kind of action, is an end, and even in the case of external actions the directing mind is most truly said to act. Neither, again, is it necessary that states which are cut off from others and choose to live alone should be inactive; for activity, as well as other 25 things, may take place by sections; there are many ways in which the sections of a state act upon one another. The same thing is equally true of every individual. If this were otherwise, the gods and the universe, who have no external actions over and above their own energies, would be far enough from perfection. Hence it is evident 30 that the same life is best for each individual, and for states and for mankind collectively.

4 · Thus far by way of introduction. In what has preceded I have

discussed other forms of government; in what remains the first point
35   to be considered is what should be the conditions of the ideal or
perfect state; for the perfect state cannot exist without a due supply of
the means of life. And therefore we must presuppose many purely
imaginary conditions, but nothing impossible. There will be a certain
number of citizens, a country in which to place them, and the like. As
1326ª1   the weaver or shipbuilder or any other artisan must have the material
proper for his work (and in proportion as this is better prepared, so
will the result of his art be nobler), so the statesman or legislator must
5   also have the materials suited to him.

First among the materials required by the statesman is population:
he will consider what should be the number and character of the
citizens, and then what should be the size and character of the
country. Most persons think that a state in order to be happy ought to
10   be large; but even if they are right, they have no idea what is a large
and what a small state. For they judge of the size of the city by the
number of the inhabitants; whereas they ought to regard, not their
numbers, but their power. A city too, like an individual, has a work to
do; and that city which is best adapted to the fulfilment of its work is to
be deemed greatest, in the same sense of the word great in which
15   Hippocrates might be called greater, not as a man, but as a physician,
than someone else who was taller. And even if we reckon greatness by
numbers, we ought not to include everybody, for there must always be
20   in cities a multitude of slaves and resident aliens and foreigners; but
we should include those only who are members of the state, and who
form an essential part of it. The number of the latter is a proof of the
greatness of a city; but a city which produces numerous artisans and
25   comparatively few soldiers cannot be great, for a great city is not the
same as a populous one. Moreover, experience shows that a very
populous city can rarely, if ever, be well governed; since all cities
which have a reputation for good government have a limit of
population. We may argue on grounds of reason, and the same result
30   will follow. For law is order, and good law is good order; but a very
great multitude cannot be orderly: to introduce order into the
unlimited is the work of a divine power – of such a power as holds
together the universe. Beauty is realized in number and magnitude,
and the state which combines magnitude with good order must
35   necessarily be the most beautiful. To the size of states there is a limit,
as there is to other things, plants, animals, implements; for none of

these retain their natural power when they are too large or too small, but they either wholly lose their nature, or are spoiled. For example, a ship which is only a span long will not be a ship at all, nor a ship a 40 quarter of a mile long; yet there may be a ship of a certain size, either too large or too small, which will still be a ship, but bad for sailing. In 1326^{b}1 like manner a state when composed of too few is not, as a state ought to be, self-sufficient; when of too many, though self-sufficient in all mere necessaries, as a nation may be, it is not a state, being almost 5 incapable of constitutional government. For who can be the general of such a vast multitude, or who the herald, unless he have the voice of a Stentor?

A state, then, only begins to exist when it has attained a population sufficient for a good life in the political community: it may indeed, if it somewhat exceeds this number, be a greater state. But, as I was 10 saying, there must be a limit. What the limit should be will be easily ascertained by experience. For both governors and governed have duties to perform; the special functions of a governor are to command and to judge. But if the citizens of a state are to judge and to distribute 15 offices according to merit, then they must know each other's charac- ters; where they do not possess this knowledge, both the election to offices and the decision of lawsuits will go wrong. When the popula- tion is very large they are manifestly settled at haphazard, which 20 clearly ought not to be. Besides, in an over-populous state foreigners and resident aliens will readily acquire the rights of citizens, for who will find them out? Clearly then the best limit of the population of a state is the largest number which suffices for the purposes of life, and can be taken in at a single view. Enough concerning the size of a state. 25

5 · Much the same principle will apply to the territory of the state: everyone would agree in praising the territory which is most self- sufficient; and that must be the territory which can produce every- thing necessary, for to have all things and to want nothing is sufficiency. In size and extent it should be such as may enable the 30 inhabitants to live at once temperately and liberally in the enjoyment of leisure. Whether we are right or wrong in laying down this limit we will inquire more precisely hereafter, when we have occasion to 35 consider what is the right use of property and wealth – a matter which is much disputed, because men are inclined to rush into one of two extremes, some into meanness, others into luxury.

It is not difficult to determine the general character of the territory which is required (there are, however, some points on which military
40 authorities should be heard); it should be difficult of access to the enemy, and easy of egress to the inhabitants. Further, we require that
1327ª1 the land as well as the inhabitants of whom we were just now speaking should be taken in at a single view, for a country which is easily seen can be easily protected. As to the position of the city, if we could have
5 what we wish, it should be well situated in regard both to sea and land. This then is one principle, that it should be a convenient centre for the protection of the whole country: the other is, that it should be suitable for receiving the fruits of the soil, and also for the bringing in
10 of timber and any other products that are easily transported.

6 · Whether a communication with the sea is beneficial to a well-ordered state or not is a question which has often been asked. It is argued that the introduction of strangers brought up under other
15 laws, and the increase of population, will be adverse to good order; the increase arises from their using the sea and having a crowd of merchants coming and going, and is inimical to good government. Apart from these considerations, it would be undoubtedly better, both with a view to safety and to the provision of necessaries, that the
20 city and territory should be connected with the sea; the defenders of a country, if they are to maintain themselves against an enemy, should be easily relieved both by land and by sea; and even if they are not able to attack by sea and land at once, they will have less difficulty in doing mischief to their assailants on one element, if they themselves can use
25 both. Moreover, it is necessary that they should import from abroad what is not found in their own country, and that they should export what they have in excess; for a city ought to be a market, not indeed for others, but for herself.

Those who make themselves a market for the world only do so for
30 the sake of revenue, and if a state ought not to desire profit of this kind it ought not to have such an emporium. Nowadays we often see in countries and cities dockyards and harbours very conveniently placed outside the city, but not too far off; and they are kept in dependence
35 by walls and similar fortifications. Cities thus situated manifestly reap the benefit of intercourse with their ports; and any harm which is likely to accrue may be easily guarded against by laws, which will

pronounce and determine who may hold communication with one another, and who may not.

There can be no doubt that the possession of a moderate naval force is advantageous to a city; the city should be formidable not only to its own citizens but to some of its neighbours, or, if necessary, able to assist them by sea as well as by land. The proper number or 1327^b1 magnitude of this naval force is relative to the character of the state; for if her function is to take a leading part in politics, her naval power 5 should be commensurate with the scale of her enterprises. The population of the state need not be much increased, since there is no necessity that the sailors should be citizens: the marines who have the control and command will be freemen, and belong also to the 10 infantry; and wherever there is a dense population of country people and farmers, there will always be sailors more than enough. Of this we see instances at the present day. The city of Heraclea, for example, although small in comparison with many others, can man a considerable fleet. Such are our conclusions respecting the territory of the 15 state, its harbours, its towns, its relations to the sea, and its maritime power.

7 · Having spoken of the number of citizens, we will proceed to speak of what should be their character. This is a subject which can be 20 easily understood by anyone who casts his eye on the more celebrated states of Greece, and generally on the distribution of races in the habitable world. Those who live in a cold climate and in Europe are full of spirit, but wanting in intelligence and skill; and therefore they 25 retain comparative freedom, but have no political organization, and are incapable of ruling over others. Whereas the natives of Asia are intelligent and inventive, but they are wanting in spirit, and therefore they are always in a state of subjection and slavery. But the Hellenic race, which is situated between them, is likewise intermediate in 30 character, being high-spirited and also intelligent. Hence it continues free, and is the best-governed of any nation, and, if it could be formed into one state, would be able to rule the world. There are also similar differences in the different tribes of Greece; for some of them are of a one-sided nature, and are intelligent or courageous only, while in 35 others there is a happy combination of both qualities. And clearly those whom the legislator will most easily lead to excellence may be

expected to be both intelligent and courageous. Some say that the
40 guardians should be friendly towards those whom they know, fierce
towards those whom they do not know. Now, passion is the quality of
the soul which begets friendship and enables us to love; notably the
1328ª1 spirit within us is more stirred against our friends and acquaintances
than against those who are unknown to us, when we think that we are
despised by them; for which reason Archilochus, complaining of his
5 friends, very naturally addresses his spirit in these words, 'For surely
thou art plagued on account of friends.'

The power of command and the love of freedom are in all men
based upon this quality, for passion is commanding and invincible.
Nor is it right to say that the guardians should be fierce towards those
whom they do not know, for we ought not to be out of temper with
10 anyone; and a lofty spirit is not fierce by nature, but only when excited
against evil-doers. And this, as I was saying before, is a feeling which
men show most strongly towards their friends if they think they have
received a wrong at their hands: as indeed is reasonable; for, besides
15 the actual injury, they seem to be deprived of a benefit by those who
owe them one. Hence the saying, 'Cruel is the strife of brethren', and
again, 'They who love in excess also hate in excess'.

Thus we have nearly determined the number and character of the
citizens of our state, and also the size and nature of their territory. I
20 say 'nearly', for we ought not to require the same accuracy in theory as
in the facts given by perception.

8 · As in other natural compounds the conditions of a composite
whole are not necessarily organic parts of it, so in a state or in any
25 other combination forming a unity not everything is a part which is a
necessary condition. The members of an association have necessarily
some one thing the same and common to all, in which they share
equally or unequally; for example, food or land or any other thing. But
where there are two things of which one exists for the sake of the
30 other, they have nothing in common except that the one receives what
the other produces. Such, for example, is the relation in which
workmen and tools stand to their work; the house and the builder
have nothing in common, but the art of the builder is for the sake of
the house. And so states require property, but property, even though
35 living beings are included in it, is no part of a state; for a state is a
community of equals, aiming at the best life possible. Now, whereas

happiness is the highest good, being a realization and perfect practice of excellence, which some can attain, while others have little or none of it, the various qualities of men are clearly the reason why there are 40 various kinds of states and many forms of government; for different men seek after happiness in different ways and by different means, and so make for themselves different modes of life and forms of 1328^{b}1 government. We must see also how many things are indispensable to the existence of a state, for what we call the parts of a state will be found among the indispensable things. Let us then enumerate the functions of a state, and we shall easily elicit what we want. 5

First, there must be food; secondly, arts, for life requires many instruments; thirdly, there must be arms, for the members of a community have need of them, and in their own hands, too, in order to maintain authority both against disobedient subjects and against external assailants; fourthly, there must be a certain amount of 10 revenue, both for internal needs, and for the purposes of war; fifthly, or rather first, there must be a care of religion, which is commonly called worship; sixthly, and most necessary of all, there must be a power of deciding what is for the public interest, and what is just in men's dealings with one another.

These are the services which every state may be said to need. For a 15 state is not a mere aggregate of persons, but, as we say, a union of them sufficing for the purposes of life; and if any of these things is wanting, it is impossible that the community can be absolutely self-sufficient. A state then should be framed with a view to the fulfilment of these functions. There must be farmers to procure food, and 20 artisans, and a warlike and a wealthy class, and priests, and judges to decide what is necessary and expedient.

9 · Having determined these points, we have in the next place to consider whether all ought to share in every sort of occupation. Shall 25 every man be at once farmer, artisan, councillor, judge, or shall we suppose the several occupations just mentioned assigned to different persons? or, thirdly, shall some employments be assigned to individuals and others common to all? The same arrangement, however, does not occur in every constitution; as we were saying, all may be shared by all, or not all by all, but only some by some; and hence arise the 30 differences of constitutions, for in democracies all share in all, in oligarchies the opposite practice prevails. Now, since we are here

speaking of the best form of government, i.e. that under which the
35 state will be most happy (and happiness, as has been already said,
cannot exist without excellence), it clearly follows that in the state
which is best governed and possesses men who are just absolutely,
and not merely relatively to the principle of the constitution, the
40 citizens must not lead the life of artisans or tradesmen, for such a life
is ignoble and inimical to excellence. Neither must they be farmers,
1329ᵃ1 since leisure is necessary both for the development of excellence and
the performance of political duties.

Again, there is in a state a class of warriors, and another of
councillors, who advise about the expedient and determine matters of
5 law, and these seem in an especial manner parts of a state. Now,
should these two classes be distinguished, or are both functions to be
assigned to the same persons? Here again there is no difficulty in
seeing that both functions will in one way belong to the same, in
another, to different persons. To different persons in so far as these
employments are suited to different primes of life, for the one
requires wisdom and the other strength. But on the other hand, since
10 it is an impossible thing that those who are able to use or to resist force
should be willing to remain always in subjection, from this point of
view the persons are the same; for those who carry arms can always
determine the fate of the constitution. It remains therefore that both
functions should be entrusted by the ideal constitution to the same
persons, not, however, at the same time, but in the order prescribed
15 by nature, who has given to young men strength and to older men
wisdom. Such a distribution of duties will be expedient and also just,
and is founded upon a principle of conformity to merit. Besides, the
ruling class should be the owners of property, for they are citizens,
and the citizens of a state should be in good circumstances; whereas
20 artisans or any other class which is not a producer of excellence have
no share in the state. This follows from our first principle, for
happiness cannot exist without excellence, and a city is not to be
termed happy in regard to a portion of the citizens, but in regard to
25 them all. And clearly property should be in their hands, since the
farmers will of necessity be slaves or barbarian country people.

Of the classes enumerated there remain only the priests, and the
manner in which their office is to be regulated is obvious. No farmer
or artisan should be appointed to it; for the gods should receive
30 honour from the citizens only. Now since the body of the citizens is

divided into two classes, the warriors and the councillors, and it is fitting that the worship of the gods should be duly performed, and also a rest provided in their service for those who from age have given up active life, to the old men of these two classes should be assigned the duties of the priesthood.

We have shown what are the necessary conditions, and what the 35 parts of a state: farmers, artisans, and labourers of all kinds are necessary to the existence of states, but the parts of the state are the warriors and councillors. And these are distinguished severally from one another, the distinction being in some cases permanent, in others not.

10 · It is no new or recent discovery of political philosophers that the 40 state ought to be divided into classes, and that the warriors should be 1329^{b}1 separated from the farmers. The system has continued in Egypt and in Crete to this day, and was established, as tradition says, by a law of Sesostris in Egypt and of Minos in Crete. The institution of common 5 tables also appears to be of ancient date, being in Crete as old as the reign of Minos, and in Italy far older. The Italian historians say that there was a certain Italus king of Oenotria, from whom the Oenotrians were called Italians, and who gave the name of Italy to the 10 promontory of Europe lying within the Scylletic and Lametic Gulfs, which are distant from one another only half a day's journey. They say that this Italus converted the Oenotrians from shepherds into farmers, and besides other laws which he gave them, was the founder 15 of their common meals; even in our day some who are derived from him retain this institution and certain other laws of his. On the side of Italy towards Tyrrhenia dwelt the Opici, who are now, as of old, called Ausones; and on the side towards Iapygia and the Ionian Gulf, in the 20 district called Siritis, the Chones, who are likewise of Oenotrian race. From this part of the world originally came the institution of common tables; the separation into castes from Egypt, for the reign of Sesostris is of far greater antiquity than that of Minos. It is true indeed that 25 these and many other things have been invented several times over in the course of ages, or rather times without number; for necessity may be supposed to have taught men the inventions which were absolutely required, and when these were provided, it was natural that other things which would adorn and enrich life should grow up by degrees. And we may infer that in political institutions the same rule holds. 30

Egypt witnesses to the antiquity of all these things, for the Egyptians appear to be of all people the most ancient; and they have laws and a regular constitution existing from time immemorial. We should therefore make the best use of what has been already discovered, and
35 try to supply defects.

I have already remarked that the land ought to belong to those who possess arms and have a share in the government, and that the farmers ought to be a class distinct from them; and I have determined what should be the extent and nature of the territory. Let me proceed
40 to discuss the distribution of the land, and the character of the agricultural class; for I do not think that property ought to be
1330ᵃ1 common, as some maintain,[1] but only that by friendly consent there should be a common use of it; and that no citizen should be in want of subsistence.

As to common meals, there is a general agreement that a well-ordered city should have them; and we will hereafter explain what are
5 our own reasons for taking this view. They ought, however, to be open to all the citizens. And yet it is not easy for the poor to contribute the requisite sum out of their private means, and to provide also for their household. The expense of religious worship should likewise be a
10 public charge. The land must therefore be divided into two parts, one public and the other private, and each part should be subdivided, part of the public land being appropriated to the service of the gods, and the other part used to defray the cost of the common meals; while of the private land, part should be near the border, and the other near
15 the city, so that, each citizen having two lots, they may all of them have land in both places; there is justice and fairness in such a division and it tends to inspire unanimity among the people in their border wars. Where there is not this arrangement, some of them are too ready to come to blows with their neighbours, while others are so cautious that
20 they quite lose the sense of honour. For this reason there is a law in some places which forbids those who dwell near the border to take part in public deliberations about wars with neighbours, on the ground that their interests will pervert their judgement. For the reasons already mentioned, then, the land should be divided in the
25 manner described. The very best thing of all would be that the farmers should be slaves taken from among men who are not all of the

[1] cf. II 5.

180

same race and not spirited, for if they have no spirit they will be better suited for their work, and there will be no danger of their making a revolution. The next best thing would be that they should be barbarian country people, and of a like inferior nature; some of them should be the slaves of individuals, and employed on the private estates of men of property, the remainder should be the property of the state and employed on the common land. I will hereafter explain what is the proper treatment of slaves, and why it is expedient that liberty should be always held out to them as the reward of their services.

11 · We have already said that the city should be open to the land and to the sea, and to the whole country as far as possible. In respect of the place itself our wish would be that its situation should be fortunate in four things. The first, health – this is a necessity: cities which lie towards the east, and are blown upon by winds coming from the east, are the healthiest; next in healthiness are those which are sheltered from the north wind, for they have a milder winter. The site of the city should likewise be convenient both for political administration and for war. With a view to the latter it should afford easy egress to the citizens, and at the same time be inaccessible and difficult of capture to enemies. There should be a natural abundance of springs and fountains in the town, or, if there is a deficiency of them, great reservoirs may be established for the collection of rain-water, such as will not fail when the inhabitants are cut off from the country by war. Special care should be taken of the health of the inhabitants, which will depend chiefly on the healthiness of the locality and of the quarter to which they are exposed, and secondly, on the use of pure water; this latter point is by no means a secondary consideration. For the elements which we use most and oftenest for the support of the body contribute most to health, and among these are water and air. For this reason, in all wise states, if there is a want of pure water, and the supply is not all equally good, the drinking water ought to be separated from that which is used for other purposes.

As to strongholds, what is suitable to different forms of government varies: thus an acropolis is suited to an oligarchy or a monarchy, but a plain to a democracy; neither to an aristocracy, but rather a number of strong places. The arrangement of private houses is considered to be more agreeable and generally more convenient if the streets are

regularly laid out after the modern fashion which Hippodamus
25 introduced,[1] but for security in war the antiquated mode of building,
which made it difficult for strangers to get out of a town and for
assailants to find their way in, is preferable. A city should therefore
adopt both plans of building: it is possible to arrange the houses
irregularly, as farmers plant their vines in what are called 'clumps'.
30 The whole town should not be laid out in straight lines, but only
certain quarters and regions; thus security and beauty will be
combined.

As to walls, those who say that cities making any pretension to
military virtue should not have them, are quite out of date in their
notions; and they may see the cities which prided themselves on this
fancy confuted by facts. True, there is little courage shown in seeking
35 for safety behind a rampart when an enemy is similar in character and
not much superior in number; but the superiority of the besiegers
may be and often is too much both for ordinary human valour and for
that which is found only in a few; and if they are to be saved and to
40 escape defeat and outrage, the strongest wall will be the truest
1331ᵃ1 soldierly precaution, more especially now that missiles and siege
engines have been brought to such perfection. To have no walls
would be as foolish as to choose a site for a town in an exposed
5 country, and to level the heights; or as if an individual were to leave his
house unwalled, lest the inmates should become cowards. Nor must
we forget that those who have their cities surrounded by walls may
either take advantage of them or not, but cities which are unwalled
10 have no choice.

If our conclusions are just, not only should cities have walls, but
care should be taken to make them ornamental, as well as useful for
warlike purposes, and adapted to resist modern inventions. For as the
assailants of a city do all they can to gain an advantage, so the
15 defenders should make use of any means of defence which have been
already discovered, and should devise and invent others, for when
men are well prepared no enemy even thinks of attacking them.

12 · As the walls are to be divided by guard-houses and towers built
20 at suitable intervals, and the body of citizens must be distributed at
common tables, the idea will naturally occur that we should establish

---

[1] cf. II 8.

some of the common tables in the guard-houses. These might be arranged as has been suggested; while the principal common tables of the magistrates will occupy a suitable place, and there also will be the buildings appropriated to religious worship except in the case of those rites which the law or the Pythian oracle has restricted to a special locality. The site should be a spot seen far and wide, which gives due elevation to excellence[a] and towers over the neighbourhood. Below this spot should be established an agora, such as that which the Thessalians call the 'freemen's agora'; from this all trade should be excluded, and no artisan, farmer, or any such person allowed to enter, unless he be summoned by the magistrates. It would be a pleasing use of the place, if the gymnastic exercises of the elder men were performed there. For in this noble practice different ages should be separated, and some of the magistrates should stay with the boys, while the grown-up men remain with the magistrates; for the presence of the magistrates is the best mode of inspiring true modesty and ingenuous fear. There should also be a traders' agora, distinct and apart from the other, in a situation which is convenient for the reception of goods both by sea and land.

But we must not forget another section of the citizens, viz. the priests, for whom public tables should likewise be provided in their proper place near the temples. The magistrates who deal with contracts, indictments, summonses, and the like, and those who have the care of the agora and of the city respectively, ought to be established near an agora and some public place of meeting; the neighbourhood of the traders' agora will be a suitable spot; the upper agora we devote to the life of leisure, the other is intended for the necessities of trade.

The same order should prevail in the country, for there too the magistrates, called by some 'Inspectors of Forests' and by others 'Wardens of the Country', must have guard-houses and common tables while they are on duty; temples should also be scattered throughout the country, dedicated some to gods and some to heroes.

But it would be a waste of time for us to linger over details like these. The difficulty is not in imagining but in carrying them out. We may talk about them as much as we like, but the execution of them will

25

30

35

40

1331[b]1

5

10

15

20

---

[a] Text uncertain.

depend upon fortune. Therefore let us say no more about these matters for the present.

13 · Returning to the constitution itself, let us seek to determine out
25 of what and what sort of elements the state which is to be happy and well-governed should be composed. There are two things in which all well-being consists: one of them is the choice of a right end and aim of action, and the other the discovery of the actions which contribute
30 towards it; for the means and the end may agree or disagree. Sometimes the right end is set before men, but in practice they fail to attain it; in other cases they are successful in all the contributory factors, but they propose to themselves a bad end; and sometimes they fail in both. Take, for example, the art of medicine; physicians do
35 not always understand the nature of health, and also the means which they use may not effect the desired end. In all arts and sciences both the end and the means should be equally within our control.

The happiness and well-being which all men manifestly desire, some have the power of attaining, but to others, from some accident
40 or defect of nature, the attainment of them is not granted; for a good
1332ª1 life requires a supply of external goods, in a less degree when men are in a good state, in a greater degree when they are in a lower state. Others again, who possess the conditions of happiness, go utterly wrong from the first in the pursuit of it. But since our object is to discover the best form of government, that, namely, under which a
5 city will be best governed, and since the city is best governed which has the greatest opportunity of obtaining happiness, it is evident that we must clearly ascertain the nature of happiness.

We maintain, and have said in the *Ethics*, if the arguments there adduced are of any value, that happiness is the realization and perfect
10 exercise of excellence, and this not conditional, but absolute.[1] And I use the term 'conditional' to express that which is indispensable, and 'absolute' to express that which is good in itself. Take the case of just actions; just punishments and chastisements do indeed spring from a good principle, but they are good only because we cannot do without
15 them – it would be better that neither individuals nor states should need anything of the sort – but actions which aim at honour and advantage are absolutely the best. The conditional action is only the

[1] *NE*, I 7, 1098a16.

choice of a lesser evil; whereas these are the foundation and creation of good. A good man may make the best even of poverty and disease, and the other ills of life; but he can only attain happiness under the 20 opposite conditions (for this also has been determined in the *Ethics*, that the good man is he for whom, because he is excellent, the things that are absolutely good are good; it is also plain that his use of these goods must be excellent and in the absolute sense good).[1] This makes men fancy that external goods are the cause of happiness, yet we 25 might as well say that a brilliant performance on the lyre was to be attributed to the instrument and not to the skill of the performer.

It follows then from what has been said that some things the legislator must find ready to his hand in a state, others he must provide. And therefore we can only say: may our state be constituted in such a manner as to be blessed with the goods of which fortune 30 disposes (for we acknowledge her power): whereas excellence and goodness in the state are not a matter of chance but the result of knowledge and choice. A city can be excellent only when the citizens who have a share in the government are excellent, and in our state all the citizens share in the government; let us then inquire how a man 35 becomes excellent. For even if we could suppose the citizen body to be excellent, without each of them being so, yet the latter would be better, for in the excellence of each the excellence of all is involved.

There are three things which make men good and excellent; these are nature, habit, reason. In the first place, every one must be born a 40 man and not some other animal; so, too, he must have a certain character, both of body and soul. But some qualities there is no use in having at birth, for they are altered by habit, and there are some gifts 1332^b1 which by nature are made to be turned by habit to good or bad. Animals lead for the most part a life of nature, although in lesser particulars some are influenced by habit as well. Man has reason, in addition, and man only. For this reason nature, habit, reason must be 5 in harmony with one another; for they do not always agree; men do many things against habit and nature, if reason persuades them that they ought. We have already determined what natures are likely to be most easily moulded by the hands of the legislator. All else is the work of education; we learn some things by habit and some by instruction. 10

---

[1] *NE*, III 4.

14 · Since every political society is composed of rulers and subjects, let us consider whether the relations of one to the other should interchange or be permanent. For the education of the citizens will necessarily vary with the answer given to this question. Now, if some men excelled others in the same degree in which gods and heroes are supposed to excel mankind in general (having in the first place a great advantage even in their bodies, and secondly in their minds), so that the superiority of the governors was undisputed and patent to their subjects, it would clearly be better that once for all the one class should rule and the others serve. But since this is unattainable, and kings have no marked superiority over their subjects, such as Scylax affirms to be found among the Indians, it is obviously necessary on many grounds that all the citizens alike should take their turn of governing and being governed. Equality consists in the same treatment of similar persons, and no government can stand which is not founded upon justice. For if the government is unjust everyone in the country unites with the governed in the desire to have a revolution, and it is an impossibility that the members of the government can be so numerous as to be stronger than all their enemies put together. Yet that governors should be better than their subjects is undeniable. How all this is to be effected, and in what way they will respectively share in the government, the legislator has to consider. The subject has been already mentioned. Nature herself has provided the distinction when she made a difference between old and young within the same species, of whom she fitted the one to govern and the other to be governed. No one takes offence at being governed when he is young, nor does he think himself better than his governors, especially if he will enjoy the same privilege when he reaches the required age.

We conclude that from one point of view governors and governed are identical, and from another different. And therefore their education must be the same and also different. For he who would learn to command well must, as men say, first of all learn to obey. As I observed in the first part of this treatise, there is one rule which is for the sake of the rulers and another rule which is for the sake of the ruled; the former is a despotic, the latter a free government. Some commands differ not in the thing commanded, but in the intention with which they are imposed. That is why many apparently menial offices are an honour to the free youth by whom they are performed; for actions do not differ as honourable or dishonourable in them-

selves so much as in the end and intention of them. But since we say 10
that the excellence of the citizen and ruler is the same as that of the
good man, and that the same person must first be a subject and then a
ruler, the legislator has to see that they become good men, and by
what means this may be accomplished, and what is the end of the
perfect life. 15

Now the soul of man is divided into two parts, one of which has a
rational principle in itself, and the other, not having a rational
principle in itself, is able to obey such a principle. And we call a man in
any way good because he has the excellences of these two parts. In
which of them the end is more likely to be found is no matter of doubt 20
to those who adopt our division; for in the world both of nature and of
art the inferior always exists for the sake of the superior, and the
superior is that which has a rational principle. This principle, too, in
our ordinary way of making the division, is divided into two kinds, for
there is a practical and a speculative principle. This part, then, must 25
evidently be similarly divided. And there must be a corresponding
division of actions; the actions of the naturally better part are to be
preferred by those who have it in their power to attain to two out of the
three or to all, for that is always to everyone the most desirable which
is the highest attainable by him. The whole of life is further divided 30
into two parts, business and leisure, war and peace, and of actions
some aim at what is necessary and useful, and some at what is
honourable. And the preference given to one or the other class of
actions must necessarily be like the preference given to one or other
part of the soul and its actions over the other; there must be war for
the sake of peace, business for the sake of leisure, things useful and 35
necessary for the sake of things honourable. All these points the
statesman should keep in view when he frames his laws; he should
consider the parts of the soul and their functions, and above all the
better and the end; he should also remember the diversities of human 40
lives and actions. For men must be able to engage in business and to
go to war, but leisure and peace are better; they must do what is 1333^b1
necessary and indeed what is useful, but what is honourable is better.
On such principles children and persons of every age which requires
education should be trained. Whereas even the Greeks of the present 5
day who are reputed to be best governed, and the legislators who gave
them their constitutions, do not appear to have framed their governments with a regard to the best end, or to have given them laws and

education with a view to all the excellences, but in a vulgar spirit have
10 fallen back on those which promised to be more useful and profitable.
Many modern writers have taken a similar view: they commend the
Lacedaemonian constitution, and praise the legislator for making
conquest and war his sole aim, a doctrine which may be refuted by
15 argument and has long ago been refuted by facts. For most men
desire empire in the hope of accumulating the goods of fortune; and
on this ground Thibron and all those who have written about the
Lacedaemonian constitution have praised their legislator, because
20 the Lacedaemonians, by being trained to meet dangers, gained great
power. But surely they are not a happy people now that their empire
has passed away, nor was their legislator right. How ridiculous is the
result, if, while they are continuing in the observance of his laws and
25 no one interferes with them, they have lost the better part of life!
These writers further err about the sort of government which the
legislator should approve, for the government of freemen is nobler
and implies more excellence than despotic government. Neither is a
30 city to be deemed happy or a legislator to be praised because he trains
his citizens to conquer and obtain dominion over their neighbours,
for there is great harm in this. On a similar principle any citizen who
could, should obviously try to obtain the power in his own state – the
crime which the Lacedaemonians accuse king Pausanias of attempt-
35 ing, although he had such great honour already. No such principle
and no law having this object is either statesmanlike or useful or right.
For the same things are best both for individuals and for states, and
these are the things which the legislator ought to implant in the minds
of his citizens. Neither should men study war with a view to the
40 enslavement of those who do not deserve to be enslaved; but first of all
they should provide against their own enslavement, and in the second
place obtain empire for the good of the governed, and not for the sake
1334ª1 of exercising a general despotism, and in the third place they should
seek to be masters only over those who deserve to be slaves. Facts
as well as arguments, prove that the legislator should direct all his
military and other measures to the provision of leisure and the
5 establishment of peace. For most of these military states are safe only
while they are at war, but fall when they have acquired their empire;
like unused iron they lose their edge in time of peace. And for this the
legislator is to blame, he never having taught them how to lead the life
10 of peace.

15 · Since the end of individuals and of states is the same, the end of the best man and of the best constitution must also be the same; it is therefore evident that there ought to exist in both of them the excellences of leisure; for peace, as has been often repeated, is the 15 end of war, and leisure of toil. But leisure and cultivation may be promoted not only by those excellences which are practised in leisure, but also by some of those which are useful to business. For many necessaries of life have to be supplied before we can have leisure. Therefore a city must be temperate and brave, and able to endure: for 20 truly, as the proverb says, 'There is no leisure for slaves,' and those who cannot face danger like men are the slaves of any invader. Courage and endurance are required for business and philosophy for leisure, temperance and justice for both, and more especially in times of peace and leisure, for war compels men to be just and temperate, 25 whereas the enjoyment of good fortune and the leisure which comes with peace tend to make them insolent. Those then who seem to be the best-off and to be in the possession of every good, have special need of justice and temperance – for example, those (if such there be, 30 as the poets say) who dwell in the Islands of the Blest; they above all will need philosophy and temperance and justice, and all the more the more leisure they have, living in the midst of abundance. There is no difficulty in seeing why the state that would be happy and good ought 35 to have these excellences. If it is disgraceful in men not to be able to use the goods of life, it is peculiarly disgraceful not to be able to use them in time of leisure – to show excellent qualities in action and war, and when they have peace and leisure to be no better than slaves. That is why we should not practise excellence after the manner of the Lacedaemonians. For they, while agreeing with other men in their 40 conception of the highest goods, differ from the rest of mankind in thinking that they are to be obtained by the practice of a single 1334^{b}1 excellence. And since these goods and the enjoyment of them are greater than the enjoyment derived from the excellences . . .^{a} and that for its own sake, is evident from what has been said; we must now consider how and by what means it is to be attained. 5

We have already determined that nature and habit and reason are required, and, of these, the proper nature of the citizens has also been defined by us. But we still have to consider whether the training of

---

^{a} Dreizehnter marks a lacuna.

early life is to be that of reason or habit, for these two must accord,
10 and when in accord they will then form the best of harmonies. Reason
may be mistaken and fail in attaining the highest ideal of life, and
there may be a like influence of habit. Thus much is clear in the first
place, that, as in all other things, birth implies an antecedent
beginning, and that there are beginnings whose end is relative to a
15 further end. Now, in men reason and mind are the end towards which
nature strives, so that the birth and training in custom of the citizens
ought to be ordered with a view to them. In the second place, as the
soul and body are two, we see also that there are two parts of the soul,
the rational and the irrational, and two corresponding states – reason
20 and appetite. And as the body is prior in order of generation to the
soul, so the irrational is prior to the rational. The proof is that anger
and wishing and desire are implanted in children from their very
birth, but reason and understanding are developed as they grow
25 older. For this reason, the care of the body ought to precede that of
the soul, and the training of the appetitive part should follow: none
the less our care of it must be for the sake of the reason, and our care
of the body for the sake of the soul.

16 · Since the legislator should begin by considering how the bodies
30 of the children whom he is rearing may be as good as possible, his first
care will be about marriage – at what age should his citizens marry,
and who are fit to marry? In legislating on this subject he ought to
consider the persons and the length of their life, that their procreative
35 life may terminate at the same period, and that they may not differ in
their bodily powers, as will be the case if the man is still able to beget
children while the woman is unable to bear them, or the woman able
to bear while the man is unable to beget, for from these causes arise
quarrels and differences between married persons. Secondly, he
40 must consider the time at which the children will succeed to their
parents; there ought not to be too great an interval of age, for then the
1335ª1 parents will be too old to derive any pleasure from their affection, or to
be of any use to them. Nor ought they to be too nearly of an age; to
youthful marriages there are many objections – the children will be
lacking in respect for the parents, who will seem to be their con-
temporaries, and disputes will arise in the management of the
5 household. Thirdly, and this is the point from which we digressed,
the legislator must mould to his will the bodies of newly-born

children. Almost all these objects may be secured by attention to one point. Since the time of generation is commonly limited within the age of seventy years in the case of a man, and of fifty in the case of a woman, the commencement of the union should conform to these 10 periods. The union of male and female when too young is bad for the procreation of children; in all other animals the offspring of the young are small and ill-developed, and with a tendency to produce female children, and therefore also in man, as is proved by the fact that in 15 those cities in which men and women are accustomed to marry young, the people are small and weak; in childbirth also younger women suffer more, and more of them die; some persons say that this was the meaning of the response once given to the Troezenians – the oracle 20 really meant that many died because they married too young; it had nothing to do with the gathering of the harvest. It also conduces to temperance not to marry too soon; for women who marry early are apt to be wanton; and in men too the bodily frame is stunted if they marry 25 while the seed is growing (for there is a time when the growth of the seed, also, ceases, or continues to but a slight extent). Women should marry when they are about eighteen years of age, and men at thirty-seven; then they are in the prime of life, and the decline in the powers 30 of both will coincide. Further, the children, if their birth takes place soon, as may reasonably be expected, will succeed in the beginning of their prime, when the fathers are already in the decline of life, and have nearly reached their term of three-score years and ten. 35

Thus much of the age proper for marriage: the season of the year should also be considered; according to our present custom, people generally limit marriage to the season of winter, and they are right. The precepts of physicians and natural philosophers about gener- 40 ation should also be studied by the parents themselves; the physicians give good advice about the favourable conditions of the body, and the natural philosophers about the winds; of which they prefer the north 1335^{b}1 to the south.

What constitution in the parent is most advantageous to the offspring is a subject which we will consider more carefully when we speak of the education of children, and we will only make a few general remarks at present. The constitution of an athlete is not 5 suited to the life of a citizen, or to health, or to the procreation of children, any more than the valetudinarian or exhausted constitution, but one which is in a mean between them. A man's constitution

should be inured to labour, but not to labour which is excessive or of
10 one sort only, such as is practised by athletes; he should be capable of
all the actions of a freeman. These remarks apply equally to both
parents.

Women who are with child should take care of themselves; they
should take exercise and have a nourishing diet. The first of these
15 prescriptions the legislator will easily carry into effect by requiring
that they shall take a walk daily to some temple, where they can
worship the gods who preside over birth. Their minds, however,
unlike their bodies, they ought to keep quiet, for the offspring derive
their natures from their mothers as plants do from the earth.

20 As to the exposure and rearing of children, let there be a law that no
deformed child shall live. But as to an excess in the number of
children, if the established customs of the state forbid the exposure of
any children who are born, let a limit be set to the number of children
25 a couple may have; and if couples have children in excess, let abortion
be procured before sense and life have begun; what may or may not be
lawfully done in these cases depends on the question of life and
sensation.

And now, having determined at what ages men and women are to
begin their union, let us also determine how long they shall continue
30 to beget and bear offspring for the state; men who are too old, like
men who are too young, produce children who are defective in body
and mind; the children of very old men are weakly. The limit, then,
should be the age which is the prime of their intelligence, and this in
most persons, according to the notion of some poets who measure life
35 by periods of seven years, is about fifty; at four or five years later, they
should cease from having families; and from that time forward only
cohabit with one another for the sake of health, or for some similar
reason.

As to adultery, let it be held disgraceful, in general, for any man or
40 woman to be found in any way unfaithful when they are married, and
called husband and wife. If during the time of bearing children
1336ᵃ1 anything of the sort occur, let the guilty person be punished with a loss
of privileges in proportion to the offence.

17 · After the children have been born, the manner of rearing them
5 may be supposed to have a great effect on their bodily strength. It
would appear from the example of animals, and of those nations who

desire to create the military habit, that the food which has most milk in it is best suited to human beings; but the less wine the better, if they would escape diseases. Also all the motions to which children can be subjected at their early age are very useful. But in order to preserve 10 their tender limbs from distortion, some nations have had recourse to mechanical appliances which straighten their bodies. To accustom children to the cold from their earliest years is also an excellent practice, which greatly conduces to health, and hardens them for military service. Hence many barbarians have a custom of plunging 15 their children at birth into a cold stream; others, like the Celts, clothe them in a light wrapper only. For human nature should be early habituated to endure all which by habit it can be made to endure; but the process must be gradual. And children, from their natural 20 warmth, may be easily trained to bear cold. Such care should attend them in the first stage of life.

The next period lasts to the age of five; during this no demand should be made upon the child for study or labour, lest its growth be 25 impeded; and there should be sufficient motion to prevent the limbs from being inactive. This can be secured, among other ways, by play, but the play should not be vulgar or tiring or effeminate. The Directors of Education, as they are termed, should be careful what 30 tales or stories the children hear, for all such things are designed to prepare the way for the business of later life, and should be for the most part imitations of the occupations which they will hereafter pursue in earnest. Those are wrong who in their *Laws* attempt to 35 check the loud crying and screaming of children, for these contribute towards their growth, and, in a manner, exercise their bodies.[1] Straining the voice has a strengthening effect similar to that produced by the retention of the breath in violent exertions. The Directors of Education should have an eye to their bringing up, and in particular 40 should take care that they are left as little as possible with slaves. For until they are seven years old they must live at home; and therefore, 1336ᵇ1 even at this early age, it is to be expected that they should acquire a taint of meanness from what they hear and see. Indeed, there is nothing which the legislator should be more careful to drive away than indecency of speech; for the light utterance of shameful words 5 leads soon to shameful actions. The young especially should never be

---

[1] Plato, *Laws*, 742A.

allowed to repeat or hear anything of the sort. A freeman who is found saying or doing what is forbidden, if he be too young as yet to have the privilege of reclining at the public tables, should be disgraced and beaten, and an elder person degraded as his slavish conduct deserves. And since we do not allow improper language, clearly we should also banish pictures or speeches from the stage which are indecent. Let the rulers take care that there be no image or picture representing unseemly actions, except in the temples of those gods at whose festivals the law permits even ribaldry, and whom the law also permits to be worshipped by persons of mature age on behalf of themselves, their children, and their wives. But the legislator should not allow youth to be spectators of iambi or of comedy until they are of an age to sit at the public tables and to drink strong wine; by that time education will have armed them against the evil influences of such representations.

We have made these remarks in a cursory manner – they are enough for the present occasion; but hereafter we will return to the subject and after a fuller discussion determine whether such liberty should or should not be granted, and in what way granted, if at all. Theodorus, the tragic actor, was quite right in saying that he would not allow any other actor, not even if he were quite second-rate, to enter before himself, because the spectators grew fond of the voices which they first heard. And the same principle applies universally to association with things as well as with persons, for we always like best whatever comes first. And therefore youth should be kept strangers to all that is bad, and especially to things which suggest vice or hate. When the five years have passed away, during the two following years they must look on at the pursuits which they are hereafter to learn. There are two periods of life with reference to which education has to be divided, from seven to the age of puberty, and onwards to the age of twenty-one. The poets who divide ages by sevens are in the main right: but we should observe the division actually made by nature; for the deficiencies of nature are what art and education seek to fill up.

Let us then first inquire if any regulations are to be laid down about children, and secondly, whether the care of them should be the concern of the state or of private individuals, which latter is in our own day the common custom, and in the third place, what these regulations should be.

BOOK VIII

1 · No one will doubt that the legislator should direct his attention 10
above all to the education of youth; for the neglect of education does
harm to the constitution. The citizen should be moulded to suit the
form of government under which he lives. For each government has a
peculiar character which originally formed and which continues to 15
preserve it. The character of democracy creates democracy, and the
character of oligarchy creates oligarchy; and always the better the
character, the better the government.

Again, for the exercise of any faculty or art a previous training and
habituation are required; clearly therefore for the practice of excel- 20
lence. And since the whole city has one end, it is manifest that
education should be one and the same for all, and that it should be
public, and not private – not as at present, when everyone looks after
his own children separately, and gives them separate instruction of 25
the sort which he thinks best; the training in things which are of
common interest should be the same for all. Neither must we suppose
that anyone of the citizens belongs to himself, for they all belong to the
state, and are each of them a part of the state, and the care of each part 30
is inseparable from the care of the whole. In this particular as in some
others the Lacedaemonians are to be praised, for they take the
greatest pains about their children, and make education the business
of the state.

2 · That education should be regulated by law and should be an
affair of state is not to be denied, but what should be the character of
this public education, and how young persons should be educated, 35
are questions which remain to be considered. As things are, there is
disagreement about the subjects. For men are by no means agreed
about the things to be taught, whether we look to excellence or the
best life. Neither is it clear whether education is more concerned with
intellectual or with moral excellence. The existing practice is perplex- 40
ing; no one knows on what principle we should proceed – should the
useful in life, or should excellence, or should the higher knowledge,
be the aim of our training? – all three opinions have been entertained.
Again, about the means there is no agreement; for different persons, 1337^{b}1
starting with different ideas about the nature of excellence, naturally

disagree about the practice of it. There can be no doubt that children should be taught those useful things which are really necessary, but
5 not all useful things; for occupations are divided into liberal and illiberal; and to young children should be imparted only such kinds of knowledge as will be useful to them without making mechanics of them. And any occupation, art, or science, which makes the body or soul or mind of the freeman less fit for the practice or exercise of
10 excellence, is mechanical; wherefore we call those arts mechanical which tend to deform the body, and likewise all paid employments, for they absorb and degrade the mind. There are also some liberal arts quite proper for a freeman to acquire, but only in a certain
15 degree, and if he attends to them too closely, in order to attain perfection in them, the same harmful effects will follow. The object also which a man sets before him makes a great difference; if he does or learns anything for his own sake or for the sake of his friends, or with a view to excellence, the action will not appear illiberal; but if
20 done for the sake of others, the very same action will be thought menial and servile. The received subjects of instruction, as I have already remarked, are partly of a liberal and partly of an illiberal character.

3 · The customary branches of education are in number four; they are – reading and writing, gymnastic exercises, and music, to which is
25 sometimes added drawing. Of these, reading and writing and drawing are regarded as useful for the purposes of life in a variety of ways, and gymnastic exercises are thought to infuse courage. Concerning music a doubt may be raised – in our own day most men cultivate it for the sake of pleasure, but originally it was included in education, because
30 nature herself, as has been often said, requires that we should be able, not only to work well, but to use leisure well; for, as I must repeat once again, the first principle of all action is leisure. Both are required, but leisure is better than occupation and is its end; and therefore the
35 question must be asked, what ought we to do when at leisure? Clearly we ought not to be playing, for then play would be the end of life. But if this is inconceivable, and play is needed more amid serious occupations than at other times (for he who is hard at work has need of relaxation, and play gives relaxation, whereas occupation is always
40 accompanied with exertion and effort), we should introduce amusements only at suitable times, and they should be our medicines, for

the emotion which they create in the soul is a relaxation, and from the pleasure we obtain rest. But leisure of itself gives pleasure and happiness and enjoyment of life, which are experienced, not by the busy man, but by those who have leisure. For he who is occupied has in view some end which he has not attained; but happiness is an end, since all men deem it to be accompanied with pleasure and not with pain. This pleasure, however, is regarded differently by different persons, and varies according to the habit of individuals; the pleasure of the best man is the best, and springs from the noblest sources. It is clear then that there are branches of learning and education which we must study merely with a view to leisure spent in intellectual activity, and these are to be valued for their own sake; whereas those kinds of knowledge which are useful in business are to be deemed necessary, and exist for the sake of other things. And therefore our fathers admitted music into education, not on the ground either of its necessity or utility, for it is not necessary, nor indeed useful in the same manner as reading and writing, which are useful in money-making, in the management of a household, in the acquisition of knowledge and in political life, nor like drawing, useful for a more correct judgement of the works of artists, nor again like gymnastic, which gives health and strength; for neither of these is to be gained from music. There remains, then, the use of music for intellectual enjoyment in leisure; which is in fact evidently the reason of its introduction, this being one of the ways in which it is thought that a freeman should pass his leisure; as Homer says –

1338ᵃ1

5

10

15

20

But he who alone should be called to the pleasant feast,   25

and afterwards he speaks of others whom he describes as inviting

The bard who would delight them all.[1]

And in another place Odysseus says there is no better way of passing life than when men's hearts are merry and

The banqueters in the hall, sitting in order, hear the voice of the minstrel.[2]   30

It is evident, then, that there is a sort of education in which parents

---

[1] Of these two lines, the first is not to be found in the text of Homer as we have it and the second roughly corresponds to *Odyssey*, XVII 385.

[2] Homer, *Odyssey*, IX 7–8.

should train their sons, not as being useful or necessary, but because it is liberal or noble. Whether this is of one kind only, or of more than one, and if so, what they are, and how they are to be imparted, must hereafter be determined. Thus much we are already in a position to
35 say; for the ancients bear witness to us – their opinion may be gathered from the fact that music is one of the received and traditional branches of education. Further, it is clear that children should be instructed in some useful things – for example, in reading and writing – not only for their usefulness, but also because many other sorts of
40 knowledge are acquired through them. With a like view they may be taught drawing, not to prevent their making mistakes in their own purchases, or in order that they may not be imposed upon in the
1338^{b}1 buying or selling of articles, but perhaps rather because it makes them judges of the beauty of the human form. To be always seeking after the useful does not become free and exalted souls. Now it is clear that
5 in education practice must be used before theory, and the body be trained before the mind; and therefore boys should be handed over to the trainer, who creates in them the proper habit of body, and to the wrestling-master, who teaches them their exercises.

4 · Of those states which in our own day seem to take the greatest
10 care of children, some aim at producing in them an athletic habit, but they only injure their bodies and stunt their growth. Although the Lacedaemonians have not fallen into this mistake, yet they brutalize their children by laborious exercises which they think will make them
15 courageous. But in truth, as we have often repeated, education should not be exclusively, or principally, directed to this end. And even if we suppose the Lacedaemonians to be right in their end, they do not attain it. For among the barbarians and among animals courage is found associated, not with the greatest ferocity, but with a gentle and
20 lion-like temper. There are many races who are ready enough to kill and eat men, such as the Achaeans and Heniochi, who both live about the Black Sea; and there are other mainland tribes, as bad or worse, who all live by plunder, but have no courage. It is notorious that the
25 Lacedaemonians themselves, while they alone were assiduous in their laborious drill, were superior to others, but now they are beaten both in war and gymnastic exercises. For their ancient superiority did not depend on their mode of training their youth, but only on the circumstance that they trained them when their only rivals did not.

Hence we may infer that what is noble, not what is brutal, should have the first place; no wolf or other wild animal will face a really noble danger; such dangers are for the brave man. And parents who devote their children to gymnastics while they neglect their necessary education, in reality make them mechanics; for they make them useful to the art of statesmanship in one quality only, and even in this the argument proves them to be inferior to others. We should judge the Lacedaemonians not from what they have been, but from what they are; for now they have rivals who compete with their education; formerly they had none.

It is an admitted principle that gymnastic exercises should be employed in education, and that for children they should be of a lighter kind, avoiding severe diet or painful toil, lest the growth of the body be impaired. The evil of excessive training in early years is strikingly proved by the example of the Olympic victors; for not more than two or three of them have gained a prize both as boys and as men; their early training and severe gymnastic exercises exhausted their constitutions. When boyhood is over, three years should be spent in other studies; the period of life which follows may then be devoted to hard exercise and strict diet. Men ought not to labour at the same time with their minds and with their bodies; for the two kinds of labour are opposed to one another; the labour of the body impedes the mind, and the labour of the mind the body.

5 · Concerning music there are some questions which we have already raised; these we may now resume and carry further; and our remarks will serve as a prelude to this or any other discussion of the subject. It is not easy to determine the nature of music, or why anyone should have a knowledge of it. Shall we say, for the sake of amusement and relaxation, like sleep or drinking, which are not good in themselves, but are pleasant, and at the same time 'make care to cease', as Euripides says?[1] And for this end men also appoint music, and make use of all three alike – sleep, drinking, music – to which some add dancing. Or shall we argue that music conduces to excellence, on the ground that it can form our minds and habituate us to true pleasures as our bodies are made by gymnastic to be of a certain character? Or shall we say that it contributes to the enjoyment

[1] Euripides, *Bacchae*, 381.

of leisure and mental cultivation, which is a third alternative? Now obviously youths are not to be instructed with a view to their amusement, for learning is no amusement, but is accompanied with

30 pain. Neither is intellectual enjoyment suitable to boys of that age, for it is the end, and that which is imperfect cannot attain the end. But perhaps it may be said that boys learn music for the sake of the amusement which they will have when they are grown up. If so, why should they learn themselves, and not, like the Persian and Median

35 kings, enjoy the pleasure and instruction which is derived from hearing others? (for surely persons who have made music the business and profession of their lives will be better performers than those who practise only long enough to learn). If they must learn

40 music, on the same principle they should learn cookery, which is absurd. And even granting that music may form the character, the objection still holds: why should we learn ourselves? Why cannot we

1339ᵇ1 attain true pleasure and form a correct judgement from hearing others, as the Lacedaemonians do? – for they, without learning music, nevertheless can correctly judge, as they say, of good and bad melodies. Or again, if music should be used to promote cheerfulness

5 and refined intellectual enjoyment, the objection still remains – why should we learn ourselves instead of enjoying the performances of others? We may illustrate what we are saying by our conception of the gods; for in the poets Zeus does not himself sing or play on the lyre. Indeed we call professional performers artisans; no freeman would play or sing unless he were intoxicated or in jest. But these matters

10 may be left for the present.

The first question is whether music is or is not to be a part of education. Of the three things mentioned in our discussion, which does it produce – education or amusement or intellectual enjoyment? – for it may be reckoned under all three, and seems to share in the

15 nature of all of them. Amusement is for the sake of relaxation, and relaxation is of necessity sweet, for it is the remedy of pain caused by toil; and intellectual enjoyment is universally acknowledged to contain an element not only of the noble but of the pleasant, for happiness is made up of both. All men agree that music is one of the pleasantest

20 things, whether with or without song; as Musaeus says,

Song is to mortals of all things the sweetest.

Hence and with good reason it is introduced into social gatherings and entertainments, because it makes the hearts of men glad: so that on this ground alone we may assume that the young ought to be trained in it. For innocent pleasures are not only in harmony with the 25 end of life, but they also provide relaxation. And whereas men rarely attain the end, but often rest by the way and amuse themselves, not only with a view to a further end, but also for the pleasure's sake, it 30 may be well at times to let them find a refreshment in music. It sometimes happens that men make amusement the end, for the end probably contains some element of pleasure, though not any ordinary pleasure; but they mistake the lower for the higher, and in seeking for the one find the other, since every pleasure has a likeness to the end of action. For the end is not desirable for the sake of any future good, nor 35 do the pleasures which we have described exist for the sake of any future good but of the past, that is to say, they are the alleviation of past toils and pains. And we may infer this to be the reason why men seek happiness from these pleasures. But music is pursued, not only 40 as an alleviation of past toil, but also as providing recreation. And who can say whether, having this use, it may not also have a nobler one? In 1340ᵃ1 addition to this common pleasure, felt and shared in by all (for the pleasure given by music is natural, and therefore adapted to all ages 5 and characters), may it not have also some influence over the character and the soul? It must have such an influence if characters are affected by it. And that they are so affected is proved in many ways, and not least by the power which the songs of Olympus exercise; for beyond question they inspire enthusiasm, and 10 enthusiasm is an emotion of the character of the soul. Besides, when men hear imitations, even apart from the rhythms and tunes themselves, their feelings move in sympathy. Since then music is pleasure, and excellence consists in rejoicing and loving and hating rightly, 15 there is clearly nothing which we are so much concerned to acquire and to cultivate as the power of forming right judgements, and of taking delight in good dispositions and noble actions. Rhythm and melody supply imitations of anger and gentleness, and also of courage 20 and temperance, and of all the qualities contrary to these, and of the other qualities of character, which hardly fall short of the actual affections, as we know from our own experience, for in listening to such strains our souls undergo a change. The habit of feeling pleasure or pain at mere representations is not far removed from the same feeling about realities; for example, if any one delights in the 25

sight of a statue for its beauty only, it necessarily follows that the sight
of the original will be pleasant to him. The objects of no other sense,
30 such as taste or touch, have any resemblance to moral qualities; in
visible objects there is only a little, for there are figures which are of a
moral character, but only to a slight extent, and all do not participate
in the feeling about them. Again, figures and colours are not
imitations, but signs, of character, indications which the body gives of
35 states of feeling. The connexion of them with morals is slight, but in
so far as there is any, young men should be taught to look, not at the
works of Pauson, but at those of Polygnotus, or any other painter or
sculptor who expresses character. On the other hand, even in mere
melodies there is an imitation of character, for the musical modes
40 differ essentially from one another, and those who hear them are
1340^b1 differently affected by each. Some of them make men sad and grave,
like the so-called Mixolydian, others enfeeble the mind, like the
relaxed modes, another, again, produces a moderate and settled
temper, which appears to be the peculiar effect of the Dorian; the
5 Phrygian inspires enthusiasm. The whole subject has been well
treated by philosophical writers on this branch of education, and they
confirm their arguments by facts. The same principles apply to
rhythms; some have a character of rest, others of motion, and of these
10 latter again, some have a more vulgar, others a nobler movement.
Enough has been said to show that music has a power of forming the
character, and should therefore be introduced into the education of
the young. The study is suited to the stage of youth, for young persons
15 will not, if they can help, endure anything which is not sweetened by
pleasure, and music has a natural sweetness. There seems to be in us
a sort of affinity to musical modes and rhythms, which makes some
philosophers say that the soul is a harmony, others, that it possesses
harmony.

20 6 · And now we have to determine the question which has been
already raised, whether children should be themselves taught to sing
and play or not. Clearly there is a considerable difference made in the
character by the actual practice of the art. It is difficult, if not
25 impossible, for those who do not perform to be good judges of the
performance of others. Besides, children should have something to
do, and the rattle of Archytas, which people give to their children in
order to amuse them and prevent them from breaking anything in the

house, was a capital invention, for a young thing cannot be quiet. The
rattle is a toy suited to the infant mind, and education is a rattle or toy   30
for children of a larger growth. We conclude then that they should be
taught music in such a way as to become not only critics but
performers.

The question what is or is not suitable for different ages may be
easily answered; nor is there any difficulty in meeting the objection of
those who say that the study of music is mechanical. We reply in the   35
first place, that they who are to be judges must also be performers,
and that they should begin to practise early, although when they are
older they may be spared the execution; they must have learned to
appreciate what is good and to delight in it, thanks to the knowledge
which they acquired in their youth. As to the vulgarizing effect which
music is supposed to exercise, this is a question which we shall have   40
no difficulty in determining when we have considered to what extent
freemen who are being trained to political excellence should pursue
the art, what melodies and what rhythms they should be allowed to   1341^{a}1
use, and what instruments should be employed in teaching them to
play; for even the instrument makes a difference. The answer to the
objection turns upon these distinctions; for it is quite possible that
certain methods of teaching and learning music do really have a   5
degrading effect. It is evident then that the learning of music ought
not to impede the business of riper years, or to degrade the body or
render it unfit for civil or military training, whether for bodily
exercises at the time or for later studies.

The right measure will be attained if students of music stop short of   10
the arts which are practised in professional contests, and do not seek
to acquire those fantastic marvels of execution which are now the
fashion in such contests, and from these have passed into education.
Let the young practise even such music as we have prescribed, only
until they are able to feel delight in noble melodies and rhythms, and
not merely in that common part of music in which every slave or child   15
and even some animals find pleasure.

From these principles we may also infer what instruments should
be used. The flute, or any other instrument which requires great skill,
as for example the harp, ought not to be admitted into education, but
only such as will make men intelligent students of music or of the   20
other parts of education. Besides, the flute is not an instrument which
is expressive of character; it is too exciting. The proper time for using

it is when the performance aims not at instruction, but at the relief of the passions. And there is a further objection; the impediment which the flute presents to the use of the voice detracts from its educational value. The ancients therefore were right in forbidding the flute to youths and freemen, although they had once allowed it. For when their wealth gave them a greater inclination to leisure, and they had loftier notions of excellence, being also elated with their success, both before and after the Persian War, with more zeal than discernment they pursued every kind of knowledge, and so they introduced the flute into education. In Lacedaemon there was a choragus who led the chorus with a flute, and at Athens the instrument became so popular that most freemen could play upon it. The popularity is shown by the tablet which Thrasippus dedicated when he furnished the chorus to Ecphantides. Later experience enabled men to judge what was or was not really conducive to excellence, and they rejected both the flute and several other old-fashioned instruments, such as the Lydian harp, the many-stringed lyre, the 'heptagon', 'triangle', 'sambuca', and the like – which are intended only to give pleasure to the hearer, and require extraordinary skill of hand. There is a meaning also in the myth of the ancients, which tells how Athene invented the flute and then threw it away. It was not a bad idea of theirs that the Goddess disliked the instrument because it made the face ugly; but with still more reason may we say that she rejected it because the acquirement of flute-playing contributes nothing to the mind, since to Athene we ascribe both knowledge and art.

Thus then we reject the professional instruments and also the professional mode of education in music (and by professional we mean that which is adopted in contests), for in this the performer practises the art, not for the sake of his own improvement, but in order to give pleasure, and that of a vulgar sort, to his hearers. For this reason the execution of such music is not the part of a freeman but of a paid performer, and the result is that the performers are vulgarized, for the end at which they aim is bad. The vulgarity of the spectator tends to lower the character of the music and therefore of the performers; they look to him – he makes them what they are, and fashions even their bodies by the movements which he expects them to exhibit.

7 · We have also to consider rhythms and modes, and their use in

education. Shall we use them all or make a distinction? and shall the same distinction be made for those who practise music with a view to education, or shall it be some other? Now we see that music is produced by melody and rhythm, and we ought to know what influence these have respectively on education, and whether we 25 should prefer excellence in melody or excellence in rhythm. But as the subject has been very well treated by many musicians of the present day, and also by philosophers who have had considerable experience of musical education, to these we would refer the more exact student of the subject; we shall only speak of it now after the 30 manner of the legislator, stating the general principles.

We accept the division of melodies proposed by certain philosophers into melodies of character, melodies of action, and passionate or inspiring melodies, each having, as they say, a mode cor- 35 responding to it. But we maintain further that music should be studied, not for the sake of one, but of many benefits, that is to say, with a view to education, or purgation (the word 'purgation' we use at present without explanation, but when hereafter we speak of poetry, we will treat the subject with more precision); music may also serve 40 for intellectual enjoyment, for relaxation and for recreation after exertion. It is clear, therefore, that all the modes must be employed by 1342ᵃ1 us, but not all of them in the same manner. In education the modes most expressive of character are to be preferred, but in listening to the performances of others we may admit the modes of action and passion also. For feelings such as pity and fear, or, again, enthusiasm, exist 5 very strongly in some souls, and have more or less influence over all. Some persons fall into a religious frenzy, and we see them restored as a result of the sacred melodies – when they have used the melodies that excite the soul to mystic frenzy – as though they had found healing and purgation. Those who are influenced by pity or fear, and 10 every emotional nature, must have a like experience, and others in so far as each is susceptible to such emotions, and all are in a manner purged and their souls lightened and delighted. The melodies which purge the passions likewise give an innocent pleasure to mankind. 15 Such are the modes and the melodies in which those who perform music at the theatre should be invited to compete. But since the spectators are of two kinds – the one free and educated, and the other a vulgar crowd composed of artisans, labourers, and the like – there 20 ought to be contests and exhibitions instituted for the relaxation of the

second class also. And the music will correspond to their minds; for as their minds are perverted from the natural state, so there are perverted modes and highly strung and unnaturally coloured
25 melodies. A man receives pleasure from what is natural to him, and therefore professional musicians may be allowed to practise this lower sort of music before an audience of a lower type. But, for the purposes of education, as I have already said, those modes and melodies should
30 be employed which are expressive of character, such as the Dorian, as we said before; though we may include any others which are approved by philosophers who have had a musical education. The Socrates of the *Republic* is wrong in retaining only the Phrygian mode along with the Dorian,[1] and the more so because he rejects the flute; for the
1342^b1 Phrygian is to the modes what the flute is to musical instruments – both of them are exciting and emotional. Poetry proves this, for Bacchic frenzy and all similar emotions are most suitably expressed
5 by the flute, and are better set to the Phrygian than to any other mode. The dithyramb, for example, is acknowledged to be Phrygian, a fact of which the connoisseurs of music offer many proofs, saying, among other things, that Philoxenus, having attempted to compose his
10 *Mysians* as a dithyramb in the Dorian mode, found it impossible, and fell back by the very nature of things into the more appropriate Phrygian. All men agree that the Dorian music is the gravest and manliest. And whereas we say that the extremes should be avoided
15 and the mean followed, and whereas the Dorian is a mean between the other modes, it is evident that our youth should be taught the Dorian music.

Two principles have to be kept in view, what is possible, and what is becoming: at these every man ought to aim. But even these are
20 relative to age; the old, who have lost their powers, cannot very well sing the high-strung modes, and nature herself seems to suggest that their songs should be of the more relaxed kind. That is why the musicians too blame Socrates, and with justice, for rejecting the
25 relaxed modes in education under the idea that they are intoxicating, not in the ordinary sense of intoxication (for wine rather tends to excite men), but because they have no strength in them. And so, with a view also to the time of life when men begin to grow old, they ought to practise the gentler modes and melodies as well as the others, and,

---

[1] Plato, *Rep.*, 399A.

further, any mode, such as the Lydian above all others appears to be, which is suited to children of tender age, and possesses the elements 30 both of order and of education. Thus it is clear that education should be based upon three principles – the mean, the possible, the becoming, these three.

The Constitution of Athens

The history of the constitution

... the accuser being Myron before a jury selected by birth who 1
had taken their oath over sacrificial victims. When it had been
decided that sacrilege had been committed, the bodies of the guilty
were disinterred and their families exiled in perpetuity. Epimenides of Crete purified the city in connection with this matter.

After this there was an extended period of discord between the II
upper classes and the people. The constitution was in all respects 2
oligarchic, in particular in that the poor, together with their wives
and children, were the slaves of the rich; they were described as
pelatae and *hektemori*, which referred to the terms on which they
worked the fields of the rich. The whole land was under the control of a few men, and if the ordinary people did not pay their
dues they and their children could be seized. Further, all loans
were made on the security of the person of the debtor until the
time of Solon – he was the first champion of the people. The 3
harshest and most resented aspect of the constitution for the mass
of the people was this slavery, although they had other complaints,
for they had virtually no share in any aspect of government.

The primitive constitution before the time of Draco, then, was III
as follows. Eligibility for office depended on birth and wealth,
while tenure was at first for life and later for a period of ten years.
The most powerful and earliest of the political offices were those 2
of the King Archon, the Polemarch and the Archon. The first was
that of the King, being traditional, while the office of Polemarch
was the first added to this because of the incompetence of some
of the kings in war; it was in this way that they sent for Ion in a
crisis. The last of the three was that of the Archon. Most people 3
say that it was established in the time of Medon, though some
say it was under Acastus, arguing from the fact that the nine
Archons swear to observe their oaths as was done under Acastus
that it was at this time that the sons of Codrus surrendered the
kingship in return for the powers granted to the Archon. Whichever of these alternatives is true, the difference of date is not great;
that the Archonship was the last of the three offices is shown by
the fact that the Archon does not control any of the traditional

ceremonies as the King Archon and the Polemarch do, but only ceremonies which are later additions; hence the importance of the
4 office is of recent origin, arising from these later additions. The *Thesmothetae* were instituted at a much later date when offices were already annual; their function is to inscribe the laws and preserve them for the decision of disputes. Because of its late date, the office of the *Thesmothetae* is the only archonship which was
5 never anything but annual. Such, then, was the chronological sequence of these offices. All nine Archons did not have the same official residences; the King Archon lived in the building now called the Bucolium near the Prytaneum, evidence for which is the fact that the union and marriage of the wife of the King Archon with Dionysus even now takes place there. The Archon had the Prytaneum, while the Polemarch had the Epilyceum, a building formerly called the Polemarcheum, but renamed the Epilyceum when it was rebuilt and furnished by Epilycus as Polemarch; the *Thesmothetae* had the Thesmotheteum. Under Solon all the archons were brought together in the Thesmotheteum. The Archons had full power to decide cases themselves, not only to hold preliminary hearings as now. Such then was the position of the Archons.
6 The Council of the Areopagus had the duty of watching over the laws, and had wide-ranging and important powers in the city since it punished and fined all offenders without appeal. Archons were chosen on the basis of birth and wealth qualifications, and they made up the Areopagus; this is the reason why this is the only office which is still held for life today.

IV The above is an outline of the first constitution. A short time after this, in the Archonship of Aristaechyus, Draco introduced
2 his legislation; this constitution was as follows. Political power had been handed over to those who provided their own armour. They chose the nine Archons and the Treasurers from those men who had an unencumbered property qualification of not less than ten minae; the lesser magistrates were chosen from those who armed themselves, while the *strategi* and cavalry commanders had to show unencumbered property to the value of at least a hundred minae and legitimate children, by citizen wives, not less than ten years old. The Prytanies had to receive sureties for them, as also for

the *strategi* and cavalry commanders of the previous year until after their *euthuna*, the sureties being four citizens from the same class as the *strategi* and cavalry commanders. There was a *Boule* 3 of 401 members, selected by lot from the citizen body. All those over thirty years old cast lots for this and the other offices, and nobody could hold the same office twice until all those eligible had held it; then the allotment started again from the beginning. If a member of the *Boule* failed to attend a sitting of the *Boule* or *Ekklesia*, he was fined three drachmae if he was a *pentacosiomedimnus*, two if he was a *hippeus* and one if he was a *zeugites*. The Council of the Areopagus was the guardian of the laws and super- 4 vised the magistrates to ensure that they acted legally. If a man were wronged, he could lay information before the Areopagus specifying the law he relied on. Loans were made on the security 5 of the person of the borrower, as noted above, and the land was under the control of a few men.

Solon

In this political situation, when the majority were the slaves of v the few, the people opposed the leaders of the state. When the 2 strife was severe, and the opposition of long standing, both sides agreed to give power to Solon as mediator, and entrusted the state to him; at that time he had written the poem which begins:

> Grief lies deep in my heart when I see the oldest of the Ionian states being murdered . . .

In this poem he champions both sides against the other, and argues their position, and then recommends an end to the prevailing rivalry.

Solon was one of the leading men by birth and reputation, but 3 'middle class' in wealth and position; this is agreed from other evidence, and Solon himself makes it clear in the following poem, where he advises the rich not to be greedy:

> Restrain in your breasts your mighty hearts; you have taken too much of the good things of life; satisfy your pride with what is moderate, for we shall not tolerate excess, nor will everything turn out as you wish.

He always attaches the overall blame for the strife to the rich; this is why he says at the opening of the poem that he is afraid of their 'avarice and overbearing pride', since this was the cause of the conflict.

VI   When he had taken power, Solon freed the people both then and for the future by making loans on the security of a person's freedom illegal; he passed laws, and instituted a cancellation of debts both private and public which men call the *seisachtheia*, for
2   they shook off their burdens. Some try to attack him in this context; it happened that when Solon was about to introduce his *seisachtheia* he told some of the leading citizens, and then (according to the democratic version of the story) he was outmanoeuvred by his friends, while those who wish to blacken his reputation say that he was a party to fraud. These men borrowed money and bought large areas of land; shortly afterwards, when debts were cancelled, they were rich. This is alleged to be the origin of those
3   who later appeared to have been wealthy for generations. However, the democratic account is more convincing. It is unlikely that Solon would have been so moderate and public-spirited in other respects, that, when he had it in his power to subject the other group and become tyrant of the city, he chose to incur the hostility of both sides, and preferred what was right and the salvation of the city to his own advantage, but yet would have sullied
4   himself with such a trivial and manifest fraud. That he had power to become tyrant is demonstrated by the perilous state of the city's affairs at the time; he himself mentions it frequently in his poems, and all other sources agree. One must therefore conclude that this charge is false.

VII   Solon established a constitution and enacted other laws; the Athenians ceased to use Draco's code except for his homicide laws. Solon's laws were inscribed on *kurbeis* set up in the portico of the King Archon, and all swore to observe them. The nine Archons used to take their oath on the Stone, and undertook to set up a golden statue if they broke one of the laws; hence the oath which
2   they still take now. Solon made his laws binding for a hundred
3   years and arranged the constitution in the following way. He divided the people into four property classes according to wealth, as

had been done before; the four classes were: *pentacosiomedimni,
hippeis, zeugitae* and *thetes*. He distributed the other magistracies
to be held by the *pentacosiomedimni, hippeis* and *zeugitae*, allotting
the nine Archons, the Treasurers, the *poletae*, the Eleven and the
cholachretae to various classes in accordance with their property
qualification. The *thetes* received only the right to sit in the *Ekklesia* and the *dikasteria*. The property qualification for a *pentacosi-* 4
omedimnus was a minimum yearly return from his own property
of 500 measures, dry or liquid. The *hippeis* had a minimum of
300, and some say that the class was also restricted to those able
to maintain a horse; they deduce this from early dedications, for
there is a statue of Diphilus on the Acropolis with the following
inscription:

> Anthemion, the son of Diphilus, made this dedication to the gods,
> having risen from the *thetes* to the class of the *hippeis*.

A horse stands by, showing the connection between the *hippeis*
and being able to maintain a horse. None the less, it is more plausible that this class should have been defined by measures of produce like the *pentacosiomedimni*. The minimum qualification for
the *zeugitae* was 200 measures, wet and dry combined, while the
remainder of the population formed the *thetes* and were not
entitled to hold office. This is why even now, when they are about
to cast lots for a magistracy and a man is asked what his class is,
nobody would say that he was one of the *thetes*.

Magistracies were selected by lot from a group previously VIII
elected by each tribe. For the nine Archons, each tribe made a
preliminary selection of ten men, and they cast lots among them;
this is the origin of the practice which survives today by which
each tribe picks ten men by lot, and then lots are cast again among
them. Evidence that Solon instituted selection by lot in accordance
with property classes is the law about the Treasurers which is still
in force; this lays down that the Treasurers shall be selected by
lot from the *pentacosiomedimni*. These were Solon's provisions 2
about the nine Archons. In early times, the Areopagus had summoned the candidates and selected the man it judged suitable for
each office itself and installed him for the year. Solon retained the 3
four tribes which already existed and the four tribal Kings; within

each tribe there were three *trittyes* and twelve *naucraries*. The officers in charge of the *naucraries* were called *naucrari*, and they controlled contributions and expenditure; this is why many of the laws of Solon which are no longer in force contain the phrases 'the *naucrari* shall collect' and 'shall be spent from the funds of

4 the *naucraries*'. Solon instituted a *Boule* of 400 members, 100 from each tribe, and he gave the Areopagus the duty of watching over the laws, analogous to its earlier position of guardian of the constitution. It had extensive supervisory powers over the important aspects of political life, and punished wrongdoers with full powers to inflict fines or other penalties; fines were deposited in the treasury, and there was no obligation to state the reason for the fine. The Areopagus tried those who conspired to overthrow the constitution under a law of impeachment which Solon introduced.

5 Solon realised that the city was often split by factional disputes but some citizens were content because of idleness to accept whatever the outcome might be; he therefore produced a specific law against them, laying down that anyone who did not choose one side or the other in such a dispute should lose his citizen rights.

IX The magistracies were reformed in this way. The following seem to be the three most popular features of Solon's constitution: first and most important, that nobody might borrow money on the security of anyone's freedom; secondly, that anyone might seek redress on behalf of those who were wronged; thirdly, the feature which is said to have contributed most to the strength of the democracy, the right of appeal to the *dikasterion*, for when the people have the right to vote in the courts they control the consti-

2 tution. The fact that the laws have not been drafted simply or clearly, but are like the provisions controlling inheritances and heirs, inevitably leads to disputes; hence the courts have to decide everything, public and private. Some think that Solon made his laws obscure deliberately to give the people the power of decision. This is not likely; the obscurity arises rather from the impossibility of including the best solution for every instance in a general provision. It is not right to judge his intentions from what happens now but by analogy with the rest of his provisions.

X Those were the democratic aspects of his legislation; before introducing his laws, he carried out the cancellation of debts, and after that the increase of the measures, weights and coinage. For 2 it was under Solon that the measures were made larger than the Pheidonian standard, and the mina, which formerly had a weight of seventy drachmae, was increased to the hundred it now contains. The old coin was the two-drachma piece. He established weights for coinage purposes in which the talent was divided into sixty-three minae, and the three added minae were divided proportionately for the stater and the other weights.

After the reform of the constitution which has been described xi above, Solon was annoyed by people approaching him criticising some parts of his legislation and questioning others. He did not wish to make alterations or to incur unpopularity while in Athens, and so went abroad to Egypt for trading purposes and also to see the country, saying he would not return for ten years; he said it was not right for him to stay to interpret the laws but that everyone should follow them as they were drafted. He had incurred the 2 hostility of many of the leading men because of the cancellation of debts, and both sides had changed their attitude to him because his legislation had been different from what they had expected. The common people had expected him to redivide all property, while the wealthy had expected him to restore them to their traditional position, or at most only to make minor alterations to it. Solon had resisted them both, and, when he could have made himself tyrant by joining whichever side he chose, had preferred to be hated by both while saving his country and giving it the best constitution possible.

That this was Solon's attitude is agreed by all authorities, and xii he himself comments on it in his poems in the following terms:

> To the people I gave as much privilege as was sufficient for them, neither reducing nor exceeding what was their due. Those who had power and were enviable for their wealth I took good care not to injure. I stood casting my strong shield around both parties, and allowed neither to triumph unjustly.

In another passage he describes how the ordinary people should 2 be handled:

The people will follow their leaders best if they are neither too free nor too much restrained, for excess produces insolent behaviour when great wealth falls to men who lack sound judgement.

3 In another passage he discusses those who wish for a redistribution of land:

They came to plunder with hopes of riches, and each of them expected to find great wealth; they thought that although I spoke soothingly I would reveal stern determination. Their expectation was vain, and now they are angry and look askance at me like an enemy. This is wrong; for with the gods I carried out what I said, and did nothing else foolishly; it does not please me to act with the violence of a tyrant nor to give equal shares of our rich country to worthless and noble alike.

4 He discusses the cancellation of debts and those who had previously been enslaved but were freed through the *seisachtheia* in the following passage:

Which of my aims did I abandon unattained, the aims for which I had assembled the people? My witness to this before the judgement of the future will be the great mother of the Olympian gods, dark Earth; I took up the markers fixed in many places – previously she was enslaved, but now is free. Many I brought back to Athens, their divinely founded city, who had been sold abroad, one unjustly, another justly, and others who had fled under compulsion of debt, men who no longer spoke the Attic tongue, so wide had their wanderings been. Those at home, suffering here the outrages of slavery and trembling at the whims of their masters, I freed. This I achieved by the might of law, combining force and justice; I carried it out as I promised. I drafted ordinances equally for bad and good, with upright justice for each. Another man holding the spur that I held, a man of evil counsel and greed, would not have restrained the people. Had I been willing to indulge the enemies of the people or do to them what the people wished to do, the city would have lost many men. That is why I set up a strong defence all round, turning like a wolf at bay among the hounds.

5 Again, of the latter attacks of both parties he says reproachfully:

If I must express my reproach of the people in clear terms, they would never otherwise even have dreamed of what they now possess. The greater and more powerful also should praise me and make me their friend.

for, he says, if anyone else had held his position,

> he would not have restrained the people nor checked them before
> they squeezed all the cream from the milk. But I stood, as it were
> in no man's land, a barrier between them.

For these reasons, then, Solon went abroad. When he had left, xiii
the city was still very disturbed; four years passed peacefully, but
in the fifth year after his Archonship they did not appoint an
Archon because of the dissension, and four years later the same
thing happened again for the same reason. After the same interval, 2
Damasias was chosen Archon, and retained the position for two
years and two months until he was forcibly removed from office.
Then the Athenians decided because of the civil strife to choose
ten Archons, five from the *Eupatridae*, three from the men of the
country and two from artisans; they held office the year after
Damasias. This demonstrates the great power of the Archon, for
the strife clearly centred round this office. In general, the Atheni- 3
ans lived in a state of continual turmoil in internal affairs, some
finding the cause and reason for dissent in the cancellation of
debts, which had reduced them to poverty, some being angered
by the great change in the constitution, and some motivated by
private feuds. There were three groups. The first was that of the 4
Shore; their leader was Megacles the son of Alcmeon, and they
favoured a middle-of-the-road policy. The second group was that
of the Plain; their aim was oligarchy, and their leader Lycurgus.
The third group was that of the Uplands; they were led by Peisistratus, and he seemed to be the most democratic leader. This fac- 5
tion had been joined by those who had lost money when the debts
were cancelled because they were impoverished, and those who
were not of pure Athenian descent because of anxiety about their
position. Evidence of this is the fact that after the abolition of the
tyranny the Athenians revised the lists of citizens on the grounds
that many were exercising citizen rights who were not entitled to
them. Each group took its name from the area in which it farmed.

Peisistratus

Peisistratus had the reputation of being a strong supporter of the xiv
people and had distinguished himself in the war against Megara;

he wounded himself, and persuaded the people that his political opponents had done it, with the result that they voted him a bodyguard on the proposal of Aristion. With the assistance of these 'club-bearers' he rose against the people and seized the Acropolis in the thirty-second year after the legislation of Solon, which was

2 the Archonship of Comeas. It is said that when Peisistratus asked for the bodyguard, Solon opposed him, claiming to be wiser than some and braver than others; he said he was wiser than those who did not realise that Peisistratus was aiming at tyranny, and braver than those who kept silent although they knew it. When he failed to persuade his hearers, he placed his arms in front of his door, saying that he had done all he could to help his country – he was already a very old man – and insisted that the other citizens should

3 do the same. Solon's appeal fell on deaf ears, and Peisistratus seized power, and ran the state more like a private citizen than a tyrant. However, when the tyranny had not yet had time to take root the groups led by Megacles and Lycurgus combined to expel him in the Archonship of Hegesias, which was the sixth year after

4 he first took power. In the twelfth year after this Megacles was hard pressed by dissensions, and opened negotiations with Peisistratus; having agreed that Peisistratus would marry his daughter, he brought him back by a primitive and very simple trick. Having spread a rumour that Athena was bringing Peisistratus back home, he found a tall beautiful woman called Phye, whom Herodotus says came from Paiania, but others say was a Thracian flower girl from Collytus, dressed her as Athena, and brought her into the city with Peisistratus. Peisistratus rode on a chariot with the woman beside him, and the inhabitants fell to the ground and accepted him with awe.

xv Peisistratus returned to Athens for the first time in this way. He was expelled for a second time in about the seventh year after his return; he did not keep his position for a long time, but, being afraid of both groups because he did not wish to treat Megacles'

2 daughter as his wife, retired abroad. First he joined in the foundation of a place called Rhaecelus near the Thermaic Gulf, and then moved to the area around Mt Pangaeus. He grew wealthy there and hired mercenaries, and so came to Eretria and made his first attempt to recover the tyranny by force in the eleventh year

after his expulsion. He received wide support, and in particular that of the Thebans, Lygdamis of Naxos, and the *hippeis* who controlled affairs in Eretria. After winning the battle of Pallene, 3 he took Athens, disarmed the people, and established his tyranny on a firm basis. He also took Naxos and established Lygdamis as 4 tyrant. He disarmed the Athenians in the following way. During a review of the people in full armour at the Theseum, he began to address the crowd, and spoke for a short while. When they said that they could not hear him, he told them to come up to the gate of the Acropolis where he would be more audible. While he continued his speech, a group who had been specially detailed for the purpose collected the people's weapons and locked them in the buildings of the Theseum, near by; when they had finished, they signalled to Peisistratus. When he had concluded his speech, 5 he told the crowd not to be surprised or alarmed by what had happened to their weapons; they should go home and look after their private affairs – he would take care of the state.

That, then, was how Peisistratus' tyranny was first established, xvi and those were the vicissitudes it passed through. As noted above, 2 Peisistratus ran the state moderately, and constitutionally rather than as a tyrant. He was benevolent, mild and forgiving to those who did wrong, and moreover he advanced money to the bankrupt to further their work so that they could make a living as farmers. He had two motives for doing this; he did not want them in the 3 city, but scattered in the country, and if they had enough to live on, and were busy with their own affairs, they would neither want to meddle with affairs of state nor have the time to do so. The 4 working of the land increased his revenues, for he took a 10 per cent tax on produce. He also had the same motive for establishing 5 the magistrates of the demes and for travelling round the country frequently, inspecting and settling disputes: it made it unnecessary for the people to come into the city and neglect their work. It was 6 on one of these circuits that there occurred the incident of the farmer on Mt Hymettus and the land later called 'tax-exempt'. Peisistratus saw someone working an area that was all stones, and, being surprised, told his attendant to ask what the land produced. 'Aches and pains,' the farmer replied; 'Peisistratus ought to take his 10 per cent of the aches and pains too.' The man made the reply not knowing that he was speaking to Peisistratus, while the latter was delighted at his frankness and industriousness, and exempted him from all taxation.

7 Peisistratus did not in general impose any heavy burdens on the people during his rule, but always preserved peace abroad and at home, with the result that it was often said that his reign was a golden age – for when his sons later took over his position their

8 rule was much more severe. The most important facet of all those discussed was that he was naturally inclined to support the common people and was benevolent. It was his aim to govern in accordance with the laws, and not to claim any superior position for himself. He was once summoned for murder before the Areopagus; he appeared in person to make his defence, but his accuser

9 panicked and failed to put in an appearance. This is why he remained in power for a long time, and when expelled recovered his position easily. He was supported by the majority of both nobles and the common people; he attracted the former by his association with them, and the latter by the assistance he gave

10 them in their personal affairs; he was liked by both. Athenian laws about tyranny were mild at the time, and in particular the law about the establishment of a tyrant, which ran as follows: 'This is the law and traditional practice of the Athenians; any man who attempts to establish, or aids in the establishment of, a tyranny shall lose his citizenship together with his family.'

XVII Peisistratus, then, grew old in office, and fell ill and died in the Archonship of Philoneus, having lived for thirty-three years since he first set himself up as tyrant, and having ruled for nineteen of

2 those years; for the remainder he was in exile. From the dates it is manifestly absurd to suggest, as some do, that Peisistratus was loved by Solon, and was general in the war against Megara for possession of Salamis; their ages make it impossible if one calculates each man's life and the date of his death.

3 After Peisistratus' death, his sons ruled, and conducted affairs in the same way. He had two sons by his citizen wife, Hippias and Hipparchus, and two by his Argive wife, Iophon and Hegesis-

4 tratus, who was also called Thettalus. Peisistratus had married Timonassa, the daughter of an Argive from Argos called Gorgilus; she had previously been married to Archinus, the Ambraciot, who

was of the family of the Cypselids. This was the origin of Peisistratus' friendship with Argos; Hegesistratus brought 1,000 men to fight with him at Pallene. Some say that Peisistratus married her during his first exile, others while he was in power.

Their position and age meant that the state was run by Hipparchus and Hippias; Hippias was the older, a natural politician and a wise man, and he presided over the government. Hipparchus was fond of amusements, and interested in love affairs and the arts – he was the man who sent for Anacreon and Simonides and their associates and the other poets. Thettalus was much younger, and violent and outrageous in his behaviour, which was the cause of all their troubles. He fell in love with Harmodius, and when his love was not returned, far from restraining his anger, he gave vent to it viciously; finally, when Harmodius' sister was to carry a basket in the procession at the Panathenaea, he stopped her, and insulted Harmodius as effeminate. Hence Harmodius and Aristogeiton were provoked to their plot, in which many took part. At the time of the Panathenaea, when they were watching for Hippias on the Acropolis (for it so happened that he was receiving the procession while Hipparchus despatched it), they saw one of the conspirators greet Hippias in a friendly way. They thought that they were betrayed. Wishing to achieve something before they were arrested, they went down into the city, and, not waiting for their fellow conspirators, killed Hipparchus as he was organising the procession by the Leocoreum; thus they spoiled the whole attempt. Harmodius was killed immediately by the guards, but Aristogeiton was captured later, and tortured for a long time. Under torture he accused many nobles who were friends of the tyrants of complicity. At first enquiries had been unable to find any trace of the plot, for the story that Hippias had disarmed those in the procession and searched them for daggers is not true, for they did not carry weapons in the procession at that time – it was a later innovation of the democracy. The democrats say that Aristogeiton accused the friends of the tyrants deliberately in order to involve them in impiety and weaken their faction if they killed their friends who were innocent; others say that he was not making it up, but did reveal those who were in the plot. Finally, when, despite all his efforts, death eluded him, he promised that he would implicate many others; having persuaded Hippias to give him his hand as a pledge, he reviled him for giving his hand to the murderer of his brother. This angered Hippias so much that his fury overcame him, and he drew his dagger and killed him.

XIX   After this the tyranny became much more severe; in avenging his brother, Hippias had killed or exiled many people, and was 2 distrusted and hated by all. About three years after the death of Hipparchus, Hippias tried to fortify Munichia because of his unpopularity in the city of Athens; he intended to move his residence there, but while this was going on he was expelled by Cleomenes, the Spartan king, because the Spartans were repeatedly receiving oracles instructing them to end the tyranny at Athens. 3 The reason was this. The Athenian exiles, who were led by the Alcmeonids, could not bring about their return unaided; a number of attempts failed. One of these unsuccessful attempts involved the fortification of Lipsydrium, a point over Mt Parnes; there they were joined by some supporters from the city, but the place was besieged and taken by the tyrants. This was the origin of the well-known drinking song about the disaster which ran:

> Alas, Lipsydrium, betrayer of friends, what heroes you destroyed, men brave in battle and of noble blood; then they showed the quality of their families.

4   Having failed, then, in all other attempts, the Alcmeonids contracted to rebuild the temple at Delphi, and in this way they obtained plenty of money to secure the support of the Spartans. Whenever the Spartans consulted the oracle, the priestess instructed them to free Athens; finally she persuaded them, although they had ties of hospitality with the Peisistratids. The Spartans were swayed no less by the friendship between the Peisi- 5 stratids and the Argives. First, they sent Anchimolus with an army by sea. He was defeated and killed because Cineas the Thessalian came to the help of the Athenians with a thousand cavalry. The Spartans were angered by this, and sent their king, Cleomenes, with a larger force by land; he defeated an attempt by the Thessalian cavalry to prevent his entry into Attica, shut up Hippias inside the so-called Pelargic wall, and besieged him with Athenian help. 6 While he was conducting the siege, it happened that the sons of

the Peisistratids were captured as they attempted to slip out of the city secretly. After their capture, the Peisistratids agreed, in return for the children's safety, to hand over the Acropolis and leave with their own property within a period of five days. This was in the Archonship of Harpactides when they had held the tyranny for about seventeen years after the death of their father; the whole period including their father's reign had lasted forty-nine years.

Cleisthenes

After the fall of the tyranny, there was a struggle between Isagoras xx the son of Teisander, who was a supporter of the tyrants, and Cleisthenes, who was of the family of the Alcmeonids. When Cleisthenes lost power in the political clubs, he won the support of the people by promising them control of the state. The power 2 of Isagoras waned in turn, and he called in Cleomenes again, for he had ties of friendship with him. He persuaded him to 'expel the curse', for the Alcmeonids were thought to be amongst those accursed. Cleisthenes retired into exile, and Cleomenes arrived 3 with a few men and expelled 700 Athenian families as being under the curse. Having done this, he tried to dissolve the *Boule* and to put Isagoras and 300 of his friends in control of the city. The *Boule* resisted and the people gathered; the supporters of Cleomenes and Isagoras fled to the Acropolis. The people surrounded them and besieged them for two days; on the third they let Cleomenes and all those with him go under a truce, and recalled Cleisthenes and 4 the other exiles. The people had taken control of affairs, and Cleisthenes was their leader and champion of the people, for the Alcmeonids had been the group probably most responsible for the expulsion of the tyrants and had stirred up trouble for them for much of the time. Even before the Alcmeonids, Cedon had 5 attacked the tyrants, and therefore his name also figures in the drinking songs:

> Pour a draught also for Cedon, boy, and do not forget him, if it
> is right to pour wine for brave men.

The people trusted Cleisthenes for these reasons. At that time, xxi as their leader, in the fourth year after the overthrow of the tyr-

2 anny which was the Archonship of Isagoras, he first divided all the citizens into ten tribes instead of the earlier four, with the aim of mixing them together so that more might share control of the state. From this arose the saying 'No investigation of tribes' as an

3 answer to those wishing to inquire into ancestry. Then he established a *Boule* of 500 instead of 400, 50 from each tribe; previously there had been 100 from each. His purpose in not splitting the people into twelve tribes was to avoid dividing them according to the *trittyes* which already existed; there were twelve *trittyes* in the

4 four old tribes, and the result would not have been a mixing. He divided Attica into thirty sections, using the demes as the basic unit; ten of the sections were in the city area, ten around the coast and ten inland. He called these sections *trittyes*, and placed three into each tribe by lot, one from each geographical area. He made fellow demesmen of those living in each deme so that they would not reveal the new citizens by usng a man's father's name, but would use his deme in addressing him. Hence the Athenians use

5 their demes as part of their names. He set up demarchs with the same functions as the previous *naucrari*, for the demes took the place of the *naucraries*. Some of the demes he named after their position, others after their founders, for not all were still connec-

6 ted with a particular locality. He left the citizens free to belong to clan groups, and phratries, and hold priesthoods in the traditional way. He gave the tribes ten eponymous heroes selected by the Delphic oracle from a preliminary list of a hundred.

XXII   These changes made the constitution much more democratic than it had been under Solon. A contributory factor was that Solon's laws had fallen into disuse under the tyranny, and Cleisthenes replaced them with others with the aim of winning the

2 people's support; these included the law about ostracism. It was in the fifth year after this constitution was established in the Archonship of Hermocreon, that they formulated the oath which the *Boule* of 500 still take today. At that time they selected the *strategi* by tribes, one from each; the Polemarch was the overall

3 commander of the army. Eleven years later, in the Archonship of Phaenippus, the Athenians won the battle of Marathon. This made the democracy so confident that after a further two years had

passed they first used the law of ostracism; it had been passed from a suspicion of those in power, because Peisistratus had started as leader of the people and *strategus*, and become tyrant. The first 4 to be ostracised was one of his relations, Hipparchus, the son of Charmus of Collytus; it was the desire to expel him which was the primary motive of Cleisthenes in proposing the law. With the customary forbearance of the democracy, the people had allowed the friends of the tyrants to continue to live in Athens with the exception of those who had committed crimes in the civil disorders; their leader and champion was Hipparchus. In the year 5 immediately following, the Archonship of Telesionus, they cast lots for the nine Archons by tribes from the 500 previously elected by the demesmen; this first happened then after the tyranny; all their predecessors were elected. In the same year, Megacles, the son of Hippocrates, from Alopece was ostracised. For three years 6 they ostracised the friends of the tyrants, the original purpose of ostracism, but in the fourth year they also removed anyone else who seemed to be too powerful. The first man to be ostracised who was not connected with the tyranny was Xanthippus, the son of Ariphron.

Two years later, in the Archonship of Nicodemus, when the 7 mines at Maroneia were discovered and the city had a surplus of one hundred talents from their exploitation, some recommended that the money should be distributed to the people. Themistocles prevented this; he did not say for what he would use the money, but recommended that a talent should be lent to each of the hundred wealthiest Athenians. If the people approved of what it was spent on, the expenditure should be borne by the state; if not, they should recover the money from those who had borrowed it. The proposal was approved on these terms, and he had a hundred triremes built, one by each man. This was the fleet in which they fought the barbarians at Salamis. Aristides, the son of Lysimachus, was ostracised at this time.

Three years later, in the Archonship of Hypsichides, because 8 of Xerxes' expedition, they recalled all those who had been ostracised; for the future they decreed that those who had been ostracised should not live nearer to Athens than Geraestus or Scyllaeum under penalty of losing their citizenship for good.

The Areopagus

XXIII Up to this point the city went on growing and developing its democracy by gradual stages, but after the Persian wars the Areopagus became strong again and ran the city, not because it was voted the position but because it had been responsible for the battle of Salamis. When the *strategi* did not know how to handle the situation, and ordered each man to see to his own safety, the Areopagus provided each person with eight drachmae and
2 embarked them in the ships. For this reason the Athenians respected the Areopagus, and were well governed at this time. At the time they paid attention to military training, were respected by the Greeks, and took the hegemony at sea despite the Spartans.
3 The champions of the people at this period were Aristides the son of Lysimachus and Themistocles the son of Neocles, the latter with the reputation of being an expert in military matters, the former a clever politician and an outstandingly just man; therefore they employed the one as a general and the other as a political
4 adviser. These two men worked together over the rebuilding of the walls of Athens despite their differences, but Aristides was the instigator of the defection of the Ionians from the Spartan alliance, when he seized the opportunity offered by the disgrace
5 of the Spartans caused by the behaviour of Pausanias. Hence he was the man who assessed the first list of contributions to be paid by the cities two years after the battle of Salamis, in the Archonship of Timosthenes. He also gave the oath to the Ionians 'to have the same enemies and friends', in the ratification of which they dropped the lumps of iron into the sea.

XXIV Athens' confidence increased and she built up a significant financial reserve; Aristides recommended them to seize the hegemony and to live in the city rather than the countryside; there would be a livelihood for all, some on expeditions, others on garrison duty, and others in government; in this way they would hold
2 the hegemony. The people agreed, took control, and treated their allies more tyrannically except for the peoples of Chios, Lesbos and Samos; they used them as guards of the empire, and so allowed them to retain their own constitutions and such possessions as they had.

The result was also affluence for the masses, as Aristides had 3
suggested. More than 20,000 men earned their living as a result
of the tribute, the taxation and the money the empire brought in.
There were 6,000 *dikastai*, 1,600 archers, and 1,200 cavalry, and
500 members of the *Boule*. There were 500 guards in the docks
and fifty others on the Acropolis; offices in the city occupied up
to 700 men, and up to 700 were employed abroad. In addition to
them, when later they were at war, there were 2,500 hoplites and
twenty guard ships and other ships to carry the tribute employing
2,000 men selected by lot. There were also those maintained by
the state at the Prytaneum or as orphans, and the guards of the
prison. All these people were paid from public funds.

Ephialtes

The people were supported in this way. For about seventeen years xxv
after the Persian wars the constitution remained the same under
the guidance of the Areopagus, although it was gradually deterior-
ating. Then, with the increase of the power of the masses, Ephialtes the son of Sophonides became champion of the people; he
had a reputation for incorruptibility and justice in public life. He
launched an attack on the Areopagus. First, he removed many of 2
its members on charges of administrative misconduct. Then, in
the Archonship of Conon, he stripped it of all its additional
powers including the guardianship of the constitution; he distributed them among the *Boule*, the *Ekklesia* and the *dikasteria*. He 3
was aided in the reforms by Themistocles, who was a member of
the Areopagus, but was facing a charge of treason with Persia.
Because Themistocles wanted the Areopagus to be ruined, he told
Ephialtes that they were intending to arrest him, and told the
Areopagus that he would lay information against certain persons
who were plotting to overthrow the constitution. Then he took a
group selected by the Areopagus to the place where Ephialtes was,
ostensibly to show them a meeting of the conspirators, and talked
with them seriously. Ephialtes was so alarmed when he saw this
that he took refuge at an altar dressed in a suppliant's single garment. Everyone was amazed at what happened, and there followed 4
a meeting of the *Boule* at which Ephialtes and Themistocles made
accusations against the members of the Areopagus. They repeated

these accusations before the *Ekklesia* until they succeeded in depriving them of their power ... Ephialtes also died shortly afterwards, murdered by Aristodicus of Tanagra.

XXVI   The Areopagus lost its supervisory powers in this way. In the years which followed, the enthusiasm of the demagogues led to an increasing absence of control in political life. It happened that at this time the better citizens were without a leader, for their principal spokesman, Cimon the son of Miltiades, was rather young and had only recently entered public life, and in addition to this the masses had been decimated in war. Military service at that period depended on the citizen rolls, and the *strategi* in charge were militarily inexperienced but respected for the achievements of their ancestors; the result was that two or three thousand of the men on any expedition were killed, and the better men from both the upper classes and the mass of the people were decimated.

2   In their administration the Athenians did not pay the same amount of attention to the laws as they had done in earlier periods; they made no innovation affecting the selection of the nine Archons, except that in the sixth year after the death of Ephialtes they decided to admit *zeugitae* to the preliminary selection of those from whom the nine Archons would be selected by lot. The first member of this class to be Archon was Mnesitheides; all previous Archons had been *hippeis* or *pentacosiomedimni*, while the *zeugitae* had held only the ordinary offices, unless any of the legal restric-

3   tions had been disregarded. Four years later, in the Archonship of Lysicrates, the thirty justices were re-established who were

4   known as the magistrates of the demes. Two years later, in the Archonship of Antidotus, because of the large size of the citizen body, it was enacted, on the proposal of Pericles, that those whose parents were not both citizens should not themselves be citizens.

XXVII   After this, Pericles became one of the leaders of the people, first becoming famous when he was a young man and prosecuted Cimon at his *euthuna* as *strategus*. With Pericles, the state became still more democratic; he deprived the Areopagus of some of its powers and turned the state particularly towards naval power, with the result that the masses had the courage to take more into their

2   own hands in all fields of government. Forty-eight years after the

battle of Salamis, in the Archonship of Pythodorus, the Peloponnesian War broke out; during this the citizens were shut up inside
the city walls, and grew accustomed to earn their living by military
service, and decided, partly consciously and partly through the
force of circumstances, to run the state themselves. Pericles intro- 3
duced pay for those serving in the *dikasteria* as a political move
to counter the effects of Cimon's wealth. Cimon possessed a kingly
fortune, and not merely performed his public liturgies magnifi-
cently but also maintained many of the members of his deme, for
any member of the deme of Laciadae who wished could come to
him every day and receive adequate maintenance, and all his
estates were unfenced so that anyone who wished could help himself to the fruit. Pericles' wealth was not adequate to match such 4
liberality, and Damonides of Oea, who was thought to have suggested most of Pericles' measures, and was later ostracised for this
very reason, suggested to him that since he could not match
Cimon in private resources, he should give the people what was
their own; Pericles accepted his advice, and arranged pay for the
dikastai. Some say that the quality of *dikastai* declined, since it
was always the ordinary people rather than the more respectable
who took care to ensure that their names were included in the
ballot for places on the juries. This was also the beginning of 5
corruption of the *dikastai*, the first instance being Anytus after he
was *strategus* at Pylos; he had been accused over the loss of Pylos,
but bribed the court and was acquitted.

Throughout the period of Pericles' ascendancy the state was run xxviii
reasonably well, but after his death there was a marked decline. It
was then that the people first got a leader who was not approved
by the respectable citizens; before this the leaders had always come
from this class. The first leader of the people was Solon, and he 2
was followed by Peisistratus, both of them aristocrats of good
family. After the fall of the tyranny there was Cleisthenes, an
Alcmeonid, and he had no opponent after the expulsion of Isagoras
and his supporters. Then Xanthippus was the leader of the people
and Miltiades leader of the aristocrats; then came Themistocles
and Aristides. After them, Ephialtes led the people and Cimon the
wealthier classes; then Pericles led the people while Thucydides, a
relative by marriage of Cimon, led the other group. After the death 3

of Pericles, Nicias, who died in Sicily, was the leader of the upper classes, while Cleon the son of Cleaenetus led the people. The latter appears to have corrupted the people more than anyone else by his violence; he was the first to shout when addressing the people, he used abusive language, and addressed the *Ekklesia* with his garments tucked up when it was customary to speak properly dressed. After them, Theramenes the son of Hagnon was leader of the other group, while the leader of the people was Cleophon the lyre-maker who introduced the two-obol payment. This was paid for some time and then was abolished by Callicrates of Paeania; he first promised to add a third obol to the distribution. Both these last two politicians were later condemned to death, for, even if the people are deceived for a while, they tend later to hate those who have induced them to follow an unsuitable course of action.

4 After Cleophon there was an unbroken series of demagogues whose main aim was to be outrageous and please the people with no thought for anything but the present.

5 The best leaders in Athens after the early period seem to have been Nicias, Thucydides and Theramenes. Almost everyone agrees that Nicias and Thucydides were not only true gentlemen and good politicians, but also that they looked after the city like fathers. There is some dispute about Theramenes because he happened to live at a time of political turmoil. If one avoids a superficial judgement, he does not appear to have destroyed all constitutions, as hostile assessments suggest, but to have supported all so long as they did nothing illegal; he was capable of taking part in politics under all forms of government – the mark of a good citizen – but refused to support and hated regimes which disregarded the law.

The Four Hundred

xxix To resume, as long as the fortunes of war were reasonably evenly balanced, the democracy was preserved, but when after the disaster in Sicily the Spartan side gained a considerable advantage because of their alliance with the king of Persia, the Athenians were forced to change their democracy into the regime of the Four Hundred. Melobius delivered the speech introducing the resolution, and Pythodorus of the deme Anaphlystus drafted the motion. The decisive consideration in winning over the majority of the people was the belief that the king of Persia would be more likely to make a military alliance with them if their government was oligarchic. The decree of Pythodorus ran as follows: the 2 people should choose another twenty men from those over forty years of age to join the emergency committee of ten already in existence; they should take an oath to formulate such measures as were in the best interests of the state, and should make proposals for its safety; anybody else was at liberty to make proposals so that they might select the best of all the suggestions. Cleitophon 3 added a rider to the proposal of Pythodorus, to the effect that those chosen should search out the traditional laws passed by Cleisthenes when he established the democracy, in order that they might assist their deliberations; the reasoning was that Cleisthenes' constitution was not democratic but similar to that of Solon.

The first proposal of the committee when selected was that it 4 should be obligatory for the Prytanies to put to the vote all proposals which related to the safety of the state; then they suspended the statute of indictment for illegal proposals and all impeachments and summonses so that any Athenian who wished could make proposals about what was being discussed. If anyone punished, summonsed or brought before a court anyone for doing so, he should immediately be indicted and brought before the *strategi*, and they should hand him over to the Eleven for execution.

After these preliminaries, they laid down the following prin- 5 ciples: all money accruing to the state was to be spent on the war and nothing else; nobody was to receive pay for any office for the duration of the war except the nine Archons and the Prytanies of the period, who should receive three obols each per day. The rest of the administration for the duration of the war should be put in the hands of those Athenians best qualified in person and property to serve the state, up to a total of not less than five thousand. They should have the power to make treaties with whomsoever they wished. The people should elect ten men from each tribe over forty years old who should in their turn select the five thousand under an oath taken on unblemished sacrificial victims.

These were the proposals which the chosen committee put for- xxx ward. When they had been passed, the Five Thousand chose a hundred of their own members to draw up the constitution. The

proposals which were drafted and put forward by them ran as
2 follows. The *Boule* is to consist of men over thirty years of age
on a yearly basis without pay. From their number should come
the *strategi*, the nine Archons, the *hieromnemon*, the commanders
of the tribal hoplite and cavalry units, the cavalry commanders
and the commanders of garrisons, as also the ten Treasurers of
the treasury of Athena and the other gods, the twenty *Hellenotamiae*, who were also to take charge of all the other sacred funds,
ten in charge of sacrifices and ten overseers. All these officials
should be chosen from a larger group elected from the *Boule* in
office at the time. All other offices should be filled by lot by men
not members of the *Boule*; the *Hellenotamiae* who actually handled
3 the finances should not sit in the *Boule*. Four *Boulai* should be
established for the future from the specified age group, and one
section, selected by lot, should act as the *Boule*; the other citizens
should be allocated among the sections. The hundred on the draft-
ing committee should divide themselves and the others as equally
as possible into four sections, cast lots between the sections, and
4 the term of office of a *Boule* should be one year. The members
of the *Boule* were to take whatever decisions seemed best to them
both to ensure the preservation of Athens' financial resources and
their use for necessary purposes, and in other fields. If they wished
to discuss a matter with a wider group, each member could call
in an associate of his own choosing from the same age-group.
The *Boule* should meet once every five days unless more frequent
5 meetings were felt to be necessary. The nine Archons were to
handle the drawing of lots for the *Boule*, while five men selected
by lot from the *Boule* should count votes, and one man should be
selected by lot from them each day to put motions to the vote.
The five selected by lot should also cast lots among those who
wished to address the *Boule* in the following order of precedence:
first priests, second heralds, third embassies, fourth any other persons. The *strategi* should have the right of addressing the *Boule*
6 on matters of war without having to draw lots for precedence. A
member of the *Boule* who failed to attend at the Bouleutereum at
the appointed hour was to be fined a drachma per day's absence
unless he had obtained permission to be away from the *Boule*.

XXXI They drafted the above constitution for the future, and put forward the following interim proposals. There should be a *Boule* of 400 according to tradition, forty from each tribe to be chosen from a group previously elected by their fellow tribesmen from those over thirty years old. The *Boule* was to appoint the office-holders and draft the oath which they were to take, and take such measures as seemed beneficial about the laws, the *euthunai* and other matters. They were to observe such laws as might be passed 2 in the constitutional field, and might not change them or enact others. The *strategi* for the moment were to be selected from all the Five Thousand; when the *Boule* had been established and had held an inspection in full armour, it was to select ten men as *strategi* and a clerk for them, and those selected were to hold office for the following year with full powers, and consult the *Boule* if they needed to. They were to choose one cavalry commander and 3 ten commanders of the tribal cavalry units; in the future the *Boule* were to choose these officers according to the proposals. Neither they nor anyone else might hold any other office more than once except for membership of the *Boule* or being a *strategus*. For the future, the hundred men are to allot the Four Hundred among the four sections so that they may take part when the citizens join the rest in membership of the *Boule*.

The hundred men chosen by the Five Thousand drafted these xxxii proposals. When they were enacted by the main body under the presidency of Aristomachus, the *Boule* of the year of Callias' Archonship was dissolved on the fourteenth day of Thargelion before finishing its year of office, and the Four Hundred took office on the twenty-second of the same month. The demo-cratically selected *Boule* for the next year ought to have taken office on the fourteenth of Scirophorion. So the oligarchy was 2 established in the Archonship of Callias, about a hundred years after the expulsion of the tyrants; the main instigators of it were Peisander, Antiphon and Theramenes, who were well born and had the reputation of being outstanding in intelligence and judge-ment. When this constitution was established, the Five Thousand 3 were only nominally chosen; the Four Hundred, together with the ten *strategi* with full powers, entered the Bouleutereum and ruled the city. They sent a proposal of peace to the Spartans on the basis that each side should retain what it held. When the Spartans refused unless Athens surrendered her maritime power, they abandoned the proposal.

XXXIII The constitution of the Four Hundred lasted about four months, and Mnasilochus of their number was Archon for two months in the Archonship of Theopompus, who was Archon for the remaining ten months. When the Athenians were defeated in the sea battle near Eretria and the whole of Euboea revolted except for Oreus, they were more incensed by the disaster than any previous defeat, for Euboea was of more service to them than Attica at the time; they therefore overthrew the Four Hundred, and handed over the conduct of affairs to the Five Thousand who provided their own armour, passing a decree that there should be

2 no pay for office. Those most responsible for the overthrow were Aristocrates and Theramenes; they did not agree with what was being done by the Four Hundred, for they decided everything themselves, and referred nothing to the Five Thousand. The constitution at this time appears to have been a good one, for they were at war, and power belonged to those who provided their own armour.

Democracy restored

XXXIV The people shortly overthrew the Five Thousand. In the seventh year after the overthrow of the Four Hundred, which was the Archonship of Callias from Angele, the battle at Arginusae was fought. Thereafter, first the ten *strategi* who won the battle were all condemned by a single vote, although some had not been present at the battle and others had been rescued by other ships; the people had been misled by those who were enraged by what had happened. Then, when the Spartans were willing to surrender Decelea and make peace on the basis of the status quo, some were in favour, but the people rejected the proposal; they were deceived by Cleophon who came into the *Ekklesia* drunk and wearing his breastplate, and prevented peace being made. He said he would not permit it unless the Spartans surrendered all the cities they

2 had taken. Their mistake was brought home to them shortly afterwards; in the next year, the Archonship of Alexias, they lost the battle of Aegospotami, as a result of which Lysander became

master of the city and established the Thirty in the following way. The peace terms specified that the Athenians should be governed 3 by their ancestral constitution; on this basis the democrats tried to preserve the democracy, while the nobles who belonged to the political clubs and the exiles who had returned after the peace wanted an oligarchy. Those who did not belong to any political club, but were in other respects admirable citizens, aimed at establishing the ancestral constitution; among them were Archinus, Anytus, Cleitophon, Phormisius and many others, and their leader was Theramenes. Lysander sided with the oligarchs, overawed the people, and forced them to vote an oligarchy into power on the proposal of Dracontides of Aphidna.

The Thirty and the Ten

So the Thirty were established in the Archonship of Pythodorus. xxxv When they had secured their power in the city, they disregarded the proposals which had been passed about the constitution except for appointing five hundred members of the *Boule* and the other magistrates from a group previously elected from the thousand, and choosing ten colleagues to govern the Peiraeus, eleven guards for the prison and three hundred whip-bearers as their attendants; in this way they controlled the city. At first they behaved with 2 restraint towards the citizens, and pretended to be aiming at the ancestral constitution; they took down from the Areopagus the laws of Ephialtes and Archestratus about the members of that body, repealed disputed laws of Solon, and abolished the power of the *dikastai*; they claimed to be correcting the constitution and removing ambiguities. For example, they made it legal for a man to leave his property to anyone he wished without restraint, abolishing the irritating provisos 'unless he be of unsound mind, incapacitated by age, or under the influence of a woman'; their aim was to eliminate opportunities for informers. They made other 3 similar reforms. They carried these measures at an early stage, and they got rid of the informers and the wicked mischief-makers who flattered the people to their disadvantage. The people were delighted, thinking they made these changes for the best of motives.

When the Thirty had tightened their grip on the city, there 4 was no type of citizen they did not attack. They killed those remarkable for wealth, family or reputation, aiming to remove any potential threat and to lay their hands on their property. After a short time they had killed no less than fifteen hundred men.

xxxvi   The city was being undermined in this way, and Theramenes was angry at what was happening; he urged the Thirty to stop behaving so outrageously, and to give the best citizens a share in government. They opposed him at first, but when stories of Theramenes' proposals leaked out, and the people supported him, they were afraid that he might become the people's champion and overthrow their regime; they therefore compiled a list of three thousand citizens who were to receive a share in the government.

2   Theramenes attacked this move too, firstly because in aiming to share power with the respectable element they restricted it to three thousand as if virtue were restricted to a body of this size, and secondly on the grounds that they were attempting two totally conflicting things, to base their regime on force and yet create a regime weaker than those it ruled. The Thirty disregarded these criticisms, but postponed publication of the list of the Three Thousand for a long time, and kept the names of those who had been chosen secret; when they did decide to publish it, they cut out some who had been included and included others who had not been on the original list.

xxxvii   When it was already winter, the Thirty led a military expedition against Thrasybulus and the exiles who had seized Phyle, and were defeated; they therefore decided to disarm the citizens and kill Theramenes. This they achieved by laying two laws before the *Boule* and ordering their approval. The first gave the Thirty full power to execute any citizen whose name was not included on the list of the Three Thousand. The second deprived of all rights under the present constitution anyone who had taken part in the destruction of the fort at Eëtioneia or had acted in any way in opposition to the Four Hundred who had established the previous oligarchy. Theramenes had done both, with the result that when the laws were passed he lost his citizen rights, and the

2   Thirty had the power to execute him. After Theramenes had been executed, they disarmed all except the Three Thousand, and the

savagery and wickedness of their regime increased considerably. They sent an embassy to Sparta which specified charges against Theramenes and asked for help; the Spartans sent Callibius as harmost, and about seven hundred men who garrisoned the Acropolis.

The exiles from Phyle then seized Munichia, and defeated an XXXVIII attempt by the Thirty and their adherents to dislodge them. The men from the city returned after the battle, met in the Agora the next day, and deposed the Thirty and elected ten citizens with full powers to bring the war to an end. After taking office, they did nothing to further the purpose for which they had been chosen, but sent to Sparta for help and to borrow money. Those 2 who had full citizen rights were angry at this, and the Ten were afraid that they might be overthrown; therefore, with the aim of terrifying the people (in which they were successful), they seized one of the most outstanding citizens, called Demaretus, and executed him. The result was that they had firm control of affairs with the backing of Callibius and the Spartan garrison and also that of a number of the Athenian *hippeis*, for some of them were particularly keen that the exiles from Phyle should not return to Athens.

Democracy finally restored

The group which held the Peiraeus and Munichia gradually 3 gained the upper hand in the war as the whole people went over to their side, and so the men in the city deposed the Ten who had first been elected, and chose another ten men with the reputation of being outstanding citizens; it was under them that the reconciliation was arranged and the democracy returned, and they worked enthusiastically to this end. Their main leaders were Rhinon of Paeania and Phaullus of Acherdus; they were negotiating with the men in the Peiraeus before Pausanias arrived, and after he had come joined in supporting the return of the exiles. 4 The peace and the end of the hostilities was brought about by Pausanias, the Spartan king and the ten mediators who later came from Sparta at his request. Rhinon and his friends were commended for their goodwill towards the democracy, and, although they had taken office under an oligarchy, they underwent their *euthuna* under a democracy; however, nobody brought a single complaint against them – neither the men who had stayed in the city nor those who had returned from the Peiraeus. On the contrary, because of what he had done Rhinon was immediately elected *strategus*.

xxxix   The reconciliation was brought about in the Archonship of Eucleides on the following terms. Those of the Athenians who had remained in the city and wished to leave should live in Eleusis, where they should retain full citizen rights, have complete self-

2 government and enjoy their incomes. The temple was to be common to both sides, under the traditional control of the Ceryces and the Eumolpidae. Those living at Eleusis were not allowed to visit the city of Athens, nor were those living in Athens allowed to visit Eleusis, with the exception for both sides of the celebration of the Mysteries. The people at Eleusis were to contribute to a defence fund from their revenues like the other Athen-

3 ians. If any of those leaving the city took over a house at Eleusis, they were to do it with the agreement of the owner; if agreement proved impossible, each was to select three assessors, and the owner was to accept the price they fixed. Any inhabitants of Eleusis acceptable to the new settlers were to live with them there.

4 Those wishing to move out to Eleusis had to register within ten days of the swearing of the reconciliation oaths if they were in the city at the time, and move out within twenty; those abroad at the time had the same periods from the moment when they

5 returned to Athens. Nobody living at Eleusis could hold any office in the city of Athens until he had been registered as having moved his residence back to the city. Homicide trials in cases where someone had killed or wounded a person with his own hands were

6 to be conducted in accordance with traditional practice. There was to be a total amnesty covering everyone except the Thirty, the Eleven and the ten governors of the Peiraeus; even they were to be immune from prosecution once they had submitted to the *euthuna*. The *euthuna* for the governors of the Peiraeus was to be held before the citizens of the Peiraeus, while those who had held office in the city were to appear before citizens with taxable prop-

erty there. On this basis those who wished to could leave the city. Each side was to repay separately the money which it had borrowed for the war.

After the conclusion of a settlement along these lines, those who XL had fought with the Thirty were afraid, and many intended to move out of the city, but put off registration until the last moment, as men always do. Archinus saw the number involved, and cancelled the remaining days for registration because he wished to keep them in the city; many were compelled to remain, much against their will, until they recovered their confidence. This was 2 a sound move by Archinus, as was his later indictment of Thrasybulus for illegal proposals when the latter tried to give citizenship to all who had had a part in the return from the Peiraeus although some were manifestly slaves. A third good move was when he seized one of the returned exiles who was attempting to disregard the amnesty, brought him before the *Boule*, and persuaded them to execute him without trial. He argued that their actions would show whether they intended to preserve the democracy and stand by their oaths; if they let the man go, they would encourage others, while if they executed him, they would establish an example for all. This is just what happened, for after his execution nobody ever again tried to flout the amnesty. The Athenians appear to 3 have handled their affairs, both private and public, as well and with as much statesmanship as any people ever have shown in a similar situation. They not only refused to entertain any charges based on previous events, but they also repaid as a state the money which the Thirty had borrowed from the Spartans for the war, although the agreement had specified that the men of the city and those of the Peiraeus should repay their debts separately; they felt that this ought to be the first step in restoring unity and concord in the state. In other states the democrats, far from making contributions themselves in similar circumstances, redistribute the land. Athens was reunited with Eleusis in the third year after the oli- 4 garchs moved there, in the Archonship of Xenainetus.

That final reconciliation happened subsequently. When the XLI people regained power they established the constitution which is

still in force, in the Archonship of Pythodorus . . . It was just that the people should take control because they had secured their
2 return by their own efforts. This was the eleventh change of constitution. The first was the modification of the original constitution when Ion and those with him came to Athens; it was then that the Athenians were first divided into the four tribes and established the tribe kings. The second change, the first after this which had the status of a constitution, was under Theseus, and moved the state a little away from absolute monarchy. After this came the constitution of the time of Draco, under which the Athenians first had written laws. The third change after the period of dissension came under Solon; it sowed the seeds of democracy. The fourth was the tyranny under Peisistratus. The fifth, after the fall of the tyranny, was the constitution of Cleisthenes, which was more democratic than that of Solon. The sixth came after the Persian wars, when the Areopagus had overall control. For the seventh, which followed this one, Aristides showed the way, but Ephialtes brought it to completion by depriving the Areopagus of power. Under this constitution the city made innumerable mistakes under the guidance of the demagogues because of their control of the sea. The eighth was the establishment of the Four Hundred, while the ninth followed it with the return of the democracy. The tenth was the tyranny of the Thirty and the Ten. The eleventh came after the return from Phyle and the Peiraeus; it has lasted to the present day with ever-increasing power being assumed by the people. They have made themselves supreme in all fields; they run everything by decrees of the *Ekklesia* and by decisions of the *dikasteria* in which the people are supreme. For the judicial powers of the *Boule* have passed to the people, which seems a correct development, for a small number are more open to corruption by bribery or favours than a large.

3   At first the Athenians declined to institute pay for attendance at the *Ekklesia*. When attendance was poor, and the Prytanies had tried many devices to encourage citizens to come so that the people might ratify proposals by their vote, payment of one obol was instituted as a first move on the proposal of Agyrrhius; Heracleides of Clazomenae, who was called 'the king', raised it to two obols, and Agyrrhius made it three.

The present constitution

The constitution of the present day is as follows. Full citizenship XLII
belongs to men both of whose parents were citizens, and they are
inscribed on the list with their fellow demesmen when they are
eighteen years old. When they are being registered, the members
of the deme vote under oath first on whether they appear to have
reached the legal age, and if they do not, they are returned to the
status of children, and secondly on whether a man is free and
born as the laws prescribe. If they decide that he is not free, he
appeals to the *dikasterion*, while the demesmen select five of their
number as accusers; if it is decided that he has no right to be
registered as a citizen, the city sells him into slavery, but if he
wins his case, the demesmen are required to register him. Then 2
the *Boule* reviews those who have been registered, and if it is
decided that a man is younger than eighteen, the demesmen who
registered him are fined. When the Ephebes have been approved,
their fathers meet by tribes and choose under oath three members
of the tribe over forty years old whom they consider best and most
suitable to take charge of the Ephebes, and from them the people
elect one for each tribe as guardian, and they elect a controller
from the rest of the citizen body for all of them. These men take 3
the Ephebes, and after visiting the temples they go to the Peiraeus
and take up guard duties, some at Munichia and others at Acte.
The people also elect two trainers for them, and two men to teach
them to fight in armour, and to use the bow, the javelin and the
catapult. The guardians receive a drachma each for their maintenance, and the Ephebes four obols. Each guardian receives the
allowances for the members of his tribe and buys what is necessary
for them all centrally (for they live together by tribes), and takes
care of everything else for them. This is how they spend the first
year of their training. At the beginning of the second, at a meeting 4
of the *Ekklesia* held in the theatre, they demonstrate to the people
their knowledge of warfare, and receive a shield and spear from
the city. For the year thereafter they patrol the countryside and 5
man the guard posts. For their two years' service they wear the
military cloak, and are exempt from all duties. They cannot pros-
ecute or be prosecuted so that there may be no reason for their
leaving their post; the only exception is to deal with matters of

inheritance or an *epikleros*, or to take up a priesthood hereditary in a man's family. After this two years, they join the main citizen body.

XLIII   That is how citizens are registered and Ephebes trained. The holders of all routine offices in the state are selected by lot except for the treasurer of the military funds, the controllers of the Theoric Fund and the supervisor of the water supply. These are elected, and hold office from one Panathenaic festival to the next. All military officials are also elected.

2   The *Boule* of 500 members is selected by lot, fifty from each tribe. Each tribe acts as Prytany in an order decided by lot, the first four for thirty-six days each, the last six for thirty-five, for

3 they work by a lunar year. The Prytanies eat together in the Tholus at the city's expense, and summon meetings of the *Boule* and *Ekklesia*; the *Boule* meets every day except for holidays, the *Ekklesia* four times in every prytany. They publish the agenda and place for each meeting of the *Boule*, and also draw up the

4 agenda for the *Ekklesia*. In each prytany the *Ekklesia* meets for one plenary session, in which there must be a vote on whether all office-holders have performed their duties well; there must also be discussions of the corn supply and the safety of Attica; those who wish to bring impeachments do so at this meeting, lists of confiscated property are read out, and also claims to inheritances and to marry *epikleroi*, so that nobody may be ignorant of any

5 unclaimed estates. In the sixth prytany, in addition to the business already discussed, they put to the vote the question of whether an ostracism should be held, and hear accusations against informers, whether Athenians or metics (with a limit of three of each), and allegations against anyone who has failed to fulfil an undertaking

6 made to the city. The second meeting must hear petitioners, and anyone who wishes may appear as a suppliant on any subject he chooses, private or public, and address the people on it. The other two meetings deal with other matters, amongst which the law prescribes the consideration of three motions about sacred matters, three concerning heralds and embassies, and three about secular matters. On occasions they also consider matters without a preliminary vote. Heralds and ambassadors report to the Prytanies first, and despatches are delivered to them.

One man is picked as chairman of the Prytanies by lot, and xliv
holds office for a night and a day; he cannot preside for longer,
nor can the same man serve twice. He holds the keys of the sanctuaries where the treasure and the public records are kept; he holds
the city's seal, and must remain in the Tholus with one-third of
the Prytanies selected by him. When the Prytanies summon a 2
meeting of the *Boule* or *Ekklesia*, he casts lots for nine chairmen,
one from each tribe except the one supplying the Prytany; he casts
lots again among the nine for the man who will actually preside,
and he hands over the agenda to them. The nine take over, and 3
are responsible for good order, put forward topics for discussion,
assess the voting, and control everything else. They also have the
right to adjourn the meeting. An individual may not preside at a
meeting more than once in a year, nor be one of the nine chairmen
more than once in each prytany.

They elect *strategi*, cavalry commanders and other military 4
officers in the *Ekklesia* in accordance with the will of the people;
the elections are held on the first meeting after the sixth prytany
when the omens are favourable. There must also be a preliminary
resolution to hold the elections.

In former times the *Boule* had powers of punishment by fine, xlv
imprisonment or execution. Once when the *Boule* had handed
Lysimachus over to the public executioner and he was already
sitting waiting for the sentence to be carried out, Eumelides of
Alopece saved him, saying that no citizen ought to be executed
without a vote of the *dikasterion*. When the *dikasterion* heard the
case, Lysimachus was acquitted and was nicknamed 'the man who
escaped the rod'. The people deprived the *Boule* of all powers of
fine, imprisonment or execution, and passed a law that if the *Boule*
condemned a man or punished him, the *Thesmothetae* were to
bring the condemnations or punishments before the *dikasterion*
and their decision should be final.

The *Boule* conducts the investigations into the conduct of the 2
great majority of the magistrates, particularly those who handle
money; their decision is not final, but subject to appeal to the
dikasterion. Private citizens can bring a charge of acting illegally
against any office-holder they wish; he has a right of appeal to

3 the *dikasterion* if condemned by the *Boule*. It also considers the credentials of the following year's *Boule* and of the nine Archons; in the past, their decision was final, but now there is a right of appeal to the *dikasterion* for those disqualified.

4 In these matters, then, the *Boule* does not have the final decision, but it holds a preliminary discussion on everything that is to come before the people, nor can the people vote on anything that has not been previously discussed by them and put on the agenda by the Prytanies. Anyone who violates this law is liable to a prosecution for an illegal proposal.

XLVI The *Boule* is in charge of the completed triremes, the tackle stores and the ship sheds, and builds new triremes or quadriremes, whichever the people vote to construct, and tackle and ship sheds for them, but the people elect the naval architects for the ships. If the *Boule* do not hand them over to the new *Boule* completed, they cannot receive the usual reward, for they receive the reward under the next *Boule*. The triremes are constructed under the 2 supervision of a board of ten members of the *Boule*. The *Boule* inspects all public buildings, and if it decides that someone has committed an offence, it reports him to the people, and hands him over to the *dikasterion* if they find him guilty.

XLVII The *Boule* also joins the other magistrates in most areas of the administration. First, there are ten Treasurers of Athena, one picked by lot from each tribe; in accordance with Solon's law (which is still in force) they must be *pentacosiomedimni*, but the man picked by lot holds office even if he is very poor. These officers take over in front of the *Boule* the image of Athena and the Victories, and the other ceremonial equipment and the money. 2 Then there are the ten *poletae* picked by lot, one from each tribe. They let out all the public contracts, sell the right to work the mines, and let the rights of collecting taxes with the treasurer of military affairs and those in charge of the Theoric Fund; this is done in front of the *Boule*. They confirm the position of anyone elected by the *Boule*, and matters concerning mining leases which have been sold, both those where rights of exploitation have been sold for a period of three years and those where special agreements cover a period of ten years. They sell the property of those exiled by the Areopagus and of other exiles before the *Boule*, and the nine Archons confirm the transaction. They list on whitened boards taxes sold for a period of a year with the name of the buyer and the price. They hand the boards over to the *Boule*. They list 3 separately on ten boards those who have to pay their instalments every prytany, on three boards those who have to pay three times a year, and on a separate list those who pay once a year in the ninth prytany. They also list the properties and houses confiscated and sold in the *dikasterion*, for they are responsible for their sale. The price of a house must be paid in five years, of land in ten; these payments are made in the ninth prytany. The King Archon 4 produces a list of the leases of the sacred estates on whitened boards; they are leased for a period of ten years, and the rent is payable in the ninth prytany. For this reason a great deal of money is collected in this prytany. Lists of the payments due are 5 deposited with the *Boule*, and the state secretary keeps them; when a payment is due, he takes from the pigeon holes the list of those whose payments are due on this particular day, and whose entry must be cancelled after payment, and hands it over to the Receivers; the other lists are stored separately so that nothing may be prematurely cancelled.

There are ten Receivers, one picked by lot per tribe; they take XLVIII the lists, and in front of the *Boule* in its chamber erase the record of the money that has been paid, and return the records to the state secretary. If anyone fails to pay an instalment, his name is recorded there, and he has to pay double the arrears under penalty of imprisonment. The *Boule* has the legal right to exact the money or imprison the defaulter. On one day they receive all the pay- 2 ments and divide the money among the magistrates, and on the next they bring a record of their actions on a board and read it out in the chamber. They also pose the question in the *Boule* whether anyone knows of any malpractice by a magistrate or a private citizen in the division; if anyone is suspected, there is a vote on the case.

The members of the *Boule* select ten of their number by lot as 3 auditors to check the accounts of the magistrates every prytany. They also select by lot one man from each tribe for the *euthuna* 4 and two assistants for each of them. They are required to sit each market-day by the statue of the eponymous hero of their tribe, and if anyone wishes to bring a charge, whether of public misdemeanour or private malfeasance, against any of those who have undergone the *euthuna* in the *dikasterion* within three days of that hearing, he records on a whitened board the names of the accuser and the defendant, the charge, and the fine which he considers 5 suitable, and hands it to the representative of his tribe. The latter takes it and reads it, and if he considers the charge justified, he hands a private suit to the deme justices who prepare cases for the relevant tribe for the courts, while if it is a public offence, he reports the matter to the *Thesmothetae*. If the *Thesmothetae* take it over, they reopen the examination of this man before the *dikasterion*, and the decision of the jury is final.

XLIX   The *Boule* also reviews the horses, and if a man appears to have a good horse but to be maintaining it badly, deprives him of his maintenance allowance. Horses which cannot keep up, or will not remain in line but run away, are branded with a wheel on the jaw, and are disqualified. They also review the mounted skirmishers to find who seem to be suitable for this, and anyone they vote against loses his horse. They also review the infantry attached to 2 the cavalry, and anyone voted against loses his pay. The cavalry are enrolled by a board of ten elected by the people for this purpose; the names of those enrolled are handed to the cavalry commanders and the commanders of the tribal cavalry units who receive the list and bring it before the *Boule*. They open the document in which the names of the cavalrymen are recorded, and erase the names of those previously enrolled who swear that they are prevented by physical disability from serving as cavalry. Then they call those newly enrolled, and if anyone swears that he is physically or financially incapable of serving, they dismiss him. Those who do not take this oath are subject to a vote by the *Boule* as to their suitability for cavalry service; if they are approved, they are enrolled, if not they are dismissed.

3   The *Boule* used to take decisions about the models and the robe, but this is now done by a *dikasterion* selected by lot, for it was felt that the *Boule* was swayed by personal feelings. The *Boule* joins the treasurer of military affairs in supervising the making of the statues of Victory and the prizes for the Panathenaea.

The *Boule* also reviews the incapable; for there is a law that 4
anyone with property of less than three minae who suffers from
a physical disability which prevents his undertaking any employment should come before the *Boule*, and if his claim is approved
he should receive two obols a day subsistence from public funds.
There is a treasurer selected by lot to handle this.

The *Boule* also cooperates with the other magistrates in most 5
of what they do.

Those then are the areas of administration handled by the L
Boule.

A board of ten are also selected by lot to take care of the sanctuaries; they are given thirty minae by the Receivers, and repair the
temples most in need of attention. There are ten city com- 2
missioners, of whom five hold office in the Peiraeus and five in
the city itself. They see that the girls who play the flute, the harp
or the lyre are not hired for more than two drachmae; if more
than one man wishes to hire the same performer, they cast lots,
and allocate her to the winner. They ensure that the dung collec-
tors do not deposit dung within ten stades of the walls, and see
that no building either obstructs or has balconies overhanging the
streets; they also prevent the construction of waste pipes with out-
falls from above into the street, or windows with shutters opening
into the road. With assistants provided by the state, they remove
the corpses of those who die in the streets.

Ten superintendents of the markets are selected by lot, five for LI
the Peiraeus and five for the city. They are required by law to
supervise goods for sale to ensure that merchandise is pure and
unadulterated. Ten inspectors of weights and measures are simi- 2
larly selected, five for the city and five for the Peiraeus, to ensure
that honest weights and measures are used by those who are selling. There used to be ten commissioners in charge of the corn 3
supply, picked by lot, of whom five were allocated to the Peiraeus
and five to the city, but there are now twenty for the city and
fifteen for the Peiraeus. They ensure first that there is no sharp
practice in the selling of unprepared corn in the market, secondly
that the millers should sell their barley flour at a price corresponding to that of unmilled barley, and thirdly that the bakers should

sell loaves at a price corresponding to the price of wheat, and containing the full weight which the commissioners have laid

4 down as the law requires them to do. They also pick by lot ten commissioners of trade to supervise trading and ensure that two-thirds of the corn imported is brought to the city.

LII The Eleven whose duty it is to take care of prisoners are selected by lot. They execute thieves, kidnappers and brigands who confess their guilt, while if they deny the charge, they bring them before the *dikasterion*, and if they are acquitted let them go, and if not put them to death after their trial. They report to the *dikasterion* land and houses listed as belonging to the city, and hand over to the *poletae* any that is judged to be public property. It is also part of their duties to bring summary indictments before the *dikasterion*, though the *Thesmothetae* also introduce some similar indictments.

2 Five men are picked by lot to introduce cases which are to be settled within a month, each of whom covers two tribes. Cases falling in this category include failure to pay a dowry which is owed, failure to repay a loan made at an interest of a drachma per mina, or a loan of capital made to finance the opening of a business in the market; prosecutions for assault, cases involving friendly loans, cooperative ventures, slaves, animals, trierarchies and bank-

3 ing matters. These officials introduce within the month cases of these classes, while the Receivers handle cases involving tax-farming, with the power to make a final decision in cases up to ten drachmae; they refer the remainder to the *dikasterion* for settlement within the month.

LIII The Forty are picked by lot, four from each tribe, and other suits are brought before them. They used to be a board of thirty, and travel round the demes to try cases, but after the tyranny of

2 the Thirty their numbers were increased to forty. They can make the final decision in cases involving up to ten drachmae, but anything above that they hand over to the Arbitrators. These officials then take the case, and if they cannot bring about a settlement, give a decision; if the decision satisfies both sides and they accept it, the case is ended. If one party appeals to the *dikasterion*, the Arbitrators place the depositions, the challenges and the relevant

laws in boxes, one for each side in the case, seal the boxes, add the decision of the Arbitrator written on a tablet, and hand everything over to the four members of the Forty who handle the cases of the tribe of the defendant. They take them over, and bring the 3 case before the *dikasterion*, cases of less than 1,000 drachmae before a jury of 201 members, those over 1,000 before 401 jurors. At the hearing it is forbidden to use laws, challenges or depositions other than those used in front of the Arbitrator and sealed in the boxes. The Arbitrators are men in their sixtieth year; their age is 4 known from the Archons and the eponymous heroes. There are ten eponymous heroes for the tribes, and forty-two for the age-groups; the Ephebes' names are recorded together with the Archon under whom they were enrolled and the eponymous hero of the previous year's Arbitrators; this used to be done on whitened boards, but they now use a bronze plaque which is set up in front of the chamber of the *Boule* by the statues of the eponymous heroes. The Forty take the list under the name of the last 5 of the eponymous heroes, and allot to those on the list the cases for arbitration and cast lots to decide which each will decide. The man selected is required to arbitrate as directed, for the law provides that if any man fails to serve as an Arbitrator when his age-group is performing this duty he shall lose his citizen rights, unless he happens to hold public office that year or to be abroad; only these categories are exempt.

Information can be laid before the Arbitrators as a body if 6 anyone is wronged by an individual Arbitrator, and the penalty laid down by law for anyone condemned under this procedure is loss of citizen rights; there is a right of appeal. They also use the 7 names of the eponymous heroes for military service; when they send an age-group on campaign, they publish a notice saying that the groups from one Archon and eponymous hero to another are called up for service.

The following offices are also filled by lot; five commissioners LIV of roads, whose duty it is to employ the slaves provided by the city to repair the roads. Ten Auditors and ten assistants for them, 2 to whom all those who have held public office must submit their accounts; this is the only body which audits the accounts of those subject to the *euthuna* and submits the results to the *dikasterion*.

If they detect anyone who has been guilty of embezzlement, the jury condemns him for theft of public money, and he is sentenced to pay ten times the amount stolen; if they demonstrate that anyone has taken bribes and the jury convicts him, they assess the size of the bribe, and again he pays ten times this amount. If they condemn him for maladministration, they assess the amount, and this is what he pays as long as he pays up before the ninth prytany; if not, the sum is doubled. Fines of ten times the amount involved in the offence are not doubled.

3   They cast lots for the officer called Clerk to the Prytanies, who is in charge of the documents, keeps the decrees which have been passed, checks the transcription of everything else, and attends meetings of the *Boule*. In earlier days this official was elected, and they used to elect the most famous and reliable men; their names are recorded on the inscribed texts of alliances, and grants of *pro-*

4 *xenia* and citizenship; now they are selected by lot. They also pick another man by lot to look after laws; he attends the *Boule* and

5 also checks all transcriptions. The people elect the clerk whose duty it is to read out documents in the *Ekklesia* and *Boule*, and this is his only duty.

6   Ten sacred officials are elected who are called 'those in charge of expiation'; they make sacrifices ordered by oracles, and if good

7 omens are required they see to it with the prophets. Another ten religious officials are selected by lot, called 'those in charge of annual rites'; they offer certain sacrifices and are in charge of all four-yearly festivals except for the Panathenaea. The four-yearly festivals are: 1. the mission to Delos (which is also celebrated every six years); 2. the Brauronia; 3. the Heracleia; 4. the Eleusinia; 5. the Panathenaea; none of these festivals occurs in the same place. The Hephaestia was added to the group in the Archonship of Cephisophon.

8   An Archon is appointed for Salamis and a demarch for the Peiraeus by lot; they celebrate the Dionysia in each place, and appoint the *choregoi*. In Salamis the name of the Archon is recorded.

LV   The holders of the above offices are selected by lot, and their duties are those listed above. As to the so-called nine Archons, I have already described their original ways of appointment; today, six *Thesmothetae* and their secretary and also the Archon, the King Archon and the Polemarch are appointed by lot from each tribe in rotation. Their qualifications for office are checked first in the 2 *Boule* of 500, except for the secretary, whose qualifications are checked only in the *dikasterion* as happens for other office holders – for all officials, whether selected by lot or elected, have their qualifications checked before they take up office; the nine Archons have to go before both the *Boule* and the *dikasterion*. In the past a man who was disqualified by the *Boule* could not hold office, but now there is an appeal to the *dikasterion*, and the final decision is taken there. When they are checking qualifications, they ask 3 first: 'Who is your father, and what is your deme? Who was your father's father, and who was your mother, and her father and his deme?' Then they ask whether the candidate is enrolled in a cult of Apollo Patroos and Zeus Herkeios, and where the shrines are, then whether he has family tombs and where they are; whether he treats his parents well, pays his taxes, and has gone on campaign when required. When these questions have been asked, the candidate is required to call witnesses to his answers. When he 4 has produced the witnesses, the question is put: 'Does anyone wish to bring any charge against this man?' If an accuser appears, the accusation and defence are heard, and then the matter is put to the vote by a show of hands in the *Boule* or a ballot if the hearing is in the *dikasterion*. If no one wishes to bring an accusation, the vote is held immediately. In former times, only one ceremonial vote was cast, but now everyone is required to vote on candidates, so that if a criminal has managed to get rid of all his accusers it is still in the power of the jurors to disqualify him. After this investigation, the candidates go to the stone on which 5 are the parts of the sacrificial victim, and standing on it they swear to administer their office justly and in accordance with the laws, and not to take bribes in connection with their office, and if they do, to dedicate a golden statue. At this stone also the Arbitrators give their decisions on oath and witnesses swear to their depositions. After taking the oath the candidates go to the Acropolis, and repeat the same oath there; after that they take up their office.

The Archon, the King Archon and the Polemarch each have LVI two assessors of their own choice, and these men have their credentials checked in the *dikasterion* before they take up their positions, and are subject to the *euthuna* in respect of their tenure.

2 As soon as the Archon takes up office, he proclaims that every man shall hold and control until the end of the year such property

3 as he held before he took office. Then he appoints for the tragedians three *choregi* who are the richest of all the Athenians; formerly he appointed five for the comedians, but now the tribes provide for them. Then he receives the *choregi* appointed by the tribes, those for the men's and the boys' choruses and the comedies at the Dionysia, and for the men's and boys' choruses at the Thargelia; those for the Dionysia are each provided by one tribe, but two tribes combine for the Thargelia, each of the tribes serving in turn. The Archon then arranges exchanges of property, and presents any claims for exemption which may arise if a man claims either to have performed this liturgy before, or to be exempt on the grounds of having performed another liturgy after which his period of exemption has not yet passed, or not to be of the required age – for the *choregus* of the boys' chorus must be over forty years old. The Archon also appoints *choregi* for Delos, and a chief of the sacred embassy to take the young people on the

4 thirty-oared vessel. He is also in charge of the procession to Asclepius when the initiated hold a vigil, and the procession at the Great Dionysia. In arranging the latter he is aided by ten assistants who used to be elected by the people and meet the cost of the procession out of their own pockets, but now are picked by lot, one from each tribe, and receive a hundred minae for their

5 expenses. The Archon also organises the processions at the Thargelia and to Zeus Soter; he organises the contests at the Dionysia and the Thargelia. These are the festivals which he organises.

6 Some civil and criminal proceedings come before the Archon; he holds a preliminary hearing, and then introduces them into the *dikasterion*. They include cases of ill-treating parents, in which the prosecutor is immune from penalty; accusations of offences against orphans, which are brought against the guardians, and of offences against *epikleroi*, which are brought against the guardians and the people living with the *epikleroi*; accusations of mismanaging the estate of an orphan, which are also brought against the guardians; charges of insanity where it is alleged that a man is wasting his substance because he is of unsound mind, and requests for the

appointment of officials to divide up property where a person is unwilling to share out what is held in common; requests to constitute or decide a wardship, for production in court, for enrolment as a guardian, and claims to estates and *epikleroi*. He also looks 7 after orphans, *epikleroi*, and widows who declare themselves pregnant after the death of their husbands. He has the power to fine offenders or bring them before the *dikasterion*. He rents out the houses of orphans and *epikleroi* until they are fourteen years old, and takes security for the leases; he exacts maintenance from guardians who do not provide it for children in their care.

These matters are the province of the Archon. The King LVII Archon supervises the Mysteries together with assistants elected by the people, two of whom are elected from the whole citizen body, one from the family of the Eumolpidae, and one from the Ceryces. Secondly he has charge of the festival of Dionysus called the Lenaea, which involves a procession and contest. The King Archon and his assistants jointly arrange the procession, but the contest is in his hands alone. He also arranges all torch-races and virtually all the traditional sacrifices. Cases of impiety come before 2 him and disputes over priesthoods. He also decides all disputes about religious matters which arise between the clans or the priests; all cases of homicide come before him, and he it is who proclaims the exclusion of an individual from customary ceremonies. Charges of murder or wounding where a man deliberately kills 3 or injures someone are heard before the Areopagus, as are cases of poisoning which result in death, and cases of arson; these are the only cases decided by that body. Charges of unintentional homicide, conspiracy to kill, and the killing of a slave, metic or foreigner are heard by the Court of the Palladeum. Where a man 4 admits to having killed someone but claims that his action was lawful, as for example if he caught an adulterer in the act, or killed unwittingly in war or in the course of the games, the case is heard in the Delphineum. If a man has retired into exile in a situation where reconciliation is possible and is then accused of killing or wounding someone, his case is heard in the court of Phreatto, and he pleads his case from a boat anchored near the shore. Except for cases brought before the Areopagus, all these cases are tried by *Ephetae* selected by lot; the case is brought before the court by the King Archon, and the hearing is held in a sacred area out of doors; during the case the King Archon does not wear his crown. At all other times the defendant is excluded from all sanctuaries, and is even barred by law from the Agora, but for the trial he enters the sacred area and makes his defence. When the offender is not known, the proceedings are held against 'the guilty party'. The King Archon and the Tribal Kings also proceed against inanimate objects and animals.

LVIII   The Polemarch makes the sacrifices to Artemis the huntress and to Enyalius, and arranges the funeral games in honour of those who have fallen in war, and makes the offerings to Harmodius
2   and Aristogeiton. He hears only private suits which involve metics, tax-exempt metics and *proxenoi*; it is his duty to take them and divide them into ten groups, and to assign by lot one group to each of the ten tribes, and the jurors of the tribe must then bring
3   them before the Arbitrators. The Polemarch himself introduces cases where a man is accused of disregarding his patron or not having one, and also cases involving inheritance and *epikleroi* of the metics; in other respects, the Polemarch performs for the metics the same duties as the Archon performs for citizens.

LIX   The *Thesmothetae* are responsible first for announcing the days on which the *dikasteria* will sit, and then for allotting the magistrates to the courts; the latter bring cases to court as the *Thesmo-*
2   *thetae* direct. They bring impeachments and motions for the deposition of magistrates before the *Ekklesia*, and they introduce all accusations brought in the *Ekklesia*, indictments for illegal proposals and accusations of having proposed laws against the interests of the state, indictments against the chairmen or president,
3   and the *euthunai* of the *strategi*. They hear cases where the prosecutor has to make a deposit, including charges of wrongly claiming citizen rights, or using bribery to this end, which arises when a man uses bribery to escape a charge of wrongly claiming to be a citizen, charges of malicious prosecution, bribery, false entry in the lists of state debtors, falsely witnessing a summons, failure to erase the name of a debtor who had paid, non-registration of a
4   debtor, and adultery. They also introduce the investigations into the credentials of all candidates for office, the appeals of those

whose registration has been refused by their demes, and condemnations sent for confirmation by the *Boule*. They also introduce 5 private suits involving trade or the mines, and cases where a slave is accused of slandering a free man. They allocate courts to the magistrates by lot for public and private suits. They validate inter- 6 national agreements and introduce cases arising under them, and also charges of bearing false witness in the Areopagus.

The selection of the jurors by lot is done by all the nine Archons 7 together with the secretary of the *Thesmothetae*, each handling his own tribe.

Such then is the position of the nine Archons. LX

Ten commissioners are also selected by lot to run the games, one from each tribe. When they have passed the preliminary examination, they hold office for four years, and they organise the procession at the Panathenaea, the musical contest, the athletics and the horse races, and they arrange the making of Athena's robe and the vases for prizes in conjunction with the *Boule*; they also give olive oil to the athletes. This oil comes from the sacred olives, and the Archon collects three-quarters of a pint per tree from the owners of the land in which they grow. In the past the city used to sell the fruit, and if anyone dug up or cut down one of the sacred olives, he was tried before the Areopagus and the penalty for those found guilty was death. Ever since the owner of the land has paid the contribution of oil, the law has remained in force, but the penalty has been allowed to lapse. The oil is now levied as a tax on the property, not collected from the trees themselves. The Archon collects the oil due in his year of office, and hands it over to the Treasurers for storage on the Acropolis; he is not allowed to take his seat in the Areopagus until he has handed over the full amount to the stewards. At other times the stewards keep the oil on the Acropolis, but at the time of the Panathenaea they measure it out to the commissioners of the games, who give it to the winning contestants. The prizes for those who win the musical contests are of silver and gold, for those who win the contests in manliness, shields, but for those who win the athletic events and the horse races, olive oil.

All military offices are also filled by elections. There are ten LXI *strategi*, who once were elected one from each tribe, but are now elected from the whole people. They are allocated by show of hands, one to the hoplites, to command on any expedition, and one to patrol Attica and to fight any enemy who invades the country; two are stationed in the Peiraeus, one in Munichia and one in Acte – their duty is to guard the Peiraeus; one is in charge of the symmories, and enrols the trierarchs, arranges any exchanges of property for them, and introduces cases where there are disputes to the *dikasteria*; the remainder are despatched to deal

2 with any situation that may arise. There is a vote in every prytany on their conduct of their office, and if the people vote against a man, he is tried in the *dikasterion*, and if condemned, the jury assesses the appropriate penalty or fine, while if he is acquitted he resumes his position. When in command of troops, they have the power to imprison anyone for insubordination, to discharge him, and to impose a fine, though this last is not usual.

3 Also elected are ten regimental commanders, one for each tribe; they lead their fellow tribesmen, and appoint the subordinate

4 officers. Two cavalry commanders are also elected from the whole citizen body; they lead the cavalry, divided into two units of five tribes each. They have the same authority over their men as the *strategi* have over the hoplites, and are likewise subject to a

5 monthly vote on their conduct. They also elect ten tribal commanders, one per tribe, to command the cavalry just as the regi-

6 mental commanders command the hoplites. They elect a cavalry

7 commander for Lemnos to command the cavalry there, and a steward for the 'Paralus' and another for the 'Ammonis'.

LXII The magistrates chosen by lot were formerly divided into two groups, those who, with the nine Archons, were selected from whole tribes, and those who were selected from the demes in the Theseum. However, when corruption affected the choices of the demes, the selection of the latter officers was transferred to the whole tribe also, except that members of the *Boule* and the guards are still selected by demes.

2 The citizens receive the following fees for public services; at ordinary meetings of the *Ekklesia* a drachma, but nine obols for the plenary session; jurors receive three obols, while members of the *Boule* receive five, and the Prytanies a sixth for their mainten-

ance. The nine Archons receive four obols each for maintenance and have a herald and *aulos*-player to maintain, and the Archon of Salamis gets a drachma a day. The commissioners of the games receive their meals in the Prytaneum in the month of Hecatombaeon during the Panathenaia, starting from the fourth day of the month. The sacred commissioners to Delos receive a drachma a day from Delos, and the officers sent out to Samos, Scyros, Lemnos or Imbros receive money for maintenance.

Military offices may be held repeatedly, but no other office may 3 be held more than once, except that a man may sit in the *Boule* twice.

The allocation of *dikastai* to the *dikasteria* is conducted by the LXIII nine Archons for their respective tribes, and the secretary of the *Thesmothetae* handles the tenth tribe. There are ten entrances into 2 the *dikasteria*, one for each tribe, twenty allotment machines, two for each tribe, one hundred boxes, ten for each tribe, and other boxes into which are thrown the tickets of the *dikastai* who have been successful in the ballot. There are two urns by the entrance to each court, and staves equal to the number of *dikastai* required; the same number of ballot balls are thrown into the urns as there are staves, and the balls have letters written on them starting with the eleventh of the alphabet, Λ, the number of letters corresponding with the number of courts to be filled. Those over thirty years 3 of age may sit as *dikastai* as long as they are not public debtors and have not lost their citizen rights. If a man who is disqualified sits, information is laid against him and he is brought before the *dikasterion*; if he is found guilty, the jury assess whatever penalty or fine seems to them appropriate, and if it is a fine, he must be imprisoned until he has paid the previous debt on the grounds of which he was indicted and the additional fine imposed by the *dikasterion*. Each *dikastes* has a ticket of boxwood with his name, 4 his father's name and his deme written on it, together with one of the first ten letters of the alphabet, those up to K; the *dikastai* of each tribe are divided into ten roughly equal sections under the ten letters. The *Thesmothetes* draws lots for the letters which are 5 to be placed by each court, and his servant puts the relevant letter up in each case.

LXIV   The ten boxes stand in front of the entrance for each tribe, and the letters up to K are inscribed on them. When the *dikastai* throw their tickets into the box which has the same letter on it as is on their ticket, the servant shakes the boxes and the *Thesmothetes*

2   draws one ticket from each. The man drawn is called the ticket-inserter, and inserts the tickets from the box into the columns over which is the same letter as there is on the box. This man is selected by lot to prevent malpractice if the same man should always make the draw. There are five columns of slots in each

3   allotment machine. When the Archon has put the cubes into the machines, he draws lots for each tribe according to the allotment machines.The cubes are bronze, some white, some black; he puts in as many white cubes as *dikastai* are needed, one per five columns, and black cubes in the same proportion. When the Archon takes out the cubes, the herald calls the men who have been selec-

4   ted; the ticket-inserter is included in their number. When a man has been called, he steps forward and draws a ball from the urns, and holds it out with the letter upwards, and shows it first to the presiding Archon. The Archon then puts the man's ticket into the box on which is the letter which is on the ball, so that he shall go to the court which he has drawn by lot, not the one he wishes to sit in, and it may not be possible for anyone to arrange to have

5   the jury he wishes. There are beside the Archon as many boxes as there are courts to be manned, each with the letter on it which has been allocated to the relevant court,

LXV   When the *dikastes* has shown his ball to the servant, he goes inside the inner door. The servant gives him a staff of the same colour as that of the court whose letter was the same as the one on his ball, so that he is compelled to sit in the court to which he has been allotted. If he goes into a different court, the colour of the staff gives him away, for a colour is painted on the lintel

2   of the entrance of each court. He takes his staff and goes into the court whose colour corresponds to his staff and whose letter is the same as that on his ball, and when he enters he receives an

3   official token from the man selected by lot to distribute them. The *dikastai* then take their seats with their ball and staff, having got into court in the manner described above. The ticket-inserters return their tickets to those who have been unsuccessful in the

ballot. The public servants from each tribe hand over the boxes 4
of each tribe, one for each court, in which are the names of the
members of each tribe who are sitting in each court. They hand
them over to those who have been selected by lot to return them
to the *dikastai* in each court, so that they may summon them by
using their tickets, and so give them their pay. There are five of
these officials.*

When all the courts have their requisite juries, two allotment LXVI
machines are set up in the first court, with bronze cubes on which
are the colours of the courts and other cubes on which the names
of the Archons are written. Two *Thesmothetae* picked by lot separately put the cubes in the machines, one putting the colours into
one machine, the other the names of the Archons into the other.
The herald announces whichever magistrate is picked first as allocated to the court which is drawn first, and the second to the
second, and so on, so that no magistrate may know where he is
to preside but each will preside over the one he draws by lot.

When the *dikastai* have arrived and been allocated to their 2
courts, the presiding magistrate in each court draws one ticket
from each box, so that he has ten, one from each tribe, and puts
these tickets into an empty box, and draws five of these, and of
the five drawn one supervises the water clock and the other four
the voting, so that nobody may interfere either with the man in
charge of the clock or those in charge of the voting, and there
may be no chicanery in these matters. The remaining five of the 3
ten drawn receive instructions detailing how and where the jury
will receive their pay in the court itself; this is done separately by
tribes after they have fulfilled their duties, so that they may receive
it in small groups and not cause trouble because there are a lot
of people crowded together.

After these preparations, they call the cases. If they are dealing LXVII
with private cases, they call four, one from each of the categories
defined by law, and the litigants take an oath to speak to the point;
when they deal with public cases, they summon the litigants, but
deal with only one case.

* The number is missing in the text.

2   There are water clocks with narrow tubes attached; they pour the prescribed amount of water into them, and this decides the length of time allowed for the speeches. They allow ten measures for cases involving over 5,000 drachmae, with three measures for the supporting speech, seven measures for those up to 5,000, with two for the supporting speech, and five and two for those under 1,000; six measures are allowed for the deciding of disputed

3 claims, and second speeches are not allowed. The man in charge of the water clock cuts off the flow of water when the clerk is going to read out a decree, law, piece of evidence or contract. If, however, parts of the day's hearing have been allocated to each side, then he does not cut it off, but an equal period of time is

4 allowed to the prosecutor and the defendant. The standard of division is the length of the day in the month of Poseideon . . . . . .

The following section of the papyrus is so badly mutilated that the text cannot be reconstructed; the only section of which something may be made is:

. . . The day is divided into proportionate parts . . . for contests where the penalty laid down on conviction is imprisonment, death, exile, loss of citizen rights or confiscation of property . . .

There follows a further mutilated section of papyrus.

LXVIII   The majority of the juries are of five hundred members . . . but when it is necessary for public suits to have a jury of 1,000, two

2 juries are combined in the *Heliaia*. The votes are cast with tokens of bronze which have a pipe through the middle, half of them pierced and half blocked. At the conclusion of the speeches, those chosen to supervise the voting give each member of the jury two tokens, one pierced and one blocked, showing them clearly to the litigants so that the jury do not receive either two pierced tokens or two blocked ones. Then the designated official takes the staffs, in return for which each *dikastes* when he casts his vote receives a bronze tag with the number three on it, for when he hands it in he receives three obols; this is to ensure that all vote, for no

3 one can receive a tag without voting. There are two containers in the court, one of bronze and one of wood; they can be taken apart

so that nobody can introduce votes into them fraudulently before the voting begins. The *dikastai* cast their votes in them, the bronze container counting while the wooden is for the vote which is not used. The bronze one has a lid with a hole in it through which only one token can pass, so that the same man may not insert two tokens into it. When the jury are about to vote, the herald first 4 asks whether the contestants wish to protest at any of the evidence, for protests cannot be lodged after voting has commenced. Then he makes a second announcement: 'The pierced token for the first speaker, the solid for the second.' The *dikastes* takes the tokens from the stand, holding the pipe in the token so that he does not show the litigants which is pierced and which is not; he places the token that counts in the bronze container, and the other in the wooden one.

When voting is complete, the servants take the container which LXIX counts and pour out the contents on to a reckoning frame which has as many holes in it as there are votes so that it may be easy to add up the tokens which count, both the pierced and solid ones. Those selected by lot for the task count them up on the board, separating the solid from the pierced, and the herald announces the number of votes cast, the pierced for the prosecutor and the solid for the defendant. Whichever gets more votes wins, while if the votes are equal the verdict goes to the defendant. If it is neces- 2 sary, they then assess a penalty by voting in the same way; for this the *dikastai* return their tags and take back their staffs. Each side is allowed half a measure of water for their speeches at this stage. When the *dikastai* have fulfilled their duties as required by law, they take their fees in the part of the building assigned to them.

Glossary to *The Constitution of Athens*

Arbitrators Adjudicators of private law-suits.

Areopagus The council which met on and took its name from the hill outside Athens. Little is known of its nature before Solon. It was constituted by retired archons (q.v.) and although it may originally have held charge of the state's government, its powers diminished after the creation of the *Boule* (q.v.) and it became a judicial body concerned principally with deciding cases of intentional homicide, wounding, arson and religious crimes.

archon Originally the supreme office in Athens, once the kingship had become an archonship. At first, there were three archons; later, probably in the seventh century, the office was made an annual one and the number of archons was raised to nine by adding the six *thesmothetae* (q.v.). In the fifth century, the archons ceased to be elected and were appointed by lot and after that suffered a diminution in influence in relation to the *strategi* (q.v.).

auditors Those who audited official accounts.

Boule The council founded by Solon, which originally consisted of 100 members from each of the four original *phylae* (q.v.). It was reformed by Cleisthenes so as to be constituted by fifty members from each of the ten newly created *phylae*. The members were chosen by lot from candidates put forward by the demes (q.v.). The *Boule* had charge of preparing the agenda for debates in the *Ekklesia* (q.v.). It also had supervision of magistrates, as well as responsibility for the running of the navy, the care of public buildings, the collection of taxes and state revenues, and meeting with ambassadors. The *Boule* was suspended in 411, when it was supplanted by the Four Hundred and, under the thirty tyrants, by a council of 500, but was restored with the democracy.

Brauronia Festival in honour of Artemis.

choregus The man who had financial charge of a chorus in a festival.

demarch The principal officer of a deme (q.v.).

demes In Cleisthenes' reforms, the deme was the basic division of the state and each deme was represented in the *Boule* (q.v.) according to its size. Once the demes had been established, membership of a deme was determined by family rather than place of residence. Every citizen of Athens had to be a member of a deme, and became so at eighteen. *See phylae, trittyes.*

dikasterion A jury-court. A juror had to be at least thirty years old, and a list of 6,000 volunteers to serve as jurors was drawn up annually. To encourage volunteers, Pericles introduced a fee for serving as a juror. The constitution of a court depended on the charge to be decided: this determined both who the presiding magistrate was and how many jurors served on the court. Which jurors served on which courts was decided by lot so as to minimise the chance of bribery.

Ekklesia The Assembly was the sovereign Athenian body. At least from the time of Solon, it was open to every adult male Athenian citizen. It met at least four times in each *prytany* (q.v.), but could be summoned by the *Boule* (q.v.) at other times. The *Boule* also provided the *probouleumata*, drafted resolutions, thus deciding what the *Ekklesia* would debate. Although the *Ekklesia* could not debate matters beyond those given by the *probouleumata*, it could instruct the *Boule* to produce a *probouleuma* for another session.

The Eleven Athenian officials, appointed by lot, who had responsibility for prisons and executions.

Ephebes Young men who had reached the age of puberty and who were engaged in military service.

Ephetae One of the Athenian juries. It consisted of fifty-one members, appointed by lot from citizens over the age of fifty, and heard those homicide cases which did not involve the intentional killing of an Athenian citizen.

epikleros The surviving daughter of a man with no sons.

Eupatridae A group of aristocratic families.

euthuna An examination of an official's conduct in office, made after his retirement.

The Five Thousand When the democracy was challenged in 412, the oligarchs originally proposed to limit the franchise to 5,000 citizens. Instead, the council of the Four Hundred was instituted. After the overthrow of the Four Hundred in 411, however, there was an assembly of Five Thousand, but full democracy was restored in 410. The *Constitution of Athens*, however, seems to suggest that there was an assembly of 5,000 before the institution of the Four Hundred.

The Forty Council concerned with deciding private law-suits.

The Four Hundred *See* The Five Thousand.

Hellenotamiae The ten treasures of the Delian League. Although originally based at Delos, they were elected Athenian officials – one from each of the ten *phylae* (q.v.) – and indeed probably moved to Athens in 454.

hieromnemon The 'sacred recorder', sent by Athens to the council of the Greek states concerned with the sanctuaries of Demeter at Anthela and of Apollo at Delphi.

hippeis The second of the four property-classes instituted by Solon.

metic A resident and free alien in Athens.

Mysteries Mystic rites which were celebrated at Eleusis in honour of Demeter. Athens had responsibility for this after the incorporation of Eleusis in the seventh century.

naucrariae Athenian districts, each originally constituted to have responsibility for providing and manning one ship for the Athenian navy.

Panathenaea Festival in honour of Athena.

pentacosiomedimnus The highest of the four property-classes designated by Solon.

phratry Literally, a 'brotherhood'. Until Cleisthenes' institution of the demes (q.v.), membership of a phratry was the condition for citizenship of Athens. Even if the phratries had originally been constituted so that membership was by family, a phratry could admit new members who had no hereditary claim to membership.

phylae Literally, 'tribes'. Originally there were four *phylae* in Athens, and these were administrative bodies of the state. As part of his democratic reforms, Cleisthenes founded ten new *phylae* (each made up of three *trittyes* (q.v.)) to replace the existing ones.

poletae Officials concerned with the disposal of confiscated property and the arrangement of state contracts.

proxenus   Someone who was a citizen of one state and officially represented the interests of another.

prytanies   After Cleisthenes' reforms, each of the ten *phylae* sent fifty men to the *Boule* (q.v.). For each tenth of the year (also known as a 'prytany') one of these groups of fifty would serve as 'presidents', *prytanies*, conducting the everyday business of the state. The leader of the prytany (newly appointed by lot each day) presided over the *Boule* and the *Ekklesia*.

Receivers   Officials concerned with collecting money for the state.

seisachtheia   The cancellation of debts effected by Solon.

strategi   Military commanders, elected from each of the ten *phylae* (q.v.). In the fifth century these had great political influence as well as military responsibility.

symmory   A group of those who were liable to become trierachs (q.v.).

The Ten   A council which replaced the Thirty (q.v.) in 403.

Thargelia   The festival held in honour of Apollo.

Theoric Fund   A fund which was instituted to help citizens buy tickets for festivals.

The Thirty   Oligarchic ruling council, 404–403.

Thesmothetae   Members of the council of archons (q.v.), who presided over jury-trials.

thetes   The fourth of the four property-classes instituted by Solon.

trierachs   Citizens who had financial responsibility for an Athenian naval ship.

trittyes   In Cleisthenes' reforms, each *phyle* (q.v.) was made up of three trittyes, which in their turn were constituted by demes (q.v.).

zeugites   The third of the four property-classes instituted by Solon.

Index of names

Brief biographical information is given in cases where this is help-ful. Generally, for those people mentioned in *The Constitution of Athens*, the author himself provides the relevant information and I have not duplicated it here.

General index

abortion, 192
Abydos, 130, 131
Achaea (Peloponnesian), 124
acquisition, 15, 19, 21–6, *see also*
    property, usury
Acropolis, 220, 221, 225, 229, 253, 257
Acte, 243, 258
admirals, 54
adultery, 131, 192, 255, 256
Aegospotami, 236
agriculture, 20
aliens, 62, 69, *see also* foreigners
alliances, 31, 73–4, 252
allotment machines, 259–61
alternation in office, 11, 27, 32, 67, 70,
    88, 90, 154, 186
ambition (*philotimia*), 44, 45, 53, 132,
    140
Ambracia, 124, 126, 141
Ammonis, 258
Amphipolis, 124, 130
anger, 144, 149, 190
animals, xxxi, 13, 17, 20, 21, 25, 73, 96,
    185, 250, 256
Antissa, 124
Apollonia (Adriatic), 96
Apollonia (Euxine), 124, 130
appetite (*orexis*), 16, 66, 190, *see also*
    desire
Arbitrators, 250–1, 253, 256
Arcadia, 32, 50, 51
archers, 164, 229
Archons, 165, 211–12, 214, 215, 219,
    227, 230, 233, 234, 246, 247, 251,

252–5, 256, 257, 258, 259, 260. *See
also* King Archon
Areopagus, 59, 126, 150, 212, 213, 215,
    216, 222, 228, 229, 230, 237, 242,
    247, 255, 257
Argos, 50, 51, 123, 126, 140
Argusinae, 236
aristocracy, 57, 58, 68, 71, 81, 86, 90,
    102–4, 117, 131–3, 134–5, *see also*
    oligarchy, constitution
army, 226
art (*technē*), xxxii, xxxv–xxxvi, 15, 24–5,
    26, 48, 70, 78–9, 91–2, 196
artisans, 30, 46, 47, 68, 94, 96, 98, 158,
    172, 183
Asia, 55, 84, 94, 175
assault, 250
assembly, 62, 86, 101, 112–13, 116–17,
    155, 160, *see also* Ekklesia
Atarneus, 45
Athens, 46, 47, 59–60, 63, 82, 98, 118,
    123, 125, 126, 128, 129, 134, 159,
    164, *see also* Draco, Peisistratus,
    Solon (in Index of names)
athletes, 191, 198–9, 257
Attica, 258
auditors, 165, 247, 251
avarice, 45, 51, 53, 58, 122

Babylonians, 40, 64, 82
bakers, 249
barbarians, 12, 22
barter, 22
body, 16–17, 19, 167, 190, 198, 199

274

Cambridge Texts in the History of Political Thought

Titles published in the series thus far

Aristotle *The Politics* and *The Constitution of Athens* (edited by Stephen Everson)
   0 521 48400 6 paperback

Arnold *Culture and Anarchy and other writings* (edited by Stefan Collini)
   0 521 37796 X paperback

Astell *Political Writings* (edited by Patricia Springborg)
   0 521 42845 9 paperback

Augustine *The City of God against the Pagans* (edited by R. W. Dyson)
   0 521 46843 4 paperback

Austin *The Province of Jurisprudence Determined* (edited by Wilfrid E. Rumble)
   0 521 44756 9 paperback

Bacon *The History of the Reign of King Henvy VII* (edited by Brian Vickers)
   0 521 58663 1 paperback

Bakunin *Statism and Anarchy* (edited by Marshall Shatz)
   0 521 36973 8 paperback

Baxter *Holy Commonwealth* (edited by William Lamont)
   0 521 40580 7 paperback

Bayle *Political Writings* (edited by Sally L. Jenkinson)
   0 521 47677 1 paperback

Beccaria *On Crimes and Punishments and other writings* (edited by Richard Bellamy)
   0 521 47982 7 paperback

Bentham *Fragment on Government* (introduction by Ross Harrison)
   0 521 35929 5 paperback

Bernstein *The Preconditions of Socialism* (edited by Henry Tudor)
   0 521 39808 8 paperback

Bodin *On Sovereignty* (edited by Julian H. Franklin)
   0 521 34992 3 paperback

Bolingbroke *Political Writings* (edited by David Armitage)
   0 521 58697 6 paperback

Bossuet *Politics Drawn from the Very Words of Holy Scripture* (edited by Patrick Riley)
   0 521 36807 3 paperback

The British Idealists (edited by David Boucher)
   0 521 45951 6 paperback

Burke *Pre-Revolutionary Writings* (edited by Ian Harris)
   0 521 36800 6 paperback

Christine De Pizan *The Book of the Body Politic* (edited by Kate Langdon Forhan)
   0 521 42259 0 paperback

Cicero *On Duties* (edited by M. T. Griffin and E. M. Atkins)
   0 521 34835 8 paperback

Cicero *On the Commonwealth and On the Laws* (edited by James E. G. Zetzel)
   0 521 45959 1 paperback

Comte *Early Political Writings* (edited by H. S. Jones)
 0 521 46923 6 paperback
Conciliarism and Papalism (edited by J. H. Burns and Thomas M. Izbicki)
 0 521 47674 7 paperback
Constant *Political Writings* (edited by Biancamaria Fontana)
 0 521 31632 4 paperback
Dante *Monarchy* (edited by Prue Shaw)
 0 521 56781 5 paperback
Diderot *Political Writings* (edited by John Hope Mason and Robert Wokler)
 0 521 36911 8 paperback
The Dutch Revolt (edited by Martin van Gelderen)
 0 521 39809 6 paperback
Early Greek Political Thought from Homer to the Sophists (edited by Michael Gagarin
 and Paul Woodruff)
 0 521 43768 7 paperback
The Early Political Writings of the German Romantics (edited by
 Frederick C. Beiser)
 0 521 44951 0 paperback
The English Levellers (edited by Andrew Sharp)
 0 521 62511 4 paperback
Erasmus *The Education of a Christian Prince* (edited by Lisa Jardine)
 0 521 58811 1 paperback
Fenelon *Telemachus* (edited by Patrick Riley)
 0 521 45662 2 paperback
Ferguson *An Essay on the History of Civil Society* (edited by Fania Oz-Salzberger)
 0 521 44736 4 paperback
Filmer *Patriarcha and Other Writings* (edited by Johann P. Sommerville)
 0 521 39903 3 paperback
Fletcher *Political Works* (edited by John Robertson)
 0 521 43994 9 paperback
Sir John Fortescue *On the Laws and Governance of England* (edited by
 Shelley Lockwood)
 0 521 58996 7 paperback
Fourier *The Theory of the Four Movements* (edited by Gareth Stedman Jones and Ian
 Patterson)
 0 521 35693 8 paperback
Gramsci *Pre-Prison Writings* (edited by Richard Bellamy)
 0 521 42307 4 paperback
Guicciardini *Dialogue on the Government of Florence* (edited by Alison Brown)
 0 521 45623 1 paperback
Harrington *A Commonwealth of Oceana* and *A System of Politics* (edited by
 J. G. A. Pocock)
 0 521 42329 5 paperback

Hegel *Elements of the Philosophy of Right* (edited by Allen W. Wood and
   H. B. Nisbet)
   0 521 34888 9 paperback
Hegel *Political Writings* (edited by Laurence Dickey and H. B. Nisbet)
   0 521 45979 3 paperback
Hobbes *On the Citizen* (edited by Michael Silverthorne and Richard Tuck)
   0 521 43780 6 paperback
Hobbes *Leviathan* (edited by Richard Tuck)
   0 521 56797 1 paperback
Hobhouse *Liberalism and Other Writings* (edited by James Meadowcroft)
   0 521 43726 1 paperback
Hooker *Of the Laws of Ecclesiastical Polity* (edited by A. S. McGrade)
   0 521 37908 3 paperback
Hume *Political Essays* (edited by Knud Haakonssen)
   0 521 46639 3 paperback
King James VI and I *Political Writings* (edited by Johann P. Sommerville)
   0 521 44729 1 paperback
Jefferson *Political Writings* (edited by Joyce Appleby and Terence Ball)
   0 521 64841 6 paperback
John of Salisbury *Policraticus* (edited by Cary Nederman)
   0 521 36701 8 paperback
Kant *Political Writings* (edited by H. S. Reiss and H. B. Nisbet)
   0 521 39837 1 paperback
Knox *On Rebellion* (edited by Roger A. Mason)
   0 521 39988 2 paperback
Kropotkin *The Conquest of Bread and other writings* (edited by Marshall Shatz)
   0 521 45990 7 paperback
Lawson *Politica sacra et civilis* (edited by Conal Condren)
   0 521 39248 9 paperback
Leibniz *Political Writings* (edited by Patrick Riley)
   0 521 35899 x paperback
The Levellers (edited by Andrew Sharp)
   0 521 62511 4 paperback
Locke *Political Essays* (edited by Mark Goldie)
   0 521 47861 8 paperback
Locke *Two Treatises of Government* (edited by Peter Laslett)
   0 521 35730 6 paperback
Loyseau *A Treatise of Orders and Plain Dignities* (edited by Howell A. Lloyd)
   0 521 45624 x paperback
Luther and Calvin on Secular Authority (edited by Harro Höpfl)
   0 521 34986 9 paperback
Machiavelli *The Prince* (edited by Quentin Skinner and Russell Price)
   0 521 34993 1 paperback

de Maistre *Considerations on France* (edited by Isaiah Berlin and Richard Lebrun)
  0 521 46628 8 paperback
Malthus *An Essay on the Principle of Population* (edited by Donald Winch)
  0 521 42972 2 paperback
Marsiglio of Padua *Defensor minor* and *De translatione Imperii* (edited by
  Cary Nederman)
  0 521 40846 6 paperback
Marx *Early Political Writings* (edited by Joseph O'Malley)
  0 521 34994 X paperback
Marx *Later Political Writings* (edited by Terrell Carver)
  0 521 36739 5 paperback
James Mill *Political Writings* (edited by Terence Ball)
  0 521 38748 5 paperback
J. S. Mill *On Liberty*, with *The Subjection of Women* and *Chapters on Socialism* (edited
  by Stefan Collini)
  0 521 37917 2 paperback
Milton *Political Writings* (edited by Martin Dzelzainis)
  0 521 34866 8 paperback
Montesquieu *The Spirit of the Laws* (edited by Anne M. Cohler, Basia Carolyn Miller
  and Harold Samuel Stone)
  0 521 36974 6 paperback
More *Utopia* (edited by George M. Logan and Robert M. Adams)
  0 521 40318 9 paperback
Morris *News from Nowhere* (edited by Krishan Kumar)
  0 521 42233 7 paperback
Nicholas of Cusa *The Catholic Concordance* (edited by Paul E. Sigmund)
  0 521 56773 4 paperback
Nietzsche *On the Genealogy of Morality* (edited by Keith Ansell-Pearson)
  0 521 40610 2 paperback
Paine *Political Writings* (edited by Bruce Kuklick)
  0 521 36678 X paperback
Plato *Statesman* (edited by Julia Annas and Robin Waterfield)
  0 521 44778 X paperback
Price *Political Writings* (edited by D. O. Thomas)
  0 521 40969 1 paperback
Priestley *Political Writings* (edited by Peter Miller)
  0 521 42561 1 paperback
Proudhon *What is Property?* (edited by Donald R. Kelley and
  Bonnie G. Smith)
  0 521 40556 4 paperback
Pufendorf *On the Duty of Man and Citizen according to Natural Law* (edited by James
  Tully)
  0 521 35980 5 paperback